THE BOY WONDERS

WAYNE ROONEY, DUNCAN EDWARDS

AND THE CHANGING FACE OF FOOTBALL

Colin Malam

Published in 2006 by Highdown,
an imprint of Raceform Ltd
Compton, Newbury, Berkshire, RG20 6NL
Raceform Ltd is a wholly-owned subsidiary of Trinity Mirror plc

A CIP catalogue record for this book is available from the British Library.

ISBN 1-905156-25-1

Cover and interiors designed by Tracey Scarlett

Printed and bound in Great Britain by William Clowes Ltd, Beccles, Suffolk

CONTENTS

ACKNOWLEDGEMENTS

THE scope of this book was so vast, I needed all the help I could get to complete it. So grateful thanks are extended to all of those who willingly gave of their time and experience to be interviewed.

For obvious reasons, the sections about Duncan Edwards' early life were the most difficult to research, and I should like to thank David Instone, Jim Cadman, Betty Cooksey, Brian Marshall and Peter Creed in particular for opening up that part of the past for me.

Wayne Rooney's life, by comparison, is an open book. Even so, it would not have been possible to read between the lines without the invaluable assistance of, among others, Diana Law, David Meek, Neil Chambers and the *Manchester Evening News* website.

Celebrated football statisticians and historians Jack Rollin, Albert Sewell and David Barber were also of enormous help when it came to chronicling the changes in the English game during the past half-century.

Ken Jones, Alex Montgomery, Hugh McIlvanney, Peter Keeling, Chris Haynes and Ron Atkin, too, eased my path in a variety of ways.

FOREWORD
BY SIR BOBBY CHARLTON

KIDS come to me now and ask what Duncan Edwards was really like. Their dads and granddads have told them about him, and they want to know more. What I tell them is that he was really, really gentle as a person, but really loud with his football. His personality changed when he got changed and was ready to play. He was massive – that's the best way I can describe him. Tough as hell he was, too, and brave as a lion.

On the pitch, he was like a big dynamo. His size and his presence were undeniable and have never been bettered since. People have tried to compare him with anybody who has had a couple of good games, and said, 'It's the new Duncan Edwards!' It happened with Bryan Robson, and the lad who was at Ipswich – Kevin Beattie – but there's nobody like him. Roy Keane was a bit of a talisman, but even he didn't have the strength, the power and the ability of Duncan. As far as I am concerned, he was the best player I've ever played with.

When I was young, I never felt inferior to any player. I thought to myself, 'Well, I've played for England Schoolboys. I've done all right.' But when I came to Manchester United, Jimmy Murphy, Sir Matt Busby's right-hand man, said to me, 'Oh, you're going to love playing with Duncan Edwards. What a player!' I thought Jimmy must be exaggerating, as everybody does from time to time, but he was right. Duncan was so good, he was just better than anybody else.

Muddy pitches meant nothing to him. You've got to remember that the old leather ball in those days got very heavy in the wet. But he would still hit 60- or 70-yard passes with his right foot or his left. On the floor or in the air – it didn't matter. He could knock little one-twos as well; he was as cute as the next person. And his tackling! He used to clatter people, but there was nothing malicious about him. Hard but fair sums him up. He just wanted the ball, and he would usually take it.

He was colossal, really. When he wasn't playing, you felt a little bit of stature and presence was missing. If he was on the field, it was different. Everybody was thinking, 'We're all right!' He was the Busby Babes' talisman. He could play in just about any position. Central defender, sweeper, right- or left-back, anywhere in midfield or attack, goalkeeper too – they all came alike to him. Whenever there was an emergency, they would move him to deal with it. And I never saw him struggle.

He was a good lad as well. He wasn't cocky, he was good fun, and he was always laughing. He liked a laugh, but never at your expense. In fact, as a sportsman, he was a great role model. But for Munich and his tragic early death, Duncan would have been one of the most famous players in the world. I miss him still, and I would just like to keep his name up there in lights. Sadly, there's not much video or film of him in action. But he was too good to be forgotten.

If you asked me if I saw any similarities between Duncan and Wayne Rooney, I would say their enthusiasm, their love of playing the game. But Wayne is different. For a start, he plays in a different position from the one Duncan usually occupied. He does things that Duncan couldn't do, and Duncan did things that he could never do; but, generally speaking, the enthusiasm and ability of players of their kind are such that you don't worry that they are not going to be there. Wayne will still be playing at 35 or 36, you know. He'll still be around.

He loves the game and he's quite a bright lad, a funny lad. The rest of the players think he's great. I think he's the best player around in this country. As soon as he picks the ball up, you think, 'I'm glad he's got it!' He can be as delicate as anything, with a little touch just to knock it out of the reach of his defender, and round the box he wants to score. It's the thing people go to football matches for, you know. You come to see somebody like him and you want to go home and say, 'What a goal! What a goal he scored today!' Certainly, Wayne Rooney is the only player that can get me off my seat.

He's a marvellous talent, and the game has to do its best to protect him. We at Manchester United will definitely protect him. He's got the right character for our game, and I feel sorry for him when he goes too far. But he'll learn. It's happened to lots and lots of players, though never with the spotlight as bright as it is today. Times have changed, society has changed, football has changed. But I don't worry about Wayne Rooney at all. I only feel sorry for myself when I can't see him, because he's a marvellous player, a potentially great player.

INTRODUCTION

THERE are some things about football that never change. Things like the sheer joy of kicking a ball about in an open space with others and knowing you are good at it. And it is that, the most fundamental of pleasures the game has to offer, which links Duncan Edwards and Wayne Rooney with an unbreakable bond. They may be light years – never mind half a century – apart in many other respects, but what unites them is an all-consuming passion for the game. In all probability, you feel, Duncan Edwards and Wayne Rooney would have played professional football for nothing if required to do so. They would have done it just for the thrill of parading their formidable skills on the big stage.

The pair share other similarities: both came from humble, working-class backgrounds; both were teenage sensations for Manchester United; and both astonished world football with their precocity. But there the similarities end. Edwards was the classic *Boy's Own* hero. Big, strong and powerful, he towered over the matches in which he played. Blessed with a fair turn of speed, apparently limitless reserves of energy, no little skill and a cannonball shot in both feet, the brawny young Midlander was a dominating force in midfield, or wherever else he was asked to play. Although fiercely competitive, too, Edwards rarely let his behaviour run out of control on or off the field of play. Mature beyond his tender years, he exuded a certain nobility as well as a natural air of authority before the Munich air disaster took him from us so cruelly at the early age of 21.

In that respect, sadly, Rooney suffers by comparison with his almost saintly predecessor at Old Trafford. Football's equivalent of an angel with a dirty face, the sublimely gifted Scouse teenager quickly developed a reputation as a foul-mouthed hothead after a series of four-letter outbursts during matches that cost him several suspensions and supposedly scandalised the nation. But allowances have to be made here for differences of temperament. Whereas Edwards was lucky enough to be born phlegmatic, Rooney is volatile. Whereas Edwards could go about his business without television cameras recording his every cough and spit, Rooney's behaviour is held up for public examination every week by the all-seeing eye that has been responsible for some of the most cataclysmic changes in English football since the Second World War. Off the field, Rooney and his fiancée, Coleen McLoughlin, are rarely left in peace by newspapers and magazines hungry for another taste of the pernicious and overwhelming cult of celebrity that helps to make today's society so different from the much simpler and more respectful one of Edwards' day. In fact, the tabloids' eagerness to dish the dirt on, and belittle, the pair of them smacks of persecution. What makes this systematic hounding so much worse is the hypocrisy of a media – television as well as newspapers – that has actually helped bring about the lower behavioural standards of which they pretend to complain.

In short, Duncan Edwards and Wayne Rooney are, as much as anything else, products of their times. And those times have changed almost beyond recognition in the past half-century. You have only to think of the difference in footballers' pay to appreciate the change: £15 to £20 a week for a top player in Edwards' heyday, £100,000-plus a week now. The massive expansion of television coverage of the game has been largely responsible for that huge hike in wages, but the players' union and Jean-Marc Bosman have played their part, too. Bosman's successful fight for complete freedom of contract, plus the European Union's insistence on the free movement of labour within its member states, has also filled English football with so many foreign players that Edwards would probably struggle to recognise it. Like Wayne Rooney, however, the Manchester United powerhouse of the 1950s would not have been fazed by, or out of place in, such challenging and exalted company.

CHAPTER ONE

TWINKLE, TWINKLE LITTLE STARS

UNDENIABLY, Duncan Edwards and Wayne Rooney have much in common. In fact, there are probably more similarities between them than differences. As is more often than not the case with famous footballers, both were born into working-class families of limited means and grew up in a council house. Neither could be called academic, either, and they directed most of their energies, mental and physical, towards football. Besotted with the game, in the classic tradition of the budding star, they could rarely be found without a ball at their feet when they were kids. All that separates them really is 50 years of change in English football and society.

'He didn't mind going to school,' recalled Duncan's mother, Sarah Ann, in later years, 'and he enjoyed drawing and history, but he always preferred to be out of doors.' He always preferred to have a ball of some sort within easy reach, too. No matter how many times his parents forbade him to take a you-know-what with him when they went visiting, he would slip outside when the adults were engrossed in conversation and bring out the tennis ball he'd hidden in his pocket. In the end, Mr and Mrs Edwards realised they were wasting their time trying to limit Duncan's obsession with the game.

'As a lad he went out with a ball, and came back with a ball, and would spend hours heading and kicking a ball against the wall,' Mrs Edwards told Geoff Warburton in his awestruck biography *Duncan Edwards: Manchester United and England*. 'Even if he was dressed up on Sunday, he couldn't help kicking stones, and when we went on holiday we always had to buy him a ball.' Duncan's mother, apparently, would watch fascinated as her son kept a tennis ball in the air with head and foot while kicking it against the wall outside her kitchen.

Equally obsessed at the same tender age, Wayne used to flirt with grandparental disapproval by kicking a ball against, and wearing a hole in, the pebbledash wall of his grandmother's house. His cousin, Thomas Rooney, reported that he would be doing it from as early as seven o'clock in the morning. Not surprisingly, their nan was not best pleased, especially when she heard the pebbledash falling off her wall, and Wayne would end up getting a slap. Sometimes the culprit would be Thomas or Stephen, another cousin; but the mischievous pair would tell her it was Wayne, and she usually believed them because he had been the guilty party so often.

Fiercely competitive the both of them, what Duncan and Wayne enjoyed most was actually playing the game, pitting their abilities against those of other players, as opposed to just kicking a ball about. Both of them, and their mates, would start a game, or join one, wherever there was an open space, be it covered in grass, concrete, mud or dust.

Duncan was lucky, in that he lived in a fairly leafy setting. Dudley, his home town in the West Midlands, may be at the heart of the industrial Black Country, but it is not by any means all grimy back-to-back houses and factories belching smoke. The Priory Park estate, where Duncan lived during his pre-teen and early teenage years, did not get its name by accident. This pleasant, working-class suburb of Dudley is dominated by a large, well-kept park in which Duncan was often to be found playing football. 'Every evening and Sunday morning,' he wrote in his posthumous autobiography *Tackle Soccer This Way*, 'I would be in the park with lads of nineteen or twenty getting used to the hurly-burly of the game and giving, I hoped, as good as I took. For most of these games I would play in my ordinary walking shoes, a fact that caused friction at home. On one occasion my mother bought me a new pair of shoes and, within a couple of hours of putting them on, I arrived home with them invisible beneath great cakes of mud. My popularity was at a low ebb that night.'

Duncan's parents had no idea at all that, at ten, their young son was playing football with teenagers. They did not find out until Mrs Edwards was passing the park one day and heard a cry of 'Go on, Duncan!' from a game involving players who were obviously much older than her son, whom she quickly identified as one of the throng. Understandably concerned, she was reassured by a couple of the older boys, who broke away from the contest to tell her she had no need to worry because the youngster, blessed with the physique of a strapping lad, was more than capable of looking after himself.

One local man who could vouch for that was retired head teacher Geoffrey Groves, who used to watch those football matches in the park. In Iain McCartney's affectionate, impressively detailed biography *Duncan Edwards – The Full Report*, Groves was quoted as saying, 'The young Edwards was never afraid to go in and tackle. He had legs and thighs already like oak trees, and yet was so amazingly light on his feet. He could almost have played blindfolded.' The rest of that quote, taken from Geoff Warburton's biography, is more revealing. 'Admittedly,' added Groves, 'he [Edwards] had a "big mouth" then, as we would say today, but he came from a rough, tough background [shades of Wayne Rooney here] and as far as I can ascertain nobody took exception to his advice, so impressive was his playing. He had quietened down considerably by the time he had reached fourteen, and by the time he was fifteen he showed an amazing maturity far beyond his years.'

Groves also recalled seeing Duncan excel in a primary school fixture. 'He'd got back from hop-picking that morning and gone straight into the school team, dominating the whole match. He told the other 21 players what to do, and the referee and linesmen as well. When I got home, I wrote to a friend and told him I had seen a boy of eleven who would play for England one day.' Prophetic words, indeed.

Duncan, nine and a half pounds at birth and brought up on Ostermilk and rusks, seems to have inherited his height and much of his football skill from his father, Gladstone, but his sturdiness, determination and fearlessness came from his mother. 'His dad was tall, but his mother was strong,' said Marjorie Perry, 81, Sarah Ann's only surviving sibling and one of the few remaining members of the clan who knew the Edwards family at first hand. 'Annie was small but strong. She could fight her own battles,' Marjorie continued in her distinctive Black Country accent. 'She wouldn't let anyone get on to her; she'd get right to the point.'

Betty Cooksey, 75, Duncan's cousin and a former schoolmate of his, also knew the family well. She explained how Gladstone and Annie, the long and the short of it, came to meet and marry. 'Duncan's dad was tall, and my granddad Edwards was ever so tall. So I suppose that's where he got his height from. I said to Aunt Nance [Mrs Edwards] once, "Where did you meet Gladstone?" and she said, "On the town." What they used to do years ago, they used to walk up and down the town in Dudley on a Sunday night, her and her friend. That's what she told me. I wanted to know because he was so tall and she was so small. She was only a bit. Gladstone was a six-footer, but I don't think she was even five feet tall.'

To illustrate just how strong and courageous Duncan's mother was, Marjorie and Betty told the story of how Annie, when in her eighties, took on a couple of burglars who had broken into her ground-floor flat. Apparently, she was watching television with the light off and the intruders thought there was nobody at home. They got in by standing on a bench outside the bedroom window and climbing in through it. When they walked into the living room she did not hesitate to have a go at them. One of them held her arms up in the air, but she broke free eventually, pulled the alarm cord – it was sheltered housing – and forced them to make their escape. 'She was a brave woman,' said Marjorie. 'They took nearly everything she'd got, though.' 'From what she told me,' added Betty, 'they went to open the bureau, but she pleaded with them not to take her lad's stuff; and I don't think they did.' So the intruders must not have lost their last shred of decency. Either that or they realised it would have put them beyond the pale with even the criminal fraternity to steal the memorabilia of a local hero from his elderly, widowed mother.

Duncan's mother and father were tough in other ways, too. Duncan had a younger sister born ten years after him, but his parents had to suffer, and get over, the emotional agony of losing Carol Anne to meningitis at only fourteen weeks.

In his younger days, Gladstone partnered his brother, George, at full-back for a local side in the Cradley Heath League. And football was in the genes on Duncan's mother's side of the family as well: his maternal grandfather had played the game at the same non-league level as his father and Uncle George. Duncan employed his native talent to transform every team in which he appeared. At Priory Road Junior School, for instance, the school side was pretty ordinary until he was introduced to it. All of a sudden, performances improved and success was achieved in local competitions. He was promoted above his age level, too: as in those free-for-alls in the park, his prodigious size and strength enabled him to play with, and hold his own against, older boys. So strong was Duncan at eleven that Roy John, another pupil at Priory Road and a second cousin to Welsh rugby union legend Barry John, marvelled at having seen him kick one of those old heavy leather balls from the penalty spot at one end of a pitch into the goal at the other end with just once bounce.

Gordon Meddings, who was later to teach at Priory Road, got his first, unforgettable sight of Duncan in an inter-school match against St John's, where Meddings was then teaching. 'Duncan was only ten years old at the time,' he recalled, 'but even then it was clearly noticeable that he possessed a talent for the game. I cannot remember what position he was meant to be playing, but he covered every inch of the park and was involved in everything from the taking of goal kicks to throw-ins and corners. He was also on hand to thwart any attacks made by my lads, playing a big part in his team winning 3–0.'

In 1948, shortly before his twelfth birthday, the man-child moved on to Wolverhampton Street Secondary School. This was a surprising choice, since most of his footballing friends preferred to continue their education at the Priory Park Secondary School. The rather startling explanation is that Duncan, believe it or not, wanted to join the very successful Morris and Sword Dancing team run at Wolverhampton Street by Miss Stella Cook, the English teacher. He showed so much natural aptitude as a dancer that he went straight into the senior dance team while still a first-year pupil. According to contemporary reports, Duncan took part in mixed, Playford (whatever that might be) and social dancing, Morris dancing, short and long sword dancing, and square dancing. He also took a leading part in some of the plays used to introduce some sword dances. Duncan was certainly light enough of foot to master all of this, although it must be doubtful whether he cared to talk of his dalliance with the dance when he reached maturity and sampled professional football's unforgiving dressing-room banter.

Nor was tripping the light fantastic his only interest outside football. At a time when Britain was recovering slowly and painfully from the ravages of the Second World War, and rationing was making life dreary, there were few ready-made forms of entertainment other than the cinema. So, like many youngsters of his age, Duncan made his own entertainment by playing cricket as well as football, riding his bike and getting the rods out for his other favourite sport of fishing. Sometimes, Duncan and his friends would ride their bikes as far as Kinver, an area of natural beauty some ten to fifteen miles from Dudley, or catch the train to do some fishing at Bewdley, near Kidderminster. He also joined the local Boy Scout troop, and, at a time when conservation was a concept for the distant future, he occasionally went birds'-nesting.

'He loved the open air,' Duncan's mother told John Roberts, author of *The Team That Wouldn't Die*, a tribute to the Busby Babes. 'He was in the scouts and loved to go camping. And animals! He had pigeons and rabbits and would have turned our place into a farmyard if we'd let him. He had a black and white collie dog, too. If there was a circus anywhere near, he'd want to go to see the animals. He liked pantomime, too. And he used to be good at sketching.'

Although Duncan, 'a natural mover', waltzed straight into the senior dance team at Wolverhampton Street, he had to be content with a place in the junior football team. Impressed by his size, they played him at centre-half and made him captain. As such, he often stood head and shoulders above team-mates and opponents in terms of performance as well as physique. It was not long, then, before his ability came to the notice of the Dudley Schools selection committee. They had no hesitation in picking him, at the age of twelve, for the representative side, even though he would be playing with, and against, boys of fifteen. The committee did baulk, however, at playing him in his usual school position of centre-half. Fearing that even this well-built lad might find the central defensive position, or indeed central midfield, too demanding physically against boys three years older, they picked him at outside-left, where he would be away from the most intense action. Eric Booth, secretary of the Dudley Schools Football Association at the time, explained that the reason behind the decision was to protect Duncan, and 'in case he was overawed'. Little chance of that, one should have thought, going by the boy's previous history. But the very fact that the committee was willing to play him so totally out of position was compelling evidence of his outstanding ability and their eagerness to make use of it.

In the event, Duncan more than justified the committee's confidence in him at a time when Dudley Boys were short of left-footed players. 'He was exactly what one wanted,' Eric Booth recalled, a touch pedantically. 'For example, I told him not to let the defenders, who were generally big, hefty lads, tackle him. Get the ball into the middle – and he did it as if he were 29 years old. Every time we were astounded at his accuracy: he centred the ball or passed to a team-mate on an exact course and height. He soon judged his own and the defenders' capabilities and took them on. He played for his junior school, his secondary school and his town at eleven-plus.'

Because Wolverhampton Street School, with about 220 boys and girls, was so small, there was no young male teacher available to deal with the boys who were keen on football. So it was arranged that, in his last two years at the school, Duncan would go to Northfield Road Secondary Modern for his games period once a week. And it was there that he was taught football by Geoffrey Groves, who was soon to become deputy head. But it was Eric Booth, head of Netherton Church of England Junior School, who was undoubtedly the major influence on Edwards in his formative years. During his lunch breaks, Duncan used to go to see his mentor, who would show him tactical moves on the blackboard. The headmaster also stressed the importance of teamwork to him, pointing out that it was his job to distribute the ball to others. Edwards acknowledged the value of this private coaching in his autobiography. 'He [Booth] taught me the rudiments of the game,' he said, 'and to my eternal delight taught them very well.'

Coincidentally, the boy who partnered him on the left wing in the Dudley Schools side, and who captained the team, was his second cousin, Dennis Stevens, known as 'Nipper'. This was the same Dennis Stevens who went on to win an FA Cup winner's medal with Bolton in 1958, and then to help Everton win the old First Division Championship in 1962/63. At Wembley that May day in 1958, of course, it was the Manchester United team decimated by the Munich air disaster, missing Duncan Edwards and other key players, that Bolton beat in one of the more emotive FA Cup finals. But more of that later.

By the time he was in his second year at Wolverhampton Street, Duncan was so much in demand as a footballer that he hardly had time to catch his breath. In addition to playing for his school and Dudley Boys, he was also turning out for the Worcester County XI, Birmingham and District XI and the England Schools U-14 team. And it was while playing in a Birmingham and District trial match that he experienced his first setback, his tackle on an opponent resulting in a broken leg for the other boy. Gordon Meddings, the teacher who followed Duncan's career closely from school to England level, insisted it was a complete accident and that no blame whatsoever could be attached to the young titan. 'Although well built and not averse to using this to his advantage,' said Meddings, 'Duncan always played the game fairly.' Nevertheless, the incident clearly had a profound effect on Duncan and showed how sensitive he could be. When, the following week, he played for Dudley Schools in Birmingham, the unfortunate lad who had broken his leg was standing on the touchline with the leg in plaster. Meddings felt this reminder of what had happened was responsible for an unusually poor performance by

Edwards. 'I think the incident remained in the back of his mind for some time,' he concluded.

Otherwise, his career went from strength to strength – quite literally. In one match for Dudley Schools against Evesham in the Worcester County Trophy that was played in a very strong wind, Duncan is said to have picked up the ball in his own penalty area, dribbled the length of the pitch with it, and then shot with such force that the ball cannoned off the opposing goalkeeper's legs and went for a goal kick at the other end of the field.

It was Eric Booth, the secretary of the Dudley Schools FA, who thought it might be worth trying to get Duncan into the England U-14 team. Not hoping for much, since the lad was still only twelve, Booth recommended him for a place in a trial match at Oldham. But word must have got around about the young colossus, because the English Schools FA had no hesitation in including him. What is more, they picked him to play at centre-forward, which suggests they had no fears he might be 'overawed' by having to take on a prominent role against older boys. It meant he was being asked to occupy his fourth different position in youth football, having played already at centre-half, left-half and outside-left.

But hold everything – there was a problem. In true Hollywood fashion, the up-and-coming young star was faced with a clash of interests and had to decide between them. On the same day as the England trial, Duncan was due to take part in the National Morris and Sword Dancing Festival at Derby with his school team. He had competed already in the Birmingham and Leamington festivals and was highly regarded by his teachers and team-mates. When it came to a choice between football and sword dancing, though, there was going to be only one winner. And it was not sword dancing that made the cut.

While his schoolmates danced in Derby, Duncan overcame in Oldham. At the end of the trial match, he was selected to make his England U-14 debut against Ireland on 6 May 1949, at the same venue, Oldham FC's Boundary Park. England won the game 5–2, which was not surprising given the abundance of talent in their forward line. To Duncan's left was team captain Ray Parry, later to become a fixture with Bolton and a winner of two full England caps, and David Pegg, another future Busby Babe who played just once for the England seniors before his life, like Duncan's, was cut short so cruelly at Munich in 1958. Those three, at least, justified the rather unwieldy but prophetic headline 'These Boys Are the Stars of Today – Keep an Eye on Them, They Will Be the Stars of Tomorrow' above the pen pictures of the players in the match programme. Of D. Edwards (Dudley), it was written, 'Worcester County Player. Strong and two-footed. Splendid distributor, especially with long cross passes to wing.' Strong and two-footed, they said. So the basic qualities that helped to make Duncan Edwards such a great player were already in place by the time he was twelve years of age.

Naturally right-footed, Duncan worked hard to make himself as adept with his left foot. Encouraged by Eric Booth to become 'left-foot conscious', and aware he was losing time and opportunity by having to transfer the ball from left foot to right, he practised endlessly to correct the weakness. 'For an hour at a stretch I would bang a ball against a rough brick wall [echoes of Wayne Rooney's grandmother's falling pebbledash here] and meet the rebound with whichever foot was suitable,' he revealed in later years. 'Then I would try bouncing the ball from one instep to the other, so that the left began to get the feel of the ball as naturally as did the right.

'The natural testing ground for my left foot was the park in the evening games among the local lads. There it was of little importance if I made an error. I could slice a left-foot clearance far behind my own goal without feeling as if the end of the earth had come. I started using my left when I was in the clear with the ball and unharried by the other side. As it strengthened, so I began to use it when I was in difficulties, and eventually I would try to go through the whole of these games [and remember, they would go on from tea until it was too dark to see the ball] using my left foot. My reward now is a left foot that I can rely upon. In shooting, it packs as much power as my right, even if the direction is not quite so finely controlled.'

The appealing thing about Duncan Edwards is that he allowed none of his success as a schoolboy footballer to go to his head. 'He was quiet in class and got on with his job with no "star" tantrums,' reported his English teacher Stella Cook. 'He never bragged about football. If we wanted to know where he was playing next, one had to ask him and got the bare bones for an answer as if it was almost a casual happening. He became shyer as he became well known. One day, he came into school and said – and he had a strong voice – "You don't want to believe what you read in the papers." Why? It was reported that he had said he had "butterflies" in his stomach before a match, and he had said nothing of the sort. He was cross about them printing "lies". If he had butterflies he kept them to himself, and he wouldn't have known the expression anyway ... Duncan came from a good home. His father Gladstone kept an eye on the lad's future and both parents saw to it that he, to use the phrase then in common usage, "behaved himself".'

The summer after his England debut as a schoolboy, Edwards' dedication took him a step nearer his destiny, though he did not know it at the time. In August 1950, he and other members of the England U-14 and U-15 teams provided the players for an FA coaching course in Blackpool attended by the trainer/manager of Dudley Boys, Gordon Meddings, and other schoolteachers intent on improving their knowledge of the game and gaining an FA preliminary coaching award. The boys were housed in a hotel on the South Shore owned by Stanley Matthews, later to be a team-mate of Edwards' in the full England side, unlikely as that must have seemed at the time given that Matthews had been capped before Duncan was born. More predictable was the attraction of Blackpool's famous Pleasure Beach. There, they would head straight for the 'Shooting at the Goalkeeper' stall and drive the owner mad by scoring all the time. In the end, he took the line of least resistance and allowed them free shots to attract other customers.

One of the instructors on the teachers' coaching course was Joe Mercer, then the England wing-half who had just captained Arsenal to victory over Liverpool in the FA Cup final. Although Mercer was there principally to help the teachers become better coaches, he could not help but notice how talented Duncan Edwards was. In a long

conversation with Meddings, Mercer singled out Duncan for special praise and predicted a big future for the youngster – a future in
which Mercer himself was to play an important part.

From that point onwards, Edwards' career as a footballer made
accelerating progress towards bigger and better things. The following year he was promoted to the England U-15 team, the first boy
from Dudley to make it that far and one of only five survivors from
the lower age level. He was accompanied by the left-wing partnership of Ray Parry and David Pegg, inside-right Alec Farrall, who was
to join Everton, and the goalkeeper, one A. J. Silver of Maidenhead.
This time, though, Duncan was given the number 6 jersey and was
selected to play in the left-half position where he later made his
name.

Already well built, he was growing fast. The match programme for
his first game, against Wales at Wembley on 7 April 1951, revealed
that, at fourteen years and six months, he stood five feet eight inches
tall and weighed ten stone twelve (68.9kgs). The game itself was
the fulfilment of a wish he had made seven years earlier. Edwards
revealed as much in a school essay entitled 'A True Wish' written on
10 December 1951, reproduced here as he penned it:

Well it all began when I was a little boy of about seven years of
age. I had heard my father talking about a place by the name
of Wembly Stadium. It was a wet day in april and my Uncle
Gorge and dad were sitting round the fire where my Uncle
Gorge said to my father, 'I see England are playing Scotland
at Wembly next saterday.' 'Are they,' my father replied. I
thought to myself now's my chance to ask them where this
Wembly Stadium is while there on the subject. So I turned
to my uncle and asked him where this Stadium was, and he
replied, 'Duncan, this Stadium as you call it is the third biggest football Stadium in the world and situated in London.'
I told my uncle I wish I could go there and he said I would
before long. I was thirteen and I still wanted to go to Wembly,
and on 7th of april I was picked to play for england against

wales (at Wembly Stadium). My uncle was right when he said I would some day go to Wembly Stadium.

By the 1951/52 season Duncan was captain of the England U-15s and led them against Scotland twice, Wales and Eire (the Republic of Ireland). In each game, too, he was usually the outstanding player on the pitch. So much so that he was beginning to excite interest from leading professional clubs all over the country. But Edwards' father had been warned early about how to deal with the scouts. 'For heaven's sake, don't let Duncan sign anything no matter what rewards are being offered,' Gladstone Edwards was told by Eric Booth. 'He'll be better still in the future, and he'll render himself ineligible to play for the English Schools FA under the amateur rules if he is attached to a professional club.'

Wayne Rooney reached that point much more quickly than Duncan Edwards. He did so because the regulations governing the age at which schoolboys could be approached by professional clubs have changed out of all recognition in the 50 years between the two boy wonders. In Duncan's day, clubs could not sign a schoolboy until he was fifteen, and if he was playing for his country, his international season was over. Now, boys as young as nine are being recruited for the youth academies on which most of the Premier League clubs, and some in the Football League, have lavished millions of pounds in a bid to save themselves similar amounts in the transfer market.

This is the consequence of an overwhelming victory for professional football and the Football Association in a long and bitter battle with the English Schools FA for earlier access to, and control of, the nation's schoolboy footballers. For years, the ESFA stubbornly refused to release their grip on the situation. Imbued, consciously or unconsciously, with the public-school ideals of amateurism that launched English football in the first place, they felt they had a duty of care to protect boys from the depredations of professionalism until they reached school-leaving age. Almost certainly, and a lot less nobly, the teachers in charge of the ESFA also rather relished the power they had to select the various England schoolboy teams, and the perks that went with it. The professional clubs, on the other hand, claimed that the age of fifteen was too late in a boy's development to start coaching him. By then, they argued, he had probably developed bad habits in his play that could have been averted had they only been able to subject him to their coaching earlier. This was a little unfair to the schoolteachers because, as we have seen in the case of Wolverhampton Street's Gordon Meddings, many of them had made a serious effort to learn the secrets of football coaching. However, from my own experience – and I was born only two years after Duncan Edwards – I have to say I did not encounter any proper coaching from the teachers in charge while playing for any of the school teams at a Liverpool grammar school. They picked the teams, but we just made it up as we went along.

Just look at the continentals, the professionals added in support of their argument; they don't let the schools dictate at what age clubs can begin coaching youngsters. In Holland, certainly, there is no tradition of school football. Boys wanting to play football make straight for their local professional club after school as soon as they are old enough to kick a ball properly. So, when the Ajax Amsterdam and Dutch national side of Johan Cruyff and Johan Neeskens began to dazzle the world with their Total Football in the 1970s, it was seen as proof positive that their system for bringing on young players was the one every other country should copy.

England began to follow suit in 1984, when the Football Association opened their National School at Lilleshall, in Shropshire, and encouraged the 92 Football League clubs to set up their own 'centres of excellence'. The latter were intended to cater for the most promising young footballers in the locality, while the National School was reserved, each year, for the *crème de la crème*, the players considered to be the sixteen outstanding fourteen-year-olds from all over the country.

Then, in 1998, came the revolution. The ESFA caved in on the age limit, those clubs who could afford it were licensed by the FA to replace their centres of excellence with plush youth academies, the FA closed down the National School as redundant a year later, and the hunt for gifted nine-year-olds was on. Thus Wayne Rooney was some six years younger than Duncan Edwards when he first made contact with professional football.

Although Rooney's journey towards their shared nirvana was much shorter than Edwards', his starting point was much the same. That is to say, a council house on a suburban estate. Wayne comes from Croxteth, a district about seven miles from Liverpool city centre jammed into the right angle between the East Lancashire Road (A580) and the M57 on the north-eastern outskirts of the city. Until the mid-1970s, it was mostly a vast private estate owned by the Earls of Sefton. But then the last earl died and the estate was taken over by Liverpool City Council. They have turned it, with the ancestral home, Croxteth Hall, as the centre-piece, into one of the north-west's major heritage centres and tourist attractions. But they also used some of the land to extend a council estate begun in 1928 and intended initially, like nearby Kirkby, to rehouse families rendered homeless by slum clearance programmes in and around the city centre. Thus Croxteth did not start out with the best of reputations, and over the years it has steadily worsened. Vandalism and crime are not unknown in the area, to put it mildly, with the result that parts of it exude a discouraging air of dereliction and menace.

Croxteth is not all like that, by any means. The nearby heritage centre provides a rural backdrop and some of the more modern housing is of quite high quality. On the whole, though, it is one of those hard, unforgiving places where you have to learn to look after yourself, the niceties of social behaviour are not always observed, and bad language is second nature. All of which ought to be taken into consideration by Rooney's critics when they accuse him now of being a poor role model for the young. It is true that many footballers have endured starts in life just as difficult as his, yet have gone on to become veritable paragons. But at the time of writing Wayne had only just celebrated his twentieth birthday. He is a work in progress.

Obviously of the Irish immigrant stock that has enriched Liverpool's cultural life and reputation over the centuries (think Paul McCartney and John Lennon for a start), the Rooney family comprises father

Wayne senior, a former labourer and amateur boxer, mother Jeanette, a school dinner lady, Wayne junior and younger brothers Graham and John. They are defined by their Catholicism, as much as anything else. Wayne, for instance, began his education at Our Lady and St Swithin's Primary School and continued it at De La Salle Catholic High School, whose other alumni include former Everton players Francis Jeffers and Mick Lyons and the current Wigan manager, Paul Jewell.

At both establishments Wayne was regarded as not particularly bright but well behaved and immensely popular with the other boys. This popularity stemmed largely, of course, from his exceptional ability as a footballer. In their lively biography *Wayne Rooney – The Story of Football's Wonder Kid*, Harry Harris and Danny Fullbrook quote Tony McCaul, Wayne's headmaster at St Swithin's, as saying, 'Wayne was always a special boy who absolutely loved his football. It was obvious from a young age he was going to become a player. Wayne was head and shoulders above the other boys in the playground and would have been out there all the time if he could have been.'

Whether McCaul meant that Rooney was head and shoulders above the other boys in terms of physical stature or talent is not clear. It is well documented, however, that precocious physical development helped Wayne, like Duncan Edwards, to play football with, and hold his own against, much older boys. His mother recalled that he played his first proper game when he was only seven. It was for a local pub's U-11 or U-12 team, and he came on as a substitute and scored – of course. Other witnesses attest to the boy's unusually large size for his age, one of them with typical Scouse black humour. Joe Henningham, Wayne's PE teacher at De La Salle, was quoted by Harris and Fullbrook as saying, 'The thing you noticed about Wayne was his size. He was the biggest lad in his class. I've always said you've got to be strong to get a muffin in the dinner queue at De La Salle.'

With his bull neck, Desperate Dan chin and powerful, squat body, Rooney is built more like a boxer than a footballer. So, given his father's background in the ring and the fact that brother Graham became a north-west schoolboy boxing champion, it is no surprise to learn that he tried his hand at pugilism himself. He appears to have been pretty good at it, too. Cousin Thomas Rooney, who sparred with him, said he 'hit like a heavyweight' and reckoned he could have made the grade as a boxer. Graham, incidentally, was also good enough at football to be on Everton's books with Wayne and their other sibling, John.

Another similarity between Wayne Rooney and Duncan Edwards is the strong personalities of their mothers. Just as Annie Edwards did not think twice about taking on a couple of burglars, Jeanette Rooney went straight down to the training ground when she heard that Everton had thrown out John, her youngest son, for being overweight. Arguing that he had the potential to be every bit as good as Wayne, she got John back in the squad with the veiled threat that Wayne would not be best pleased to hear his brother had been dumped by the club.

Jeanette, who terrified everyone at Everton, was also regarded as formidable at De La Salle, where she was known as a very strict lunchtime supervisor. But friends of the family insist that she is not a pushy mum, just a strong character who believes in her three sons and wants the best for them. She also understands football and knows if somebody is playing well or badly. But, unlike some parents, she always went out of her way to praise her son, not to criticise him. 'She was a very strong woman, a lot like Wayne in many ways,' observed Peter McIntosh, Rooney's first agent. 'She was a very silent, independent type who just got on with life.'

The welfare of her family is clearly of paramount importance to Jeanette Rooney, a lady not afraid of responsibility or self-sacrifice. When her husband was out of work, she took on another job in the evening to make ends meet. Actually, not just to meet, but to overlap, because McIntosh recalled that Wayne never lacked for anything, be it trainers or money for going out. Both parents, he added, went without so that their sons could have a better chance in life.

A BMX bike, certainly, is not cheap, and one of them seems to have been Wayne's constant companion as he grew up in Croxteth with his mates. Trying out stunts on the bike, playing table tennis and listening to pop music (the Stereophonics and Jennifer Lopez are said to have been among his favourite artistes, although subsequent events appear to indicate that controversial American rapper 50 Cent has shouldered all opposition aside) filled in the little spare time not devoted to football. Kickabouts in the local park, or just about anywhere, remained the staple of his young life. Cousin Thomas Rooney remembered that the first thing he and Wayne would do when they went on holiday to a caravan park in Wales was find a gang of other boys and arrange a game of football. Indeed, recognising that their new client was that rarity, a modern boy who had learnt to play in the old-fashioned way, Proactive, his current agents, shrewdly began marketing him as 'Wayne Rooney – Street Striker'.

Agents ... marketing ... we get ahead of ourselves with words that would have sounded like a foreign language to Duncan Edwards back in the 1950s. They are among the changes to be discussed in due course. For the moment, let us just concern ourselves with those seminal moments in the history of English football when Duncan and Wayne achieved their hearts' desire. When, in other words, Edwards signed for Manchester United and Rooney was asked to join Everton.

CHAPTER 2

DISCOVERY

OF THE two 'boy wonders' of this book, only Wayne Rooney could truly be said to have been 'discovered', and then only because he was so young when it happened. Most of the leading professional clubs in the land were well aware of Duncan Edwards' awesome potential long before he joined Manchester United. Two factors saw to that: his own eye-catching performances for the England schoolboy teams, and the rules preventing clubs from signing boys until they were fifteen. The scouts might have salivated on the touchlines, but there was nothing conclusive they could do about it until Duncan came of age.

He was not fifteen until 1 October 1951, and nobody could persuade him to put pen to paper until 1 June 1952, when his international season with England would be over. Bolton Wanderers, then famous for having the newly anointed 'Lion of Vienna', Nat Lofthouse, at centre-forward, made all the early running. Frank Pickford, their chief scout, and George Taylor, the chief coach, had watched Duncan on numerous occasions, and they decided to make contact after seeing him play in a trial match at Dudley Port. But they missed him at the end of the game and had to get police directions to his home.

At 31 Elm Road, and at a nearby pub, they chatted up Duncan's parents so persuasively that an invitation for the boy to visit Burnden Park, Bolton's old ground, was accepted. There were obvious attractions here for Duncan because his second cousin, Dennis Stevens, and England Schoolboys team-mate Ray Parry had already joined the Lancashire club. Parry even accompanied Duncan back down to Dudley when Frank Pickford drove him home from Bolton, but all to no avail. Although his family very much wanted him to join one of the local clubs – Wolverhampton Wanderers, Aston Villa,

West Bromwich Albion or Birmingham City – Duncan had made up his mind that there was only one destination for him: Manchester United.

Edwards' single-mindedness on this issue is all the more remarkable in view of the fact that he was a Wolves fan as a boy and trained at Molineux at a time when manager Stan Cullis was developing a youth policy to rival United's. Don Howe remembers it well. Howe, who went on to have a distinguished career as a full-back with West Bromwich Albion, Arsenal and England and as a coach with Arsenal and England, said, 'I was just a year or two older than Duncan, but I knew him quite well because he lived in Dudley and I lived in Sedgley, which is on the edge of Wolverhampton and quite near Dudley. He went to school in Dudley and I went to school in Wolverhampton, but we all knew about Duncan because he was training at Molineux once a week. The Wolves, in those days, used to have these schoolboy sessions, and when I went to my session on a Wednesday afternoon we went round the pitch. That was for the Wolverhampton Schoolboys team, which I played in for two years. But I'm almost certain the Wolves were trying to get Duncan to sign for them as a schoolboy or an apprentice, or whatever they used to call them in those days. Groundstaff boys, I think they used to call us.

'I don't know why we both didn't go to the Wolves. West Brom came for me and the scout asked if I'd go across and see the manager at The Hawthorns. I don't know why Duncan didn't go to Molineux; I suppose Man United went in and courted his family and got him to join them. He was going to the Wolves: that's what we all thought in the Midlands. Then, all of a sudden, it was United. Obviously, United convinced him, did a super job on him, to go there. We lost touch then. The next time I saw him in terms of saying "How are you doing?" was with England!'

It is not difficult to see why Duncan might have preferred United. The first of the three great teams built by Matt Busby had won the FA Cup in 1948 and finished as First Division runners-up four times before finally winning the old league championship in 1951/52. They were the team of the moment, and they played the game stylishly enough to capture the imagination of a boy as talented and ambitious as Duncan Edwards. Not only that, but Wolves' great days – the three league titles of the 1950s and their thrilling floodlit victories over Spartak Moscow and Honved – still lay ahead.

Even so, there was more disappointment at Molineux over Edwards' preference for Manchester United than there was at Bolton. 'Of course questions were asked at Wolves as to why on earth we did not have him,' said Bill Slater, the experienced player who filled the left-half position in the Wanderers team and eventually took over from Duncan in the England side. 'Manchester United's scouting scheme was very good, but so was Wolves', and I think there was some disappointment in the area that he was lost to the Midlands, as it were. Then, as now, United had a very strong pull on ambitious young players, but Wolves competed quite strongly with them in the fifties. I think they won the league three times and we won it three times in a ten-year spell when either one or the other of the teams was challenging for or winning the championship. I suppose Manchester United was attractive for him, but we felt at the Wolves that we had something to offer him, too.'

The attraction United must have had for Duncan, and other youngsters at the time, was captured vividly by Gordon Clayton, a goalkeeper from Cannock who played for Birmingham Boys with Duncan and was signed by United at the same time as him. 'This was it – Manchester United, the 1948 Cup final, [Johnny] Carey, [Stan] Pearson, [Jack] Rowley ... there was something different about them, something vital and exciting,' Clayton told Eamon Dunphy in the former United player's gloriously passionate homage to manager and club *A Strange Kind of Glory – Sir Matt Busby & Manchester United*. 'Of course they'd just won the league, but it was the people, the idea of Matt Busby, who was a god.'

But where were United now that the youngster had played his final match for England Schoolboys, against Eire in Dublin on 31 May 1952? Busby's backroom staff – assistant manager Jimmy Murphy, coach Bert Whalley and chief scout Joe Armstrong – had all watched Duncan play and were unanimous in their view that United should sign him. They did not at first because, initially, Busby was more interested in another member of the England Schools team, inside-right Alec Farrall. That was partly because Farrall was seven months older than Edwards and therefore more immediately available. Or so Busby thought.

The United manager changed tack following a conversation with his old friend Joe Mercer. Mercer, who came from Merseyside and began his long and distinguished career with Everton, made it clear to Busby that the Wirral-born Farrall had eyes for only the Goodison Park club. Mercer was aware of this partly because he had got to know the England Schools players while conducting that FA coaching course for schoolteachers at Blackpool in the summer of 1950. Duncan was among them, remember, and Mercer suggested the outstandingly talented boy from Dudley would be a more than acceptable alternative to Farrall.

The crucial role played by Mercer in the signing of Duncan Edwards was confirmed by Busby in his 1973 autobiography *Soccer at the Top – My Life in Football*. 'Sometimes we got news from surprising sources,' he said while talking about his and Jimmy Murphy's methods for finding talented youngsters. 'Joe Mercer, the Everton, Arsenal and England wing-half and later Sheffield United, Aston Villa, Manchester City and Coventry City manager, was still playing when he was asked to coach the England schoolboy team. When we were chatting one day Joe said that among the many promising boys one was outstanding. This was a boy called Duncan Edwards. Joe had heard Duncan say in the dressing room that he wanted to go to Manchester United. So when people ask me how we came to sign Duncan Edwards, one of the greatest all-round players in history, when the boy came from Dudley, in Worcestershire, the answer is, he wanted to come.'

Nonetheless, United had to monitor the situation carefully. Their Midlands scout, Reg Priest, had kept the club informed about the attempts of any rivals to sign Duncan. So when Priest got wind of a final effort by Bolton to snatch the boy from under everyone's noses, he rang Old Trafford and urged United to make their move before it was too late. They responded by despatching Bert Whalley immediately by car. But his vehicle broke down before he got anywhere near the Midlands, and he had to hitch-hike his way back to Manchester. No sooner had the weary Whalley returned than he was met by an anxious Jimmy Murphy and told they were both to drive down to Dudley that same night in a hire car. Fearing they might already have missed their chance, Murphy and Whalley were relieved to find no rival clubs in attendance when they arrived at Elm Road in darkness. It was the early hours of the following morning by now, but the United pair felt they had no alternative but to knock on the Edwards' door loudly enough to wake the family, though not the neighbourhood.

Gladstone Edwards answered the knock sleepily in his pyjamas, but the household was soon wide awake when the late-night visitors identified themselves. Duncan was brought downstairs, rubbing the sleep from his eyes, and signed as an amateur for Manchester United minutes later at two a.m. on 2 June 1952. He could not understand what all the fuss was about because, according to the most reliable account, he had told Matt Busby already that United was the only club he wanted to join.

I say 'most reliable account' because there are conflicting versions of the signing. One claimed that Busby himself made that dash through the night to Dudley; but Jimmy Murphy did not mention the manager in his account of the signing when he published his autobiography, *Matt, United and Me*, in 1968. The most puzzling version of all, though, came in Duncan's own book, *Tackle Soccer This Way*. It read as follows:

> Came the day of my sixteenth birthday I retired to bed after the usual round of celebrations and over eating. At two o'clock in the morning the family was awakened by a knock at the door. I heard my father go downstairs but I was too tired to take much notice. I turned over and tried to go to sleep again. A few minutes later my bedroom door opened and my father said, 'Slip something on and come downstairs. There's somebody to see you.'

Still half dazed, I made my way into the light of the sitting room to come face to face for the first time with Matt Busby, the manager of Manchester United. He had known better than I about the interest other clubs had taken in me, and he wanted to be the first to talk to my parents. So he had driven through the night from Manchester.

For a long time my father and Mr Busby discussed my chances of making good in the game. They discussed such things as pay and benefits and a second career in case I failed as a footballer. They satisfied each other on such points, and then my father turned to me and said, 'It's up to you, Duncan. Do you want to join United?' Of course I said, 'Yes.' There was never any real question that I wouldn't.

This version of events is so wide of the mark factually as to be almost comical. For a start, if Edwards had signed for United on his sixteenth birthday it would have been 1 October 1952, not 2 June. The June date is not at issue because a piece in the *Manchester Evening Chronicle* of 4 June confirms that Duncan Edwards was among United's recent schoolboy signings. What is more, there is plenty of evidence that he arrived in Manchester on 9 June and was playing for United as an amateur at the start of the 1952/53 season.

Not only that, but it's extremely unlikely that this signing scenario was the first time Duncan met the then unknighted Matt Busby. According to Eamon Dunphy in *A Strange Kind of Glory*, the boy from Dudley and his parents had accepted United's invitation to visit Old Trafford long before it came to signing for them. Dunphy also quoted goalkeeper Gordon Clayton as saying that Duncan had urged him to follow suit after going up to Manchester with his mum and dad and being treated well. So Edwards' ghost-writer appears to have got hold of the wrong end of the stick entirely.

There is even some doubt as to whether Murphy, never mind Busby, accompanied Whalley on that fateful nocturnal drive from Manchester to Dudley. The phrasing of a signed piece the assistant manager did for the *People* in 1968 suggested that Whalley had made the trip on his own. 'Perseverance brought him [Edwards] to United,' said Murphy. 'The perseverance of my old chum Bert Whalley who, when his car broke down, returned to our ground and then set off again through the night to get Duncan out of bed. The big fellow came down the stairs in his pyjamas to sign the forms that made him a Manchester United player. "What's all the fuss about?" he asked, still brushing the sleep out of his eyes. "I have said all along Manchester United is the only club I want to join."'

Wayne Rooney's 'discovery' in the autumn of 1994 was far more serendipitous. Everton scout Bob Pendleton was acting mainly in his capacity as registrations and fixtures secretary of the Walton & Kirkdale Junior Football League when he went to the Long Lane playing fields in suburban Liverpool to collect an unpaid fee. There, Pendleton got talking to the manager of one of the teams, a man he knows to this day only by the name of Big Neville. Big Neville was in charge of Copplehouse Juniors, a pub team, and playing for them was a boy who immediately caught Pendleton's eye.

'He was only eight, going on nine, but he was playing in an eleven-a-side game on a big pitch against lads of eleven or twelve, and he was playing so very, very well,' recalled the scout. 'Everything about the boy was that little bit special. When he gave the ball to a teammate, he expected it back. When he didn't get it back – frustration. But when he did get it, he didn't waste it. My heart jumped when I saw him. You know when you've got someone, like, and I know it may sound soft, but you looked at him and he was enjoying it. You know what I mean? It didn't matter what was going on around him; he was enjoying it and making sure he got the ball back – and from much older boys, remember. He loved scoring goals, too.'

Although Big Neville protested that he had only just signed the lad, he did take Pendleton to meet the boy's parents, who were watching the game on the other side of the pitch. They readily agreed to accompany their son to Bellefield, the Everton training ground, where Pendleton persuaded academy manager Ray Hall to enrol him. Hall did not take much persuading, it seems. 'I did not need his scoring record as proof, or even one training session,' he was quoted as saying in the biography of Rooney by Harry Harris and Danny Fullbrook. 'You get an experienced scout sitting there with his tea cup quivering while you're talking to the lad and you know he's special.'

Talking to Hall subsequently, another anecdote emerged. 'When Bob came in with Wayne, I can picture it as if it were yesterday. I have an office at Bellefield and Joe Royle was manager at the time. Wayne came in with his father and sat opposite me. If I'm right, he was eight years of age and we couldn't actually sign him until his ninth birthday, which was about a week away. But we made arrangements to do that, and the beam on his face was unbelievable. Just at that moment, Joe passed by and I asked him to come in and meet the new boy who was about to sign for us. I told him we had heard a lot about Wayne and were excited we were signing him. So Joe said to Wayne, "Smashing, son. Where are you from?" "Croxteth," Wayne replied; but because his diction at that time wasn't too immaculate, Joe thought he had said Toxteth. "Well, you'll be all right if you finish up as good as Fowler!" said Joe, referring to Robbie Fowler, who comes from Toxteth, of course.'

Scouting itself has had to change over the past half century. The essential requirement of being able to spot a player remains the same, but it has been made more difficult by the lowering of the age at which clubs can sign boys (which is now nine), the introduction of academies and the insistence of the Football Association on smaller-sided games for pre-teens. 'It is scary,' confessed Bob Pendleton of the business of trying to decide whether some little mite who is dribbling rings round everyone will grow up to have a real chance of making it as a professional footballer. 'I've got a little lad in there now. He's only seven and an advanced kid for his age – you should see him pull a ball down. We were having a laugh about it the other day. I said, "I'm not being funny, but if he plays in the first team at seventeen I'll be friggin' 76!" I'll be honest with you, though, there's a few boys come in here at seven all of similar talent.'

At the time of this interview in 2005, Pendleton had been scouting for Everton for sixteen years. Everything about him is unusual, everything from his background (he is a former train driver who never played football of any consequence) to the fact that he took over from a chap with the wonderful Dickensian name of Tommy Fairfoul ('a rough lad, but a smashing fellow'). Pendleton became Everton's scout in the Aintree area of Liverpool when Fairfoul fell foul of the grim reaper. At first, Pendleton was reluctant to accept the invitation to succeed Fairfoul because he had become involved with one of the youth leagues. But, persuaded to give it a try, he came to realise he was in an ideal position to spot promising youngsters. As fixtures and registrations secretary of the Walton & Kirkdale League, certainly, he had access to more than 2,000 young footballers. Better still, managers of the teams and referees of the matches would tip him off about any outstanding performers.

Even so, he said, the job is a lot harder now than it was sixteen years ago, when fourteen was the earliest age at which youngsters could be signed by professional clubs, and only on schoolboy forms. 'The beauty of it then was that boys had played in the local leagues and been hurt at times. What I mean by that is they'd been beaten in semi-finals and finals. But you take a boy into the academy now at the age of eight, say, and if he goes right through he doesn't experience the sort of disappointment you get from losing a semi-final or final.

'When I started, the boys you were looking for were twelve or thirteen and had been playing for a couple of years in eleven-a-side league football on big pitches. That made it a bit easier to spot certain talent. I know they've introduced small-sided games to make sure the boys get more touches of the ball – in an eleven-a-side you might get a left-winger who only sees the ball four or five times in the whole game – but with small pitches and small goals you don't always get the best out of young players, you know. It's seven-a-side now for the young ones and, as a scout, you can't always watch everything you want to watch in the small-sided game.'

What has not changed about football scouts in 50 years is the sheer thrill they get from unearthing a little diamond. It is not a well-paid occupation: most of them out in the field are part-timers who do it just for expenses and the bonus they get for finding a youngster their club decides to sign. Discovering Wayne Rooney certainly did not change Bob Pendleton's life financially. 'Once the boys sign you get a reward,' said Pendleton, who also found right-back Tony Hibbert for Everton, 'but you're never going to retire on it, as the saying goes. It's something I enjoy, though. As I say to the parents of the boys I take to Everton, my job now is to go out and find someone better than your son. I don't mean that in a bad way; it's just the nature of the job. And if I could find another Wayne Rooney, I'd be over the moon. It's nice to be related to Wayne in this way, and I enjoy all the interviews about it, but I don't think it's going to happen again in my lifetime. I'm an Evertonian, and I hope that one or two come through the academy; but I can't see anybody at the moment. I mean, Rooney was a Rooney, wasn't he? Like a Bestie or a Gazza. But you never know.'

As with Duncan Edwards and Manchester United, there was only ever going to be one club that Wayne Rooney would join initially. His family were all staunch Evertonians and his bedroom in Croxteth was a shrine to the club. In fact, the whole house was painted blue, metaphorically speaking. Wayne's father bought him an Everton shirt on the day he was born, 24 October 1985, and a piece of the Goodison Park turf is a prized family possession. So is a framed photograph of Wayne, aged eleven, standing alongside the then Everton captain, Dave Watson, and his Liverpool counterpart, John Barnes, in the centre circle at Anfield. That day in November 1996, only ten years ago, the boy wonder-to-be was the Blues' mascot for a Merseyside derby that ended in a 1–1 draw. The speed of his development since then is difficult to comprehend.

Liverpool would very much have liked it to take place under their protective wing, but there was never any chance that Rooney would copy the likes of Michael Owen, Robbie Fowler and Steve McManaman, all of whom joined Liverpool despite having supported Everton as boys. When he was nine, Rooney reluctantly agreed to go for a trial for the Reds, but insisted on wearing his blue Everton shirt under the strip that was provided. As he later told the *Evertonian* magazine, 'I actually had a trial for them. I was playing for Copplehouse U-9s at the time and after the game I was approached by a Liverpool scout who invited me to Melwood [their training ground]. I went along, but after going there just once I got the phone call from Bob Pendleton. It was the call I had desperately wanted, and that was it for me. I gave Liverpool a "swerve" after that. As a young lad wanting to be a professional footballer, I had to go to Liverpool when I was asked because there was no other club interested in me then. But as soon as Everton came in there was never a single doubt in my mind.'

Once signed by the club at nine, Wayne was soon barred from playing in the local leagues where he had been discovered. His response was to score 99 goals in one season for the academy's U-10s. Allowed to go on playing in schools football for a time, he did so to great effect. His form for De La Salle was so impressive that it was not long before he was chosen to play for the representative side, Liverpool Schoolboys, who have produced so many outstanding players for the city's two clubs, and others, down the years.

Everton's academy manager Ray Hall has a memory of that point in Rooney's development which lives with him still. 'Wayne was playing for our U-9s, and I think it was the first season we had small-sided games. It was an eight-a-side game with smaller goals, because these were only small kids that were playing. We were playing at Manchester United's training ground, Frickleton Road, and all the parents were on one side of the field.

'It was glorious weather, the sun was shining, and the game started. The coaches and the substitutes were on the other side of the field, and I was watching with them. All of a sudden, a cross goes in that actually went behind Wayne. But he shifted his body, and did an overhead kick – a bicycle kick – from about ten yards out, which is a long distance for a nine-year-old. Even so, the ball flew into the top corner.

'There was silence, an absolute silence, but suddenly somebody – I don't know who it was – started clapping. And – I swear this is true – before anything else happened, everybody on the far side of the field was clapping, Manchester United families included. I've never seen anything like it before, and I've never seen it since. It just stopped the game. At that point, one of the coaches looked at me in astonishment and went, "Who the fucking hell is he?" That's when we began to realise we had something special.'

Needless to say, Rooney took the step up in class to representative football in his confident stride. In the 1996/97 season, he broke the individual scoring record for Liverpool Schools U-11s with 72 goals out of a team total of 158. The record had been held since the late 1970s by Steve Redmond, who went on to become a fixture in the Manchester City defence, oddly enough, and to win fourteen England U-21 caps. That same season, Wayne also won his first European trophy with Liverpool Schools in an international tournament in Holland.

At twelve, Rooney had a growth spurt and began to develop the sturdy physique that was to serve him so well in adulthood. Initially, however, this rapid physical development and the onset of adolescence threw his burgeoning football career off course. Fast-tracked through the Everton academy to such an extent that he played for the club's U-15 side while still only thirteen, he suddenly found it more difficult to apply the balance and skill that had made him such a formidable prospect. 'He's always played above his age group,' explained Ray Hall, 'and when he was twelve or thirteen he was a little bit heavy. People who saw him then wondered what all the fuss was about. But they forgot he was actually playing two or three years out of his age. He had a year or so where he was growing and developing physically and you wouldn't have thought he was going to be the player he is now. His progress didn't go in a straight line; it went up and down. But something happened around his fifteenth year, when he suddenly became so much better than anybody else.'

By the time he reached fifteen, then, Wayne and his body were well and truly back on track. So much so that he was promoted first to the academy's U-17 side, then to the U-19s. The following season, 2001/02, promised silverware but brought a disappointing end to his career as a youth team player with Everton. Not that Wayne himself could be blamed.

Outstanding in just about every round, Rooney was the Toffees' inspiration as they beat West Ham United, West Bromwich Albion,

Manchester City, Nottingham Forest and Tottenham Hotspur on their way to the final of the FA Youth Cup. He scored twice against West Brom, City and Spurs, his double in the second leg of the semi-final at White Hart Lane so sensational that Glenn Hoddle, then manager of the London club, hurried from his seat in the stand to tell Colin Harvey, Everton's youth coach, that Wayne Rooney was the best player he had ever seen at youth level. Hoddle is also said to have gone through the understandable, but futile, motions of asking whether he had any chance of buying the boy wonder.

Ray Hall remembers being so carried away by Rooney's performance in that semi-final second leg that he ignored directors' box etiquette. 'People talk about his goals now,' he said, 'but you should have seen those two at White Hart Lane that day. It was ten minutes into the game and we got a free-kick about 25 or 30 yards out. Wayne wasn't supposed to take the kick, but he pulled the ball off the young lad who was, put it down, ran up and smashed it into Spurs' defensive wall. The lad it hit was pole-axed and the ball rebounded back to Wayne. So he controlled it on his knee and smashed it into the top corner. And I swear that their goalkeeper was only just starting to move as the ball came back out from the net. And, you know, I jumped up, forgetting you don't do that in the directors' box. Glenn Hoddle and David Pleat were in the same row, but on the Tottenham side, and David Pleat looked at me and said, "No, you go ahead, son. If we had a player like that, I'd jump out of the stand!"

'Fifteen minutes later, he did it again but in a different way. He split two defenders with a back-heel, then, as the goalkeeper came out, he just dinked the ball over him. And this is a boy of sixteen. I wouldn't for one minute suggest that Wayne was a one-man team, because we had a very good goalkeeper and were competent elsewhere; but he was as capable then, as he is now, of winning games out of nothing. I think we were offered a massive amount of money by Tottenham that night to try and sign him.'

The final of the FA Youth Cup was against Aston Villa. By now, word had got round Merseyside that Everton had discovered an exceptional young player; but Rooney, in that typically self-deprecating way of his, tried to restrain the rising tide of expectation among the club's supporters. 'One player cannot win the games on his own,' Wayne was quoted as saying before the first leg at Goodison Park, 'and without the efforts of everyone involved we wouldn't have achieved what we have done so far. It's the biggest game I will have played in. I think we deserved to get there and hopefully we can get the result everyone wants. It's going to be a tough game, but if we can get a lead at Goodison and take that to Villa Park we are capable of winning it.'

The 15,000 fans who turned up to catch a first glimpse of the boy wonder were rewarded with a goal by him, the first of the final, after 25 minutes. So delighted was he that he pulled off his jersey to reveal a T-shirt bearing the words 'Once a Blue, Always a Blue'. It was a display of loyalty to Everton that was to come back to haunt him, and also a premature act of celebration. A four-goal reply by Villa, three of them scored by the brothers Stefan and Luke Moore, effectively ended the final as a contest.

Perhaps Rooney would have had a greater influence on that crucial first leg had he not just returned from a draining three weeks in Denmark, where he helped the England U-17 team to finish third in the European Championship for that age group. Colin Harvey, Everton's director of coaching at the time, certainly felt the boy might have been a little tired. And no wonder. Wayne had come back from Denmark with more rave notices after scoring five goals in five games, the last three of them in a 4–1 victory over Spain, the pre-tournament favourites, in the third-place match.

With Rooney a little more rested, Everton won the second leg of the FA Youth Cup final 1–0, but it amounted to little more than a face-saving exercise in front of a crowd of 20,000 at Villa Park. There was no doubt whom many of them had gone to see. Despite the result, Rooney was voted Player of the Final for his titanic efforts to see Everton home. In both legs he had rained shots on the Villa goal, only to find their goalkeeper, eighteen-year-old Wayne Henderson, in inspired form. Tony McAndrew, the Villa coach, was so impressed by the Everton prodigy that he echoed Glenn Hoddle and described him as the best attacking player of sixteen he had ever seen.

Sensing the first stirrings of Rooney-mania, the experienced Colin Harvey did his best to hold the hysteria in check. 'There has been an awful lot of hype about him,' said the man who had been a member of the club's famous Kendall–Ball–Harvey half-back line (with Howard Kendall and Alan Ball). 'It is now up to the coaches and the people who deal with him to see that this talent comes to fruition. Obviously we don't want him to fall by the wayside in any way. We've just got to make sure he gets to play in Everton's first team and that we see the fruits of that. He's a level-headed lad, and to play in the team he knows he has to play as a team member, which he does. It's up to him how far he goes. He's got a special talent, but he's got a long, long way to go.'

Privately, though, Harvey could barely conceal his excitement. Ray Hall remembers talking to his distinguished academy colleague one afternoon and saying of Rooney, 'You know, Colin, I've been involved with Everton as a part-time coach and as head of the youth programme for twenty years and I've not seen anything like him.' To which Harvey replied, 'Well, I've been involved here for 40 years and I haven't!'

Like most other people who saw Rooney play as a schoolboy, Harvey has never forgotten the moment he first clapped eyes on the prodigy. 'I saw him when he was about eleven,' he said. 'I used to go every Sunday morning to watch the U-14s and U-16s just to see what the next batch coming through was like. Anyway, there was a break in one of the games, so I started to look at an U-11 game. What I saw was this lad picking up a ball on the halfway line, going past about four players and blasting it in. That was me finished for watching any other game!

'When he was about fourteen, they used to get him off school to train a couple of days a week, and every day he was in training he'd do something you hadn't seen before. When he was still only fourteen, I saw him hit the opposition's crossbar from inside his own half. It wasn't a sort of Beckhamesque shot; it was hit with pure power.

He must have been ten yards inside his own half and somehow he'd spotted the goalkeeper was off his line. There was a pass on out wide, and I was thinking he was going to pass it out there. But he just let the ball run across him and blasted it.

'I don't think anyone else but his mum and dad can claim any credit for him. He's just a God-given – well, a parent-given – talent. I think Ronaldo or Ronaldinho has said the same thing, but the player Wayne's always reminded me of is Maradona. I've likened him to Kenny Dalglish, too, only Wayne's quicker. If he continues progressing the way he is, he will become one of the all-time greats.'

While acknowledging readily that Rooney was born with the sort of ability most footballers can only dream about, Ray Hall feels the part played by the Everton academy in his development should not be overlooked. 'Wayne would always have been self-motivated,' he said, 'but the academy did play a major part in his development. He is fortunate in that he has a real supportive family and a structure to his life, to which we added. You'd give him an idea, and if he could use it he would. He'd get it into his hard drive.

'The irony is that his progress was so fast, our involvement with him actually finished in terms of day-to-day contact when he was in his U-15 year. We got him off school two or three days a week in his final year, but he was training with the first team reserves as a schoolboy. Wayne kind of missed out a little bit because as soon as he left us, he went straight in with the first team. It's only an observation, but I think the difficulty then was that you had a sixteen- or seventeen-year-old boy going into a man's world and almost missing out on a transition. Because of the nature of the dressing room then, the young players were people like Kevin McCleod, Nick Chadwick, Tony Hibbert and Leon Osman, who were four or five years older than Wayne. So there was that age gap, even there. My young players weren't anywhere near as young as Wayne, so he almost missed out on two or three years in terms of his development socially and culturally.'

CHAPTER 3

ARRIVAL

DUNCAN Edwards arrived in Manchester on Monday, 9 June 1952 to begin his career with United. He was accompanied on the train journey from the Midlands by Gordon Clayton, the goalkeeper from Cannock he had met and become firm friends with when they played together for Birmingham Boys. Duncan caught the train at Dudley, and Gordon got on further up the line at Stafford. He says he will never forget the train pulling into Stafford station and seeing Duncan hanging out of the window waving to him. 'He'd saved me a seat,' Clayton told Eamon Dunphy incredulously. 'The train was empty, but he saved my seat!'

The two fifteen-year-old boys were met at Manchester's London Road station by Bert Whalley, United's chief coach, and taken to Mrs Watson's, the players' 'digs' that have gone down in the club's folklore. Mrs Watson ran a boarding house in Birch Avenue alongside Lancashire Cricket Club's Old Trafford and within walking distance of the football version. It consisted of two big houses knocked into one and could cater for about twenty lodgers. Future Busby Babes Jackie Blanchflower, Mark Jones and David Pegg were already in residence when Duncan and Gordon arrived.

Although Mrs Watson's itself was warm and welcoming, the reception the youngsters got from the earlier arrivals was not. 'We were a bit disturbed somebody had broken into our little circle,' Blanchflower admitted. 'We were a bit jealous, probably a bit too hard on them.' Duncan soon discovered that the celebrity status he had acquired in Midlands football cut no ice at Old Trafford, where gifted young players were two a penny. Largely ignored by their prospective team-mates, Duncan and Gordon had also to contend with another problem that would not even begin to register on the radar of a young player today settling in at a big club.

On the Wednesday after their arrival, 11 June, both the boys started work. Gordon went to a factory in Altrincham and Duncan began an apprenticeship as a carpenter – a trade he had always fancied – in Trafford Park, the industrial area near Old Trafford. Combining a job with playing for a professional football club was not unusual before the lifting of the maximum wage in 1961, and even for some time after it. Footballers did not earn nearly enough in those days to set them up for life and clubs tried to give them an occupation to fall back on if they failed to make it as a professional, or when their playing days were over.

Gordon lasted eighteen months at the factory, but Duncan hated the carpentry and soon abandoned it in favour of 'the brush' – the players' shorthand for working on the groundstaff at Old Trafford. Gordon's feeling was that Duncan could afford to take the risk because his outsize talent guaranteed him a future in the game. Not so sure about his own prospects, Clayton was hardly reassured when one of the other factory workers told him that, as he was Church of England, he had no chance of making progress at Old Trafford. This, of course, was a reflection of the popular belief that, since both Matt Busby and Jimmy Murphy were Catholics, only players of that religion could expect to get ahead at United. Gordon took comfort from the fact that the other member of the club's 'Big Three', Bert Whalley, was a staunch Methodist, and soon discovered to his relief that the accusations of religious prejudice were not well founded. Indeed, the career of Duncan Edwards, as Church of England as the Archbishop of Canterbury, is as complete an answer to the canard as you can get. Nonetheless, the perception of United as a predominantly Catholic club was still so strong in the 1970s that Busby felt it necessary to tackle the subject in his autobiography:

> Here I might dispel an illusion which continued to get back to me over many years of my managership. Often I have heard that a man has said of some player, 'Oh, he'll be all right. He's

a Roman Catholic.' This, of course, because I am a Roman Catholic. But it is a most unChristian thing to say for a start. And I should not have to reply to it, as I do now, that never has a man's religion influenced anybody's decisions at Manchester United in any way. I have always believed that a person's religion is in his mind and in his heart.

As with Wayne Rooney, it was in the FA Youth Cup that Duncan Edwards first began to cause a stir at his club. The tournament had just been introduced that very season, 1952/53, and Duncan was delighted to be named captain of the United side that would take part in it. Playing at The Cliff, United's old training ground at Lower Broughton, in October 1952, they beat Leeds United 4–0 (a certain Jack Charlton scored an own-goal) in the first round before thrashing Nantwich 23–0 and then disposing of Bury 2–0 in the following rounds.

Edwards scored five of the 23 goals United put past poor non-league Nantwich and gave the sort of commanding display that began to make people sit up and take notice. 'The greatest junior prospect I have ever seen – that is no exaggeration,' gushed one reporter excitedly. 'He is as big and almost as strong as a man,' wrote another, Edgar Turner, 'and I cannot recall one pass, long or short, by Edwards that could not be described, to conjure up a phrase from the past, as a daisy cutter. His delivery of the ball to his forwards, even from well back, was equal to the best I have seen anywhere, league games and internationals included, for a very long time. When I say his tackling was strong and his covering excellent, it is still not the end of the story. He also scored five goals!'

Entranced by the thrilling young prospect, Turner made sure he attended the third-round tie against Bury in November. After it, he came to the conclusion that Duncan was ready to play in United's first team. Busby was not quite of the same mind, but he did agree that promotion of some degree was called for. Having stood out again in a friendly against leading amateur side Northern Nomads on 3 December, Duncan was disappointed to find he had been omitted from the A team, for which he had been playing regularly. Disappointment turned to delight, however, when he learnt he was to make his reserve-team debut at Burnley on 6 December instead.

Edwards then shuttled between the reserve and A teams before finally laying claim to a permanent place in the reserves by the following February. In addition, he took the youth team into the fifth round of the FA Youth Cup by scoring the only goal of a fourth-round tie against Everton. So Duncan was entitled to feel pretty pleased with the progress he had made in his first season at Old Trafford as the spring of 1953 came round. But he did not know the half of it.

On Friday, 3 April, Edwards was summoned unexpectedly to Matt Busby's office. Laying down his groundstaff brush and making his way to see the great man, he wondered nervously what he might have done wrong. His sense of shock can be imagined, then, when instead of castigating him the smiling United manager announced he was to make his first-team debut against Cardiff City the following day. After recovering his composure, Duncan asked Busby for permission to use his telephone to break the good news to his parents. Then he ran all the way back to 'Ma' Watson's to tell her, 'the best landlady anyone could wish for', and the United youngsters staying there what had happened.

George Follows, then of the now defunct *News Chronicle*, must have read Busby's mind, or perhaps been tipped off about his intentions. On 1 April, the then famous football reporter had written portentously, and not a little floridly:

> Like the father of the first atom bomb, Manchester United are waiting for something tremendous to happen. This tremendous football force they have discovered is Duncan Edwards, who is exactly sixteen and a half this morning.
>
> Though nobody can tell exactly what will happen when Edwards explodes into First Division football, one thing is certain: it will be spectacular. Take these testimonials from chief coaches of other clubs after a recent Youth Cup game. 'Don't say I said so, but this boy Edwards is the finest thing

on two legs.' 'Don't say I said so, but this boy Edwards has got the lot.'

What can you expect to see in Edwards? Well, the first important thing is that this boy Edwards is a man of 12st and 5ft 10in in height. That gives him his first great asset of power. When he heads the ball, it is not a flabby flirtation with fortune, it is bold and decisive. When he tackles, it is with a man trap bite, and when he shoots with either foot, not even Jack Rowley – the pride of Old Trafford – is shooting harder.

After that kind of over-heated build-up, Edwards' first-team debut turned out to be something of a let-down. The final result – Manchester United 1 Cardiff 4 – says it all about the general quality of the home side's performance. The newspapers tried hard to make allowances for the young newcomer, but the truth of the matter was that Matt Busby's first great post-war team was in serious decline. Edwards got his big chance so early not only because he was so obviously talented, but also because Busby had realised he was going to have to rebuild the ageing side that had won the FA Cup in 1948 and the league championship in 1951/52.

Duncan went home to the Black Country to lick his wounds in the way he knew best. 'I can speak to his character,' W. H. Perry, his old headmaster at Wolverhampton Street School, said. 'He grew in the years I knew him into a quiet, unassuming boy of outstanding character. That his success as a footballer never went to his head is best illustrated by the fact that in the week following his signing for Manchester United and immediately following his first game with that famous club versus Cardiff City in a Division One match, I saw him back in Dudley and still playing football in the street with the lads he had known at school.'

Between August and the end of October 1952, the waning league champions had been stuck at the wrong end of the First Division table. But Busby had been planning for just this eventuality, as he reflected in his 1973 autobiography:

By then [1952/53] the 1948 team was no longer intact. And the future for a manager is fraught with danger, especially a manager of a championship team. Lucky is the manager who does not worry. Or should I say slap-happy is the manager who doesn't worry. If he wins the First Division championship he cannot go any higher (Europe was remote from us then) and the odds are he will go lower. And, given five years or so, he will go straight down and out, he on his backside, the club into a division or two below. Unless he has made other arrangements. Like thinking ahead, at least five years ahead.

All teams, especially teams with players of a like age, are apt to be over the top within five years of reaching it. Buying players piecemeal is at best a chancy business, at worst a financial disaster. Buy them, yes. I have never had any doubts about that. But only to fit into a scheme that planning should have provided for.

From the start of my managership, and even before, I had envisaged my own, my very own, nursery or creche. The pre-war method of team-building was to wait for a weakness to occur and try to repair it by buying a player or finding an outstanding one from junior football. Teenagers were a sensation if they made a First Division team. Even now Cliff Bastin is known as Boy Bastin because he got into Arsenal's team as a youth.

Now it doesn't raise a single eyebrow if half a dozen teenagers make their First Division debut in two weeks. And I like to think that I was the first to recognize and organize vital young talents as soon as they left school ... In 1946 it was revolutionary even to *think* about getting boys straight from school. Get them early enough, I thought, and they would be trained according to some sort of pattern; in my case, the pattern I was trying constantly to create at Manchester United, in the first team and any other team, was that if a boy came through as far as his ability, courage, speed and character were concerned, he would fit into the pattern without feeling like a stranger among people painting pretty pictures he did not understand and had never seen before. This plan I began at once.

In the early post-war years, Busby's youth policy was frustrated by a lack of sufficiently talented youngsters. The six years of hostilities, during which only ersatz league football was played and most young men were required to help the war effort, had seen to it that few new players had been properly introduced into the game. But by 1951, the supply line was beginning to function again. At 22, Roger Byrne could hardly be called a kid, but he was still young enough to be considered new blood when United signed him from a local team, Ryder Brow Boys Club, as a left-winger. Jackie Blanchflower, the younger brother of Danny and a wing-half from Protestant East Belfast, was recruited at about the same time as Byrne. So was another eighteen-year-old, centre-half Mark Jones, a big, solid country boy from Barnsley. Also from Yorkshire was the Doncaster-born David Pegg. Described vividly by Eamon Dunphy as 'a cocky lad, a flash dresser with an eye for the girls', Pegg arrived at Old Trafford in the summer of 1950. Just a year older than Duncan Edwards, outside-left Pegg had been one of Duncan's team-mates in the England Schools sides and, like Edwards, a target for most of the big clubs. Bill Foulkes, twenty, a strapping defender from St Helens, and Dennis Viollet, nineteen, a Mancunian inside-forward of deadly gifts in front of goal, made their first-team debuts for United in the same season, 1952/53, as Edwards. So did Tommy Taylor, twenty, a battering-ram centre-forward of rare quality, who cost £29,999 to buy from Barnsley and combined beautifully with the more stealthy Viollet.

Busby was certainly not averse to buying youthful talent when he could not produce it himself. Additional proof of that had been the purchase in 1949 of goalkeeper Ray Wood, then only eighteen, from Darlington. Nor did he flinch from getting out the cheque-book to acquire older players he felt were required. Hence the signing in 1951 of winger Johnny Berry, 25, from Birmingham City for £25,000.

Thus, by the time Duncan Edwards began playing for Manchester United, most of the players who became famous the world over as the

Busby Babes were in place. Still to come, of the better-known, front-rank names, were Liam 'Billy' Whelan, a tall, elegant inside-forward from Dublin; cheeky little Eddie Colman, a wing-half from Salford known affectionately as 'Snakehips' on account of his devastating body-swerve; speedy Mancunian left-winger Albert Scanlon; and, last but hardly least, Bobby Charlton, who needs no introduction.

Although Busby could see his youth policy beginning to bear fruit, others could not. It seems hard to believe now, but United's first legendary manager had to face down criticism at the club's annual general meeting in 1953 about the disappointing form of the first team. He responded to it by arguing that the youngsters in the reserve and youth teams were worth £200,000 – a lot of money in those days. But this extravagant claim put a lot more pressure on the youth team, in particular. It meant that, more than ever now, United needed to win the FA Youth Cup.

As a result, Duncan Edwards found himself back at youth level soon after making his solitary first-team appearance of the 1952/53 season. He and his team-mates beat Brentford 2–1 at Griffin Park in the first leg of the Youth Cup semi-final, and then finished off the job at Old Trafford four days later. So United were now, at least, in the final of the competition. There, thanks to one of those strange quirks of fate football is famous for, their opponents were Wolverhampton Wanderers, the local club Duncan had supported as a boy and had been expected to join.

The first leg was at Old Trafford on 4 May and a crowd of nearly 21,000 were delighted to see United simply overwhelm Wolves. They won 7–1 with two goals each from Eddie Lewis and Noel McFarlane and one apiece from more familiar names, David Pegg, Albert Scanlon and Liam Whelan. United were so superior, there was just no way back for their opponents. With the FA Youth Cup already won, to all intents and purposes, the second leg at Molineux was something of a formality. Wolves saved a little face by drawing 2–2, but United's youngsters had backed up Busby's boast in spades and had warned the football world that something extraordinary was beginning to happen at Old Trafford.

Although Duncan did not score any of United's nine goals in the two-leg final, reports of the match indicate that he was their mainspring. Under the headline 'Dudley Boy the Inspiration in Manchester United's Youth Cup Lead', the man from Wolverhampton's *Express and Star* newspaper raved about him after the first leg. 'If I thought that I was certain of seeing Duncan Edwards give another such polished display as he gave last night,' he wrote, 'wild horses would not keep me from Molineux. Edwards was to all intents and purposes the complete wing half-back. A strong man in a strong side, he failed only once in the whole game to make good use of the ball and, if for nothing else, I would remember him for the uncanny accuracy of a series of long, raking passes across the field on the inside of the full-back, not to mention the urgency with which he played throughout.'

A hidden bonus of that stylish Youth Cup triumph was that it persuaded Wilf McGuinness to join United. Since McGuinness is a Mancunian, you might have thought it a formality he would gravitate towards Old Trafford. But he had followed both Manchester clubs as a boy and, as captain of England Schoolboys in 1953, he was coveted by Wolves as well as United, City and most of the big Lancashire clubs. In the end, it was United's 7–1 win against Wolves that made up his mind for him. 'United murdered them,' McGuinness recalled in conversation with Eamon Dunphy. 'They had Duncan, Eddie Colman, David Pegg, Albert Scanlon and Billy Whelan. I looked, and I knew Eddie Colman had played for Salford Boys and Lancashire, but hadn't played for England. I thought, if they can improve me that much I'm bound to make it. I thought they would make me play better than him because I had played for England and he hadn't. When I saw Duncan I thought thank God I am not playing in his position. I thought if they can get a side to play this great, this is what I want to be in with. They must make me. That decided me.'

McGuinness's silent prayer of thanks about Edwards proved a little premature. Although he joined United as a right-half, he found himself cast as Duncan's understudy at left-half. Consequently, his first-team chances were limited initially by the overwhelming excellence of his rival. Even the Munich tragedy did not guarantee him a place, since Stan Crowther was signed from Aston Villa to replace Edwards. McGuinness finally forced his way into the side at the start of the 1958/59 season and became a regular until a broken leg effectively cut short his first-class career the following season. Eventually, of course, McGuinness succeeded Busby as manager of United for a short, traumatic time. 'I was very proud to be Duncan's understudy,' McGuinness told me. 'I also played alongside him and went on tours with him to Switzerland and Germany when we were youth players. It was wonderful. It's a bit of an exaggeration, but it wasn't like having an extra player – it was like having an extra team!

'There are lots of stories to tell, but one that sticks in the memory is of Jimmy Murphy's team talk before one youth game. It was against Chelsea in the semi-final of the FA Youth Cup, I think [in 1955]. What Jimmy said was, "You're all great players, so don't have an 'Edwards' complex. David Pegg, you could play for England. Bobby [Charlton], you're going to play for England. Wilf, you and Eddie [Colman], you can play. So don't have this 'Edwards' complex." Duncan was playing at centre-back, I think, and it was 0–0 at half time. But when Murphy came into the dressing room he told us we were not doing the right thing. "Duncan, you play up front," he barked. Then he turned to the rest of us and ordered, "Whenever you get the ball, give it to Duncan!" And we did, and we beat them. I think he scored three altogether. He was something special, he was.'

Murphy himself absolutely worshipped Duncan, calling him 'the Koh-i-noor diamond amongst our crown jewels'. He recalled for Edwards' biographer Geoff Warburton an FA Youth Cup match in which United were losing at half-time. 'I went into the dressing room for a word of advice and a chat and Duncan said to me, "Don't worry, son. I'll get a goal or two for you this half." And he did – from winghalf, too. That's what I loved about that kid. He always called me "son"!'

As with United and Duncan Edwards, Everton found it difficult not to rush Wayne Rooney into their first team. But in contrast to Matt Busby and his deliberate policy of building a young team, manager David Moyes did all in his power to delay Rooney's debut until he felt absolutely sure the boy was ready to cope with a Premiership that was twice as fast and physical as the old First Division had been in Edwards' day.

The temptation to call up Rooney must have been strong, given that Everton were in the bottom half of the table during most of the 2001/02 season and word had got round Merseyside that the club had a possible messiah in the youth team. But Moyes, who had not long taken over from Walter Smith as manager and needed to consolidate his own position as well as keep Everton clear of relegation, manfully resisted the urge to place so much responsibility on shoulders so young. Indeed, he went on record as saying it was his intention to introduce Rooney as carefully as Sir Alex Ferguson had the emerging Ryan Giggs at United. 'He scored another great goal this week and was unlucky not to score against Manchester United in the reserves,' Harris and Fullbrook quoted Moyes as saying as the manager wrestled with the problem. 'This experience will help him, but we will continue to be careful with him. We've been playing him for 45 minutes or so for the reserves. We can't just throw him in ... It's a new experience for me, too, and you've got to be careful with young players that you don't place too much expectation on their shoulders.'

The nearest Wayne got to the senior side in 2001/02 was the substitutes' bench. But at least he made the breakthrough into the first-team squad when Moyes included him for the trip to Southampton for the third-last game of Everton's season. Had he gone on, at sixteen years and 178 days he would have broken by 104 days Joe Royle's 36-year-old record as the youngest player in the club's history. There was to be no further chance of a debut that season, either, because of Rooney's selection for that England U-17 team which took him away to Denmark for the European Championship while Everton were losing their final two games, at home to Blackburn and away to Arsenal. Ominously, it meant they finished fifteenth, just seven points clear of relegation.

Still Moyes refused to be budged. 'I would have liked to have Wayne Rooney involved on Sunday,' he said of the Blackburn fixture.

'It would have been nice for him to be involved in our last home game, but I can also see reasons why perhaps it's a good thing for him to wait a little longer. It will keep expectation levels down. People must realise he is still only a baby in football terms. The fans showed on Saturday they are already aware of him, although I think most people in football are already aware of him. Wayne has the ability to be involved in the first team now, but we have to be mindful of his age and monitor his progress accordingly.

'He is a fine talent, and like most people I would like to see him included in the senior side, but you also have to ask when is the right time for the boy. Wayne Rooney has a long-term future here and we have to protect that. He will definitely be involved with us during our pre-season preparations, but we will have to wait and see about the first team before then.'

As for Rooney himself, he just accepted the situation with the calm, philosophical attitude that, in contrast to his volatile behaviour on the pitch, has come to characterise his public utterances. He said that, while he very much wanted to play for the first team of the club he had supported all his life, he had not set out to realise that ambition by the end of the 2001/02 season. All he had hoped to do was play a few reserve games, so it did not really bother him that he had not broken the record for being Everton's youngest player. You could almost hear David Moyes dictating the speech as Wayne added that the club did not want to put him in too early or play him in too many games because it would have a detrimental effect in the long term. Since the games at that level were much more physical, he said, he expected to be introduced just for twenty-minute spells. The main thing, he stressed loyally, was to take his chance when it came and play well enough to stay in the team.

As it turned out, the wait for Rooney to make his first-team debut lasted only a couple of months. During Everton's 2002 pre-season tour of Austria, he scored his first senior goal against lower-league side SC Bruck. He followed that with a hat-trick against SC Weiz and, on his club's return to domestic warm-ups, another three against Queens Park Rangers. To put it all into revealing context, Rooney was still only sixteen at that stage, had played only four times for the reserves and had only just left school.

Moyes, meanwhile, continued to strive desperately to protect the youngster. In one memorable outburst, he said he was not worried about Rooney becoming the youngest player in Everton's history; he was more concerned about him becoming the best player in the club's history. But others, like deputy chairman and theatre impresario Bill Kenwright, were more eager to let the world know that Everton had unearthed one of the finest young talents English football had ever seen. Lifelong fan Kenwright, whose takeover of the club had saved it from impending financial disaster, joked, 'We've all decided at Everton we've got to play down the fact that Wayne Rooney is probably going to be the greatest goalscorer in England. He's awesome. Walter Smith said to me two years ago that he'd seen something he'd never seen before on a football pitch. He's just got everything. He's far and away the best I've ever seen.'

In the end, there was just no holding Rooney back. Despite all his qualms about blooding the boy too early, Moyes could no longer ignore the evidence of his own eyes ('Wayne is incredibly quick in training,' he had admitted, 'he is very strong for his age, he has great awareness, and a footballing brain which normally doesn't come until later on in years') or the growing clamour from the Everton fans to be allowed to see their very own boy wonder in action in the Premiership.

The supporters' wish was finally granted on 17 August, the first day of the 2002/03 season, when Wayne Rooney made his league debut for Everton at Goodison Park against Tottenham Hotspur. He played as an attacking midfielder in a 4–4–2 line-up that read as follows: Wright; Hibbert, Stubbs, Weir, Naysmith; Li Tie, Gravesen, Rooney, Pembridge; Campbell, Radzinski. Since Everton could only draw 2–2, his first taste of the real thing was almost as inauspicious as Duncan Edwards' had been at Manchester United 49 years earlier. Rooney did not score and was substituted before the end. But at least Everton, unlike Edwards' United, did not lose.

CHAPTER 4

BLOSSOMING

AS the 1953/54 season began, Duncan Edwards had a more immediate concern than when he might play for Manchester United's first team again. Like any young player approaching his seventeenth birthday then, he worried whether he would be offered a professional contract on 1 October. There was no need to fret, of course. When the day arrived, the document was duly produced for him to sign. Matt Busby would have been out of his mind to let such a multitalented player go, a player he later described as 'incomparable'.

By the time Duncan put pen to paper, he had established himself as a regular member of United's Central League team. They had started off with a 3–2 victory over Liverpool Reserves and were playing well, so it was with mixed feelings that he found himself named as twelfth man for the senior side against Tottenham Hotspur at White Hart Lane on 26 September. While delighted to be considered part of the senior squad again, Edwards did not relish the thought of a nonplaying role, which is what twelfth man usually was at a time when substitutes were not allowed in the Football League. Like a lot of footballers then and now, Duncan hated watching football when he could be playing.

He was perfectly happy, therefore, to return to the Central League and the FA Youth Cup. Since United were the cup holders, the junior knockout tournament had real significance for the club and their first-round tie with Everton was keenly anticipated. They won it 1–0 with a goal by Eddie Colman, Edwards' partner at wing-half and his great friend. The little and large of midfield, Colman and Edwards made an odd couple but formed a partnership with massive potential for England as well as for Manchester United.

Then, on 28 October, four days after that Youth Cup victory over Everton, came a turning point in Edwards' career and United's history. Selected as twelfth man again for the first team, he travelled up to Kilmarnock for a floodlit friendly, not expecting to play against the Scottish club. The game itself was something of a novelty, since the first FA Cup tie under lights (Kidderminster Harriers v. Brierley Hill Alliance) was still two years off and the first Football League fixture (Portsmouth v. Newcastle) to be played at night was another five months beyond that. None of this mattered much to Duncan Edwards, one imagines, as he moped on the sidelines at Rugby Park watching Henry Cockburn put the visitors ahead from twenty yards with a rare goal. But then United's England international wing-half sustained an injury that forced him to go off and Edwards was called upon to replace him. Here was another novelty: it was not until 1965 that the Football League allowed teams to use just one substitute in competitive matches. Fortunately for Duncan, however, Kilmarnock and United had come to an informal agreement beforehand that substitutes could be used in the event of injury.

After Edwards' introduction, United tightened their control on the match. Two further goals, by Dennis Viollet and Tommy Taylor, clinched the victory and gave Busby food for thought. At that point, the first team was very much in transition. Veterans of the 1948 side such as John Aston, Allenby Chilton, Henry Cockburn, Stan Pearson and Jack Rowley were still commanding places in it, but a series of disappointing results suggested that changes were long overdue. Of their opening fifteen games in that 1953/54 season, United had won only four, another six having been drawn.

So for the next First Division fixture, away to Huddersfield, Busby decided to act. Impressed by their performances against Kilmarnock, the United manager retained three of the seven young, up-and-coming players he had blooded in the Scottish friendly: Jackie Blanchflower, Dennis Viollet and Duncan Edwards. Although the game at Huddersfield was goalless, this more youthful United side played well enough to be hailed in the *Manchester Evening Chronicle* with a banner headline that gave them the nickname they were to be known by for ever more: 'Busby's Bouncing Babes Keep All Town Awake'. Ironically, Busby himself disliked the famous soubriquet. He thought it implied naivety and vulnerability. The Manchester United manager preferred the more macho 'Red Devils' tag that came later. 'It was unheard-of then for sixteen-year-olds to be put in the first team,' Bobby Charlton pointed out. 'No manager had ever tried that before. But the old man [Busby] had a way of doing it. He waited for a really bad performance and then he would get rid of the bad five or six to teach them a lesson, to shake them up. People said he must be mad when he put in sixteen- and seventeen-year-olds; but it's amazing, young lads are very resilient, you know, and why should they not get the chance? And they came in and they took it and changed the whole thing.'

The Babes kept bouncing as the United manager realised he had done exactly the right thing to start easing out the veterans and bringing through the youngsters. 'The pieces dropped out, the pieces dropped in,' was the deceptively simple way Busby put it. Of their remaining 27 First Division fixtures, United won fourteen and drew six. Those 34 points (only two for a win in those far-off days, remember) hoisted them up the table to fourth place, where they finished the season nine points behind the eventual champions, Wolves. Even a 5–3 defeat by Burnley in the third round of the FA Cup could not dampen the growing sense of optimism at Old Trafford about the future of the club.

That feeling was reinforced by more success in the FA Youth Cup. Because he had become a regular member of United's senior side, Duncan Edwards had not played in rounds two and three. Since the junior side beat Wrexham 5–0 and Bradford 6–0, he does not appear to have been missed too much. However, when Rotherham held United to a goalless draw in round four, Duncan was drafted back into the side for the replay at The Cliff. United won it 3–1, all their goals coming from Edwards.

Generously, the man from the *South Yorkshire and Rotherham Advertiser* raved about the man of the match's performance, calling him 'amazing' and comparing him to the great John Charles. But he also made a valid point about the ethics of recalling such an outstanding and, by now, battle-hardened player to oppose mere boys. 'I think it was a pity,' he wrote, 'that Manchester, in their eagerness to make sure of retaining this cup, which they won last season, found it necessary to bring into the side Duncan Edwards, who played in the England U-23 side against Italy last week and has made 24 First Division appearances. I know Edwards is only seventeen, but I think it is against the basics of the Youth Cup to introduce professional players.'

This perfectly legitimate complaint cut no ice with Busby. The United manager was too intent on proving the worth of his youth policy to be shamed into not picking Edwards for the youth team. So back came Duncan for the quarter-final, which was against Bexleyheath and Welling at the Kent side's modest little ground. To their credit, the underdogs refused to be overawed by their illustrious opponents. The game was goalless until Duncan, as if reacting to a contemptuous cry from the crowd of 'Where's this great Edwards of yours? We ain't seen him yet!', thrashed the ball into the Bexleyheath net from long range. The home side fought back and equalised before the interval, but United proved just too strong and experienced for them. In the end, David Pegg sent the visitors into the semi-finals with a late winner.

There, with Edwards now seconded semi-permanently to the youth team, they coasted past West Bromwich Albion 7–1 on aggregate. Back in the final of the Youth Cup once more, United found themselves facing the same opponents as the year before. Wolves were as proud as United of their youth policy, and this was obviously an opportunity for them not only to gain revenge for the previous season's defeat but to prove their recruitment of youngsters superior to their rivals'.

They certainly stretched United to the limit in the first leg, which was at Old Trafford. Watched by a crowd of 18,246, Edwards put the home side ahead; but Wolves hit back so hard that they led 3–1 at the interval. A ding-dong battle ensued in the second half, which saw United battering away at the Wolves' goal and the visitors retaliating spiritedly on the break. Switching from inside-right to centre-forward, Duncan made it 2–3 with a powerful header. Then, shortly afterwards, Pegg equalised. Despite being penned in their own half for most of the time, Wolves managed to go ahead again; but another goal by Pegg brought the scores level once more at 4–4. And that is the way they stayed as Wolves hung on for the draw in the face of United's all-out assaults on their goal.

The return at Molineux three days later was watched by a bigger crowd of 28,651 and Edwards was again an influential force back in his native West Midlands. Drifting between inside-right and centre-forward, he caused the Wolves' defence endless trouble. So much so that when he was involved in an aerial clash with two defenders in the 33rd minute, the referee awarded United a controversial penalty. The prolific Pegg tucked the kick away to give his side a lead that won them the game and secured the FA Youth Cup for a second successive year.

But there was still more glory to come for the United youngsters. At the end of that 1953/54 season, they headed for the prestigious Blue Star international tournament in Zurich and triumphed. They did so by winning four of their games and drawing the other, all without conceding a single goal. It was another opportunity for Edwards to demonstrate his extraordinary versatility. Busby played him in his normal position of left-half in the first three games, but moved him to centre-forward in the later stages of the third one. Duncan stayed there for the semi-final and final, more than justifying the switch of positions by scoring what Busby called a 'magnificent' hat-trick in the final, which United won 4–0 against Red Star of Zurich.

Nor was that the end of it for United's all-conquering youth team. As winners of the tournament, they met a Swiss Youth select side in the national stadium as a prelude to a full international between Switzerland and Holland. Needless to say, they won that one as well, Pegg (two), Whelan and, of course, Edwards scoring the goals in another 4–0 victory.

That trip was rather more than a jolly. As his insistence – in the face of official disapproval – on United's first team competing in the European Cup three seasons later was to prove, no manager was more aware than Matt Busby of the need for British footballers to be exposed to the different demands of the continental game, and as early in their careers as possible. So important did the manager consider the Zurich tournament to be to his young players' education that not only he, but Jimmy Murphy and Bert Whalley accompanied the squad on that first, ground-breaking trip to Switzerland.

By that time Wilf McGuinness and Bobby Charlton had joined Edwards, Colman, Pegg, Scanlon and company in United's all-conquering youth team. It was Charlton's first trip to Europe, and he had no doubts about its value. 'The Zurich tournament was a vital part of our education,' he told Eamon Dunphy. 'We played against Italians, Germans and Yugoslavs and learnt about their different ways of playing. We went three years on the trot and won the first two tournaments. Then we lost 1–0 to Genoa in the final. They never came out of their own half, except once, and we thought, "There's something not right here." We'd never encountered anything like this at home. But they knew what they were doing, defending in typical Italian style. They wouldn't let you past. It was frustrating, but an amazing education.'

United's participation in, and winning of, the 1954 Blue Star tournament also needs to be evaluated against the startling evidence of the time that English football could no longer regard itself as the best in the world simply by virtue of the fact that it had invented the game. That illusion had been shattered painfully and for ever by two seminal results. In November 1953, the superb, unforgettable Hungarian side of Puskas, Bozsik, Kocsis, Hidegkuti and company had come to Wembley and thrashed England 6–3. That made them the first foreigners to win at the famous old stadium, and they proved it no fluke by handing out another hammering, 7–1, in Budapest when England tried to gain revenge in May 1954. So times they were a-changin', and Busby knew it.

The international background to Wayne Rooney's introduction to senior English football was rather more encouraging. Two months earlier in Japan, England had reached the quarter-finals of the 2002 World Cup, where they lost 2–1 to the eventual winners Brazil. It was not the most convincing of performances, England having led 1–0 and Brazil having been reduced to ten men in the second half by the sending-off of the hugely influential Ronaldinho, but at least there was some evidence of progress to show for 36 years of trying to regain a position of pre-eminence in world football. Rooney had not gone to those World Cup finals with England, of course. Not yet seventeen, he was still trying to establish himself in Everton's first team. But the world did not have to wait much longer for him to give notice of his phenomenal talent. Another six Premiership matches came and went without the boy doing anything remarkable. A substitute for the most part, he started in only two of those games as Moyes stuck firmly to his promise to introduce the youngster judiciously.

Then, on 1 October 2002, with Rooney still 23 days short of his seventeenth birthday, the Everton manager gave him a run-out in a second-round Worthington Cup tie against lower-division Wrexham (the Worthington Cup, of course, was one of the League Cup's six sponsored name changes since 1982, the others being Milk Cup, Littlewoods Cup, Rumbelows League Cup, Coca-Cola Cup and Carling Cup). Rooney responded by scoring twice in seven minutes after coming on as a 64th-minute substitute. The first of his goals made him the youngest scorer in Everton's history (the record, held by the legendary Tommy Lawton, had stood since 1937), and the brace, added to an earlier goal by Kevin Campbell, carried the Merseysiders comfortably into the third round for the first time in four years.

Typically, Moyes tried to keep his post-match reaction low-key. 'Wayne is delighted to have got his goals,' he said. 'He's been a bit anxious over not scoring so far, but you expect that of a sixteen-year-old. He took his goals well, showed what he is capable of, and hopefully there is a lot more to come in the future.' But just how much there was to come, and how soon, the Everton manager could not possibly have imagined in his wildest dreams.

Eighteen days later, Arsenal came to Goodison Park as defending champions and league leaders; unbeaten in 30 Premiership matches, they were beginning to be regarded as virtually invincible. So when Freddie Ljungberg put the London club ahead after only eight minutes, the Everton faithful feared the worst. They perked up a bit when Tomasz Radzinski equalised before half-time, though, and the game looked to be petering out into a draw. Wayne Rooney was sent on as a late substitute for Radzinski, but still nothing unusual occurred. Then, in the very last minute of the contest, the ball fell to Rooney some 30 yards out and slightly to the left of goal. He took aim immediately and, almost without trying, it seemed, his right foot sent the ball whistling over David Seaman, the Arsenal and England goalkeeper, in a deadly arc. For an instant, no one could quite believe the evidence of their own eyes. Then Goodison became bedlam as the Everton players and fans realised that they had not only won the game but acquired a superstar.

Not even previous examples of Seaman's growing fallibility against shots from long range could devalue the quality of Rooney's majestic first goal in the Premiership, a goal that made him the youngest scorer in that competition as well for a short time. While it was legitimate to criticise the veteran goalkeeper for the goals he had conceded notoriously to Real Zaragoza's Nayim in the 1995 European Cup Winners' Cup final and to Brazil's Ronaldinho in the 2002 World Cup quarter-final, few thought him to blame for not stopping an audacious shot that entered his net like a shell.

Up in the stands, Wayne's family and Bob Pendleton, the scout who had recommended him to Everton, were among the fans going potty over the sudden explosion of the *wunderkind*'s virtuosity. Even Arsène Wenger, the Arsenal manager, was ecstatic. Swallowing his disappointment at Everton's ending of his team's unbeaten run, Wenger gushed of Rooney, 'He is the biggest English talent I've seen since I arrived in England. There has certainly not been an under-twenty player as good as him since I became a manager here. We were beaten by a special goal from a very special talent. You do not need to be an expert to see that he is a special talent, very special.'

Rooney himself seemed a little dumbfounded by what he had done. When asked if he had known exactly what he was doing when he scored that sensational goal, he said, 'I knew that I was aiming for the top corner, but I didn't think it would go in. When it beat Seaman I didn't know what to do. In fact, I don't know why I ran over to where I did [the stand where his family were sitting], but it was a great feeling and it was made even more special because it was against the then champions who had been having an unbelievable run.'

Inevitably, David Moyes' reaction was more guarded than most. 'He is not particularly mature yet on or off the pitch,' he said of Rooney. 'We need to protect him, and I hope our fans understand that.' Even so, he was shrewd enough to realise that the cat was out of the bag now so far as other, predatory clubs were concerned, and Everton needed to tie him to the club contractually as quickly as possible. 'Wayne's contract is done and dusted,' Moyes added. 'He will sign a three-year deal with a two-year option.'

That bit of business brought Rooney a wage rise so steep that it reflected accurately the speed of his climb from academy starlet to first-team regular inside four months. At the start of the 2002/03 season he was earning a modest £80 per week. By the beginning of 2003, after he had finally put pen to paper on his delayed new contract, his weekly take-home pay – if you can call it that – had shot up to £13,000.

Nobody could argue that Wayne did not deserve to be rewarded so handsomely. After all, his winner against Arsenal boosted Everton's confidence to such an extent that they won their next five Premiership matches as well. And just in case anyone wondered whether 'that' goal against the Gunners had been a fluke, Rooney demonstrated two games later at Leeds that he was anything but a one-trick pony.

Coming on again as a late substitute for Tomasz Radzinski, he picked up the ball about 35 yards from goal. Not shooting this time, he went on a run that left midfielder Eirik Bakke flat on his back and centre-back Lucas Radebe tackling thin air. Only once he was inside the Leeds penalty area did Rooney drive an angled shot past Paul Robinson, now David Seaman's established successor in England's goal. It was such a breathtaking demonstration of strength, speed and artistry that many of Everton's travelling fans watching from behind that goal could not contain themselves. Briefly, they spilled on to the pitch to mob their hero.

That he was still one of them at that stage – just an ordinary Scouser and Everton fan at heart – there could be no doubt. Not long after scoring that wonderful goal against Leeds, Rooney was spotted playing football in the street with his mates, just like Duncan Edwards before him. Worried Evertonians reported this remarkable fact to his manager, who told them he didn't mind Wayne kicking a ball about. Moyes added jocularly that if they saw him doing something he really ought not to, they should send him home. But not too many seem to have responded to that request, as we shall see.

Everything went swimmingly for Rooney during most of the first half of the 2002/03 season. Still playing regularly as a substitute, he showed nerves of steel to score from the spot when Everton beat Newcastle on penalties at St James's Park in the third round of the Worthington Cup. Then, when preferred to Radzinski in mid-December after Everton had lost twice in succession, he had an enraptured Goodison chanting his name as he helped make the first goal and scored the winner in a 2–1 victory over Blackburn.

Off the field, too, his career was prospering. In the club shop, replica shirts with his name and number on the back were flying off the shelves. Nine out of ten sold in the first part of the season were his, making him the most popular player with the fans and toppling Duncan Ferguson from the top spot. Beyond Goodison, too, football lovers were clamouring to hail this apparent heir to George Best and Paul Gascoigne. In December 2002, BBC TV viewers voted him Young Sports Personality of the Year, although he offended some by accepting the award chewing gum and with loosened tie askew.

Discordant notes began to be heard on the field as well as the year drew to a close. At Birmingham on Boxing Day came the first serious blot on his disciplinary record and the consolidation of doubts about his temperament. Back on the bench again, Rooney did not come on for Radzinski until the second half. Fifteen minutes later, he injured Birmingham's Steve Vickers quite badly when, having let the ball run away from him, he lunged into a tackle on the defender. Vickers needed eight stitches in a gash on his foot and was out of action for three weeks. The referee was the vastly experienced David Elleray, then in his final season as a Premier League and FIFA official, and he showed the youngster a straight red card.

Rooney, who insisted he had been trying to play the ball, was distraught at being sent off for the first time in his career. Moyes backed him up and asked Elleray to look at the incident again on the club's TV monitor. Reluctantly, the referee agreed to do so, but refused to comment afterwards. That sparked a paranoiac outburst by the Everton manager. He cited a couple of other instances that led him to believe his club was being treated unfairly by the authorities: Everton's failure to have David Unsworth's controversial sending-off against Chelsea overturned, and the officials' failure to punish Steven Gerrard for his bloodcurdling, two-footed tackle on Gary Naysmith in the Merseyside derby four days earlier. Much less convincingly, Moyes tried to argue that Rooney had been punished solely because of his growing reputation for hot-headedness. By then, just nineteen matches into his Premiership career, this boy of seventeen had been booked four times and was already starting to become as notorious for his foul mouth and occasional recklessness in the tackle as he was famous for the sublime things he could do with a football. He worked himself into such a fury at the first sign of perceived injustice that Germaine Greer, the famous feminist and commentator on human behaviour, was moved to describe his tough, contorted face as being 'like a clenched fist'.

Even so, the Everton manager saw no reason to crack down severely on Rooney. 'Maybe a little bit of reputation has gone before him and maybe the referee has been looking at that,' Moyes was quoted as saying. 'We have to tell him that he has to be a little bit more careful. We have told Wayne already this year and we'll tell him again ... But I won't let the sending-off affect my handling of Wayne ... I'm delighted with the way Wayne is progressing. It was a decent attempt at a challenge ... which possibly deserved no more than a yellow card. One thing is certain, I'm not going to ask Wayne to change his style, because aggression and strength are big qualities, together with the boy's obvious ability.'

Oddly enough, on the day Rooney set yet another record by becoming the youngest player to be sent off in the Premiership, he was replaced by Leeds trainee James Milner, then aged sixteen years and 357 days, as the competition's youngest scorer. Wayne's unwanted milestone meant an enforced four-week break from football but Moyes was relieved, no doubt, to see the teenager given a rest from the pressures, physical and mental, of English football at its highest and most demanding level.

Because the programme over Christmas and New Year was so concentrated, Rooney played two more games before serving his suspension. And when he came back, he had to be content with a place on the bench again for four matches. But by the time he was restored to the starting line-up at Arsenal on 23 March 2003, he had ended all speculation about his future and calmed Everton's jangling nerves by committing himself to the club for three and a half years. That it was all done in front of television cameras at a late-night press conference is a measure of the international fame Rooney had acquired in the space of little more than a year.

When he eventually signed that first professional contract, on 18 January, it was revealed that complicated negotiations over his image rights had been the reason for the delay. Speaking on behalf of Rooney's Proactive Sports Management team, agent Paul Stretford explained that they and Everton had arrived at an arrangement where both club and player would be marketed by a joint operation. Some of us find that concept difficult to grasp even now; and Duncan Edwards, in his 1950s innocence, would certainly not have had a clue what Stretford was talking about. His words would have sounded like a foreign language to a former superstar who probably would have thought image rights had something to do with standing in front of the bathroom mirror. All credit, though, to Proactive for latching on to an additional source of income unfamiliar in English football, but commonplace on the continent – as David Beckham and Michael Owen discovered to their considerable enrichment at Real Madrid.

'I am delighted everything has been sorted out,' said the boy himself. 'It means everything for me to play for Everton, so this is a dream come true. I can't really explain what it means to me to sign. It is the best feeling in my life. Just playing for Everton gives me a buzz. It's a bit weird because I used to look up to players like Duncan [Ferguson] and now I am playing alongside them every day. I have been watching Everton since I was a kid, so there was never any doubt I would sign. It was very important for me and my family that I stayed here.'

Under FA rules, three and a half years was the maximum length of time for which a player of seventeen could commit himself to a professional contract. But provision was made in the agreement for Rooney to sign an extended, five-year deal as soon as he turned eighteen that October. So everybody was happy. Well, everybody except Wayne's original agent, Peter McIntosh, and his associates, that is. But more of that later.

Rooney completed his first senior season strongly, scoring three goals in Everton's last eight Premiership matches as they finished seventh, just outside the European places. It made a nice change from the previous season, when the Toffees had been unable to climb any higher than fifteenth place and seven points clear of relegation. Those three late goals, one of them against Arsenal at Highbury, took his total for 2002/03 to six in the Premiership and two in the Worthington Cup. It was not a bad return for a rookie, considering that his 37 appearances in league and cup included only 17 starts.

He had certainly done enough to impress England coach Sven-Goran Eriksson. In common with many other good judges, the Swede felt that this strongly built, supremely talented teenager was ready for international football after little more than half a season in the Premiership. And, in that sense, Wayne Rooney was well ahead of Duncan Edwards when it came to the development of their careers.

CHAPTER 5

THE ARMY GAME

BECAUSE of the 1954 World Cup, the 1954/55 season started a week later than usual in England. It did not begin at all promisingly for Manchester United, either: they got off on the wrong foot with a 3–1 home defeat by Portsmouth. But it was a temporary glitch. Over the next month or so, United went on a nine-game unbeaten run that was ended by reigning First Division champions Wolves, who gained a measure of revenge for those two FA Youth Cup final defeats by beating them 4–2 at Molineux.

Soon afterwards, United had a battle royal with the champions-to-be, Chelsea, beating them 6–5 in an extraordinary match at Stamford Bridge. From then on, though, their results were so mixed that they could finish only fifth, one place lower than the previous season. Worse still, they lost all bragging rights to Manchester City, who beat them 3–2 at Maine Road, knocked them out of the FA Cup at the fourth-round stage, then completed a league double by hammering them 5–0 at Old Trafford.

Despite United's variable form, Duncan Edwards' reputation continued to grow. Even in that heavy defeat by City, he stood out. 'It is not too much to say that the youthful dynamo Edwards, supported in spasms by Gibson and Whitefoot, pretty well faced Manchester City by himself,' concluded the man from *The Times*. For the most part, there was nothing but praise for the contributions he made to United's cause from left-half or inside-forward; but Duncan himself was not satisfied. What irked him, as a regular scorer at other levels of the game, was his failure to find the net for United's first team.

That problem was solved at Old Trafford on New Year's Day, 1955. After a season and a half of seeing his many shots saved, blocked, strike the woodwork or go just wide, he finally hit the mark late in a 4–1 win against Blackpool. The moment was described vividly by the inimitable Don Davies, otherwise known as 'An Old International', of the *Manchester Guardian*, as the *Guardian* was called then. In his characteristically ornate style, Davies wrote:

> By common consent, the outstanding incident of a somewhat desultory second half was the scoring of Edwards' first goal for United.
>
> Ever since he first pulled a red jersey over his muscular frame, this seventeen-year-old has dreamt of one thing only: namely to smite a ball so hard that it either bursts in transit or defies the effort of any goalkeeper to intercept it. On Saturday, with about twenty minutes remaining for play, Edwards at last detected his opportunity.
>
> Darting forward, he put every ounce of his prodigious strength into the mighty, uninhibited swipe. There was a sharp crack of boot on leather – a veritable detonation, this – and a clearing of the atmosphere by a blurred object which first soared over Farm's upraised arms then dipped suddenly and passed in under the crossbar.
>
> A scene of great commotion followed. Spectators hugged each other, then threw back their heads and brayed their approval. Edwards leaped and gambolled like a soul possessed, until his adoring colleagues fell upon him and pinned him down with their embraces ... It was all very touching and not the least bit spoiled when Perry broke away and scored for Blackpool.

That extract tells us many things, not least the way the reporting of football matches has changed. But sticking out a mile is the affection the United supporters and players felt for Duncan. The reaction of the crowd to his first goal can be judged from Don Davies' piece; and it is abundantly clear from the testimonies of his contemporaries at Old Trafford that, despite a natural shyness and obsession with football, he was an extremely popular member of the group of young men who came to be known as the Busby Babes, then the Red Devils. 'He was fiery when he played, but he was a very gentle person,' Bobby Charlton told me. 'Off the field, he was soft – a real soft thing, you know. In those days, I never thought of him as being hard and businesslike, or anything like that. If you asked him to do anything, he would have said, "Yes, I'll do it." There was nothing to dislike about him at all. As long as he had his talent and he had his football, that was all he ever talked about. But he was good fun. He was always laughing; he liked a good laugh. I knew him well because we were in digs together down the road for a long time and then we did our National Service together.'

Wilf McGuinness is another former contemporary and team-mate who was struck by the sharp contrast between Edwards' persona on the pitch and off it. 'He was very, very modest,' said McGuinness. 'He was bubbly, but he was modest. He was a nice guy – one of those unassuming sort of guys. He didn't talk a lot and was quietly spoken in that broad Black Country accent of his; but when he did say something, you'd look at him and you'd think, "Well, I'm not going to argue with him!"

'We all thought of him as a giant, but I think we were a lot smaller years ago. He wasn't all that tall – five foot eleven, maybe, or close to six foot – but I remember him standing out. He stood out in schoolboy football, he stood out in youth football, and he stood out in league football. It wasn't just a question of his height: he was powerfully built with it. He used that power when he was playing, but he didn't go in and just barge everybody. Other players bounced off when they tried to barge him, that's what I mean.

'The other thing about him that stood out was his fitness. We used to loosen up with a lap of the ground and moves to the side and things like that. But Duncan, he'd do anything up to ten laps in his warm-up, and those thunderous thighs of his would bounce – the muscles in them! I wouldn't say we were in awe of him exactly, but we admired him for what he could do. We tried to copy him and, instead of doing just one lap, we started doing four; but he was still far ahead of us.'

The amazing thing is that there was apparently no resentment among the other players of what might have been interpreted as sucking up to teacher. Football club dressing rooms are hardly the most forgiving places on earth, yet nobody thought to try to take the mickey out of him. '"Oh, here he comes!" we'd say,' recalled Charlton of the moment when Duncan would start his protracted solo warm-up. 'The rest of us would all be talking about different things, the way you do at the start of training; but nobody ever thought he was creeping or anything. It was just that that was what he wanted to do. He felt it was the thing to do – train, get your body right, fit. God, he was strong, though.'

There was admiration from afar, too. Back in his native Midlands, the boys he had grown up with were marvelling at Duncan's progress. 'He went off to Man United and he was such a powerful lad that within twelve months he was actually in the first team,' said Don Howe. 'But he was very down-to-earth. He didn't get carried away with himself. He wasn't going around, like, saying, "Look at me – I'm in the first team!"

'We were all surprised it had happened so quickly, but when you think about it now he was like Wayne Rooney in many ways. He was naturally stocky and strong, he had natural pace, and he had so much ability I wouldn't think there was really any need to do a coaching job on him at Man U. They would have just let him play, because that's what you do with those types of players.

'He was a midfield player, but if you asked him to play right-back, he'd play there and make a hell of a good job of it. If you asked him to play centre-forward, he'd play there because he could do it. So, as he was coming through into the Man United team, he was playing in various positions. In the end, as we all thought, he settled down as a midfield player, but he was so powerful and so naturally gifted he could play anywhere.

'He could "see" the game, too – just like Rooney. Rooney sees things that a lot of people don't see, even people who are watching the game. He's just got this natural gift of footballing vision. He can see people and knows what to do about it. Duncan was very similar

– terrific vision. Rooney's powerful, but Duncan Edwards was even more powerful. He was taller for one thing and a naturally built person in terms of body weight.

'With a lot of players, you know they'll have to work with the weights so that they can hold people off. Rooney never has a problem holding people off because he's a powerful little lad. Well, Duncan was as good as that at doing the same thing. His upper body was so naturally powerful that, if you got near him, he would put his arm out and you wouldn't get anywhere near the ball. Gazza was good at that, too: he'd kind of shield the ball and put his arm across anyone who challenged him. Duncan was the same. You couldn't get near him.'

The startling thing about those training sessions at which Edwards would put everyone else to shame is how limited and unstructured they were by comparison with today's exercises in sports science. 'You had to do your own training in those days,' said Charlton. 'The little track around the outside of the Old Trafford pitch was where we used to train; we didn't train on a big pitch. We had The Cliff then, but they played matches there. In any case, there were no changing rooms where you could take a load of people for training seven days a week. So we used to train at Old Trafford itself. They just let us go out and we would talk about what we'd done the night before as we walked round and round that little track. We would walk and we would walk and we would walk. Then the trainer would come out and you would run a little bit. Then you'd stop again. You waited until about eleven o'clock, when they threw a few balls out. Then, sometimes, the old man or Jimmy Murphy would come out and do little bits with players individually. And that, generally, was that.

'There must have been qualified coaches then, but Matt Busby wasn't one and neither was Jimmy Murphy. They knew the game, though, and how to talk to people to get the best out of them. They certainly taught us how to play the game properly. Support, control, work with your technique – they were the watchwords. But they expected you to have the technique when they signed you. These days, of course, you need your European coaching badge before you can take that sort of job, and I think that's right.'

For the second season running, Duncan Edwards had been playing for United's youth team in the FA Youth Cup as well as for the first team in the First Division. He had helped the club win the Youth Cup in the previous two seasons, and in the spring of 1955 United – with Edwards, who was still only eighteen – were in the semi-finals of the tournament once again. Their opponents were Chelsea, another club that had a fruitful youth policy, and they were expected to make it tougher than usual for United, who had scored 26 goals in the five previous rounds.

And so it proved. Despite having Charlton, Colman, McGuinness and Shay Brennan in their line-up as well as Edwards, United found themselves a goal down at half-time in the first leg at Stamford Bridge on 16 April, watched by a crowd of more than 20,000. Once again, the instructions during the interval were 'Give the ball to Duncan', and they worked like a charm. Hardly had the second half started than Edwards took possession, turned and hammered a shot into the Chelsea net to make it 1–1. Then, ten minutes later, he began to run with the ball some 40 yards from goal. Brushing aside all challenges, he steadied himself 25 yards out before belting home the winner. It was a similar story in the second leg at Old Trafford two days later, Duncan scoring both goals in another 2–1 win.

Bobby Charlton remembers those games vividly, even today. 'We played matches where he won them on his own,' he said. 'I remember, particularly, [those] two matches against Chelsea in the semi-finals of the Youth Cup. Chelsea had a reputation down south like United had up north for coaching kids and concentrating on them. But we beat them 2–1 at Chelsea, 2–1 up here at Old Trafford, and he scored all four of our goals. And I tell you, they were hard games because Chelsea did have some good players then. I remember taking a corner kick in the second leg and thinking "I'll just hang it up", because I knew he'd get there. Sure enough, he scored the winning goal by blasting through about ten people – bang. He was massive.

'If Duncan was playing against today's massed defences, he'd simply knock them down. I see teams playing against a defensive formation now and, because there's so many players and no space, they eventually finish up having to go on the outsides. If they're lucky, they'll then get a cross in. That means you need a player up front who's going to score, but most people don't have that any more because that's not the way that they play it. The long-ball game is not there any more. But Duncan would have beaten that sort of defensive system by ploughing straight through it, and nobody would have stopped him.'

The chorus of protest about United fielding a first-team player and a full England international, as Edwards was by then, against 'ordinary' youth team players was growing louder. So loud did it become that Matt Busby was moved to defend himself against accusations of unfairness from the south of England. Writing in the 'Saturday Pink' edition of the *Manchester Evening Chronicle*, the United manager referred to 'a London friend' who had told him the general opinion at a meeting of referees he had addressed was that Edwards should not be included in United's youth team. Busby responded thus:

So that's what some people think. It annoys me! Duncan is eligible to participate in the Youth Cup. And, what is more, is keen to play. He is no seeker of cups and medals, but he is just as anxious as any other United young player to have the United name inscribed on the Cup for the third successive season. It would be an achievement which perhaps may never be equalled. He may be 'outsize' in juniors, but he will probably tell you that he has to work just as hard, if not harder, in the Youth Cup competition as in senior football.

He is, as they say, 'football daft'. He dreams football and loves to talk about it and is eager to learn everything he can from the game. Duncan Edwards has not become a great footballer by bulldozer tactics. He is undoubtedly one of the greatest examples we have ever had of a footballer maturing at an early age.

But if the rules of the competition mean that he is eligible to take part, then I see no earthly reason to quibble. I don't doubt that if other clubs had the opportunity, they would willingly include him in their Youth side.

Duncan Edwards has come to the front the hard way. That is by constant training and coaching. The United youngster never needs to be told what to do – though he is not alone in that respect.

He, like others, is determined to make a success of his career as a footballer. He is willing to listen to advice and put that advice into practice on the field. Here is an eighteen-year-old whose example can be a lesson to every soccer-thinking youth.

I am happy to think that Duncan is getting so many honours from the game. I am glad to know that he remains as keen a player in junior soccer circles as in representative games. But to suggest that because of his exceptional talent he should not play in Youth games is in my opinion ridiculous.

So there was never any chance of Busby taking pity on West Bromwich Albion, United's latest victims – er, opponents – in the final of the FA Youth Cup. It was virtually ritual slaughter, United taking a 4–1 lead in the first leg at Old Trafford to which Edwards did not contribute a goal. He did score in the return at The Hawthorns, though, as United won 3–0 and claimed the cup 7–1 on aggregate.

It was Duncan's last goal at that age level, because he was too old to play in the Youth Cup from then on. But his enforced absence from the team did not bring other clubs the relief for which they had hoped, since United went on to win the trophy twice more without him in the next two seasons, 1955/56 and 1956/57. Which just goes to show how many talented youngsters Busby and Murphy had accumulated at Old Trafford. It also answered in the most emphatic terms, of course, the claim that United were just a one-man team.

In June 1955, at eighteen years and eight months of age, Edwards may have been too old to play in the FA Youth Cup, but he was eligible for something far less palatable. National Service, an institution Wayne Rooney's generation may never even have heard of, was a rite of passage most fit young men had to go through in the fifties. Because Britain needed a peacetime force for the occupation of West Germany after the Second World War and for dealing with other trouble spots around the world, men between the ages of 18 and 25 were called up to do two years' service in the army, navy or air force – and footballers were not exempted.

Edwards went into the army and was posted to Nesscliffe, near Shrewsbury, with the Royal Army Ordnance Corps. He was joined there, a year later, by Bobby Charlton, who was a year younger. 'That was so we could get to Old Trafford quickly on a Saturday for the match,' said Charlton, who did not try to disguise the fact that both he and Duncan received preferential treatment because they were Manchester United footballers. 'We got home Friday nights,' Charlton added. 'One of the COs was a big United fan and I think, somehow or other, they managed to get Duncan and me into his battalion so that he could guarantee that we would be available on Saturdays. We used to get the train back from camp every Friday night at half-past five and sit with the same person every time. He was an old man who used to travel back with us. He was coming back to Manchester for the weekend, like us, after working in Shrewsbury during the week. We didn't have cars until we were out of the service, really.'

It was quite early in his National Service that Charlton realised strings were being pulled by United. 'I did my six weeks' basic training at Portsmouth and, after that, you're told where you are going. Most of them went out to Malaya, where there was a war going on. Then it came up that I had to go to Malaya as well. It said "Charlton – Malaya" and I thought, "Jesus!" I phoned Old Trafford straight away and they said, "Oh, no. Don't worry about it. We've been told that you'll be going to Shrewsbury. Wait for a day, and if it's still the same, call me." I waited another three hours and went to look at the orders again. It said, "Report Nesscliffe, Shrewsbury".'

He has, too, a vivid memory of arriving at Nesscliffe and being greeted agitatedly, and solicitously, by Edwards. 'When I got to the billet, it was during the day, so most people were working. But Duncan hadn't gone to do his job because he was waiting for me.

"Where have you been, where have you been?" he said. To which I replied, "I'm tired. I've been travelling for about ten hours to get here." "OK," he says, "which bed do you want?" "I'm not bothered," I said, "they're all the same." But he went and shook them all, and none of them were good enough in his opinion. So he went out and I could hear him in one of the other billets, clattering around; and he brought a bed in – a whole bed – and said, "That one's all right." He took the other one out. "You'll be all right, now," he said when he came back in.'

Charlton has mixed feelings about the two years taken out of his life by National Service, and you imagine Edwards must have felt much the same. 'I did resent it when it started, and I hated it when I was in [the army],' he said, 'but when I came out, I was glad I'd done it. For the first time in your life you had to think for yourself: there was no mother and dad to look after you. You've got to look after yourself, and it gives you something. It gives you an idea of how to work with other people. It's so old-fashioned to say this, but you can't help wondering whether they should bring it back. All older people say that, but it'll never happen.'

The experience was softened considerably for Charlton and Edwards by the football – not just the weekends they were given off to play for Manchester United, but the games they were asked to play for the Army XI. 'We played for the army team a lot, and it was magical,' Charlton recalled. 'We were lucky in as much as we did get off for weekends and we travelled to play for the army during the week – which everybody called a skive, of course. We were lucky in that respect, but we both wanted to be at Old Trafford in midweek because it was just the start of European football then for Manchester United. I missed European matches because the army were a bit reluctant to let you go in the middle of the week. I remember the first time United went to play in Bilbao [on 16 January 1957]. I was watching these aeroplanes flying over Shrewsbury – there weren't many – and I was thinking, "Is that them on their way?"'

The advent of the European Cup in 1955/56 was, of course, one of the most important and far-reaching changes in the history of

European football. It would be foolish to suggest that the English would be playing just domestic football now had the European Cup not come into being, because somebody else would undoubtedly have come up with the idea during the next half-century. But England's clubs would have had a lot more ground to make up on their continental rivals had Manchester United not insisted on ignoring blinkered opposition from the Football League and taken part in the second season of the new knockout tournament for the champions of Europe.

We run ahead of ourselves, however. The 1955/56 season had not begun promisingly for United. They won only three of their opening eight fixtures, losing three and drawing two of the others. Not surprisingly, perhaps, in view of the distraction of National Service, it also took Edwards time to find his best form. Then, just when he was starting to play well and score goals, he was struck down by a bout of influenza so severe that he was admitted to Manchester's Davyhulme Park Hospital and kept under observation.

It took Duncan over a month to recover fully from the illness and United's results continued to be mixed during his absence. But his return in mid-October helped them chalk up two consecutive victories, against Huddersfield and Cardiff, that took them to the top of the First Division. It was not until early February 1956, however, that United went on the sort of unbeaten run that marks out true champions. Starting with a 2–0 victory over Burnley at home, they won all but four of their last fourteen league matches and eventually claimed the title by eleven points. It was effectively theirs, though, when they beat Blackpool, their nearest challengers, 2–1 in a tense encounter at a packed and heaving Old Trafford on 7 April, which put United beyond reach with two games remaining.

So, Matt Busby and his directors now had to decide whether or not to follow the example of Chelsea, the previous season's English champions, who had declined to take part in the inaugural European Cup competition (launched as the European Champion Clubs Cup) despite having attended the formative meeting of leading clubs in Paris and having been drawn at home against Djurgaarden of

Sweden in the first round. Chelsea backed out largely because their chairman, Joe Mears, was also a member of the Football League management committee, who were firmly opposed to the introduction of additional matches to the English fixture list. Attendances for Saturday matches in the First Division were dropping, and the committee believed one reason was the televised friendlies against high-class foreign opposition such as those Chelsea and Wolves had been arranging. According to John Battersby, Chelsea's secretary at the time, Mears was torn between wanting to see his club in the prestigious new tournament and wanting to do his duty to the Football League. In the end, he bowed to the League's pressure.

Unencumbered by such divided loyalties, Manchester United decided to defy the Football League and go it alone. One factor in their decision was the enjoyment Hibernian had derived from taking part in the inaugural tournament, with the blessing of the Scottish Football Association, as Scotland's representatives. 'At the time I was very friendly with Harry Swan, the chairman of Hibernian, and he was full of it,' recalled Busby later. 'I had the feeling at this time that football was no longer an English game or a British game but a world game. I said this to the board, and of course they were very happy about it. The invitation to compete had arrived from UEFA via the Football Association, who had no objections. But the next thing was that the League management committee wrote a letter to the club saying they did not like the idea of us going in. We had a meeting again and I felt very strongly about it, that this was the new avenue to go into, and we just went on with it.'

According to Eamon Dunphy in his study of Busby and Manchester United, *A Strange Kind of Glory*, there were other, more practical considerations behind the decision:

His [Busby's] rationale for engaging in European competition was threefold. First, it would provide money to pay for the floodlights United had still to install, and for the large, ever-expanding wage bill rising in proportion to the number of First Division quality players on United's books. Second, the extra competition, seen as a problem by the Football League, was a blessing to Busby – players could be kept happy and gain experience playing in the Champions Cup. His final reason was more abstract than practical. He understood how irrevocably the balance of power was shifting away from the English game, and saw that football in the future would be an international game. The world was contracting, travel was easier, people were curious about abroad. As a football man he was intrigued by the international game. Football as played by the Hungarians was his kind of game.

As a result of United's European adventure, Duncan Edwards faced an ever-increasing workload. Despite what Bobby Charlton said about the army's reluctance to release National Servicemen in mid-week to play for their clubs, Edwards made seven appearances for United in the European Cup in the 1956/57 season. In fact, he played 56 games at the highest level when you also take into consideration his league and FA Cup appearances for United and representative appearances for England's U-23 and full international sides. On top of that was an unknown number of games for the British Army XI and Western Command, because he was not due to be demobbed until the summer of 1957. But it is known that it was not unusual for him, at nineteen or twenty, to be playing two or three times a week; sometimes as many as four times. They are figures to make today's sports scientists blanch, but Edwards just seemed to take it all comfortably in his massive stride.

Domestically, United began the 1956/57 season like true champions. They won ten of their first twelve First Division fixtures and drew the other two. In fact, they lost only six times in all and won the title for the second year running by finishing twelve points ahead of runners-up Tottenham Hotspur. This, too, despite the additional playing burden of reaching the semi-final of the European Cup and the final of the FA Cup. In other words, it was the Busby Babes' *annus mirabilis*.

In addition to getting off to that whirlwind start in the First Division, United found little barring their way when they made their debut in the European Cup. On 12 September 1956 they went to play Anderlecht in Brussels and came away from the first leg of this preliminary round tie with a useful 2–0 lead. Duncan Edwards had missed the match because of a toe injury, but he was fit a fortnight later for the return, which was played at Maine Road because of the lack of floodlights at Old Trafford.

Edwards' inclusion at the expense of Jackie Blanchflower was not chiefly responsible for what followed, however. Unusually, he was overshadowed by other players as United slaughtered the Belgian champions 10–0 with a devastating display of attacking football. The goals were shared between Dennis Viollet (four), Tommy Taylor (three), Liam Whelan (two) and Johnny Berry (one). David Pegg, the only member of the forward line not to score, helped make most of them. It was a performance that put the rest of Europe on notice that a remarkable team had taken shape at Manchester United. Sportingly, the Anderlecht players applauded United all the way to the dressing room, and a delighted Busby reached for the superlatives. 'It was the greatest thrill in a lifetime of soccer,' he said at the time. 'It was the finest display of teamwork I have ever seen from any team, club or international. It was as near perfect football as anyone could wish to see.' Josef Mermans, Anderlecht's veteran captain and a seasoned Belgium international, was equally impressed. He said even Hungary's best teams had not given Anderlecht a beating like that and reminded everyone his club had recently beaten Arsenal. Finally, Mermans recommended that the whole United team should be picked to play for England, an honour that would have been possible for all but Irishman Whelan. But, if it came to that, United had none other than Bobby Charlton in reserve.

Delusions of grandeur may have set in, because United's young team found their next European Cup assignment a great deal more difficult. Drawn at home against the West German club Borussia Dortmund, they struggled to win the first, home leg of the first-round tie 3–2 and then had to fight a difficult rearguard action on a frozen pitch to secure a goalless draw in the return. Frank Taylor, of the *News Chronicle*, was critical of United as a team and Duncan as an individual, suggesting the runaway victory over Anderlecht had made them a little too cocky.

Further proof that Edwards was, after all, only human came three days after the first leg against Borussia Dortmund. At home to Everton, he was as guilty as anyone else of a nightmarish performance that enabled the Merseysiders to win 5–2. But as his and United's form picked up again, Duncan underlined his value to the team by demonstrating his versatility. Having turned out at left-half and inside-left, as well as an emergency centre-half, on 29 December he was asked to replace the injured Tommy Taylor at centre-forward against Portsmouth. Needless to say, he scored one of the goals in a 3–1 win.

Edwards even played in goal that season. It did not happen in any old match, either. Duncan volunteered to squeeze his substantial frame into the goalkeeper's jersey when Ray Wood was injured after 37 minutes of the annual FA Charity (now Community) Shield match between the league champions and the FA Cup holders. In 1956/57, that meant a local derby between United and Manchester City played at Maine Road. Edwards was relieved of the jersey eventually by United's junior goalkeeper, David Gaskell, who had been attending the game as a spectator; but he had played his part in keeping an important clean sheet, Viollet having scored the only goal of the game.

Progress in the European Cup began to be really hard to make when United faced Athletic Bilbao in the second round. Northern Spain in January is anything but the Costa del Sol, and the first leg was played in a blizzard and on a sea of mud. Not only that, but Bilbao were an extremely tough nut to crack. Beaten only once at home in three seasons, they had just seen off the Honved of Ferenc Puskas and company 6–5 on aggregate in the previous round.

So it was hardly surprising when the Basques, quick and strong, took a 3–0 lead by the interval. United clawed back most of the deficit with goals by Taylor and Viollet, only for Bilbao to go 5–2 in front. The visitors were in a virtually hopeless position until Whelan came up with a late face-saver that gave them a glimmer of hope for the second leg. Duncan made the most of it with a shot the Bilbao goal-keeper could only block; Viollet pounced on the rebound and United were back in the tie. Second-half goals by Taylor and Berry then saw them home as the Babes found their finest form again in front of an ecstatic 70,000 at Maine Road.

Soon after winning that trial of strength with Bilbao, United had to turn their attentions to the FA Cup. By 16 February 1957 they had reached the fifth round by beating Hartlepools United 4–3 away and Wrexham 5–0 away. Now, at home to Everton, they faced First Division opponents for the first time. They found it tough, too, as the Merseysiders, who had thrashed them 5–2 at Old Trafford in October, refused to yield in a tight, tense contest. Eventually, however, Edwards' driving presence brought a winning goal. When Whelan's shot was crowded out in the 67th minute, Duncan picked up the rebound on the edge of the penalty area and drilled the ball just inside a post.

A fortnight later, United found themselves on the south coast playing Bournemouth in the sixth round. As for Edwards, he found himself occupying two totally different positions during an unex-pectedly difficult tie against giant-killers from the old Third Division South. Starting again as a replacement for the injured Taylor at cen-tre-forward, Duncan had to switch to centre-half when Mark Jones got hurt after only ten minutes. He did not play well in his defensive role, and United were grateful to Berry for scoring the two goals that enabled them to scrape through to the semi-finals for the first time since 1949 with an unimpressive 2–1 win.

United were now being quoted at 5/1 to complete the remarka-ble new treble of league championship, FA Cup and European Cup. They were not particularly generous odds, given that this was their debut season in European football, but the bookmakers' miserliness reflected the respect and optimism this outstanding young team had inspired. Anyone who had taken the bet must have cursed under their breath, though, when United won only one of their next four First Division fixtures. In between, they overcame Birmingham quite easily in the semi-finals of the FA Cup, goals by Charlton and Berry deciding the game in the first twenty minutes.

There was a shock waiting for them at the same stage of the European Cup, where they faced a Real Madrid team in the process of becoming a legend. Puskas had yet to join them after defecting from Hungary following the uprising of 1956, but maestros like Alfredo di Stefano, Francisco Gento and Raymond Kopa were already in place. Having beaten Stade de Reims in the European Cup's first final, Real were the defending champions; as such, they simply knew too much for Busby's young, inexperienced side. Edwards admitted as much following Real's 3–1 first-leg victory in Madrid. 'We simply did not get going until Real Madrid went 2–0 in front,' he said, 'and by then it was a little too late.' It was a similar story in the return. Madrid were 2–0 up before United got going. A second-half revival produced goals by Taylor and Charlton, but they were not enough to stop Real going through 5–3 on aggregate to the second of the five successive finals they won so famously at the start of the European Cup. So bang went that unlikely treble for United.

There was still the FA Cup final to come, of course. Nine days after going out of the European Cup at the semi-final stage, United faced Aston Villa at Wembley. Having wrapped up the championship for the second season on the trot with a 4–0 victory over Sunderland on 20 April, four games from the end of the season, the Babes, or Red Devils – call them what you will – were hot favourites to complete the more familiar league and FA Cup double. After all, so the thinking went, they had taken three points off Villa in the First Division (for a win and a draw) and the Birmingham club had had a much harder struggle to reach the final. Three times they had needed a replay to get past First Division opponents Luton, Burnley and West Bromwich Albion.

Unfortunately for United, Wembley finals have a nasty habit of upsetting the odds; and such was the case on this occasion. Only six minutes into the match came its decisive moment. Chasing his own header into the United penalty area, Peter McParland, Villa's Northern Ireland international winger, just kept running as Ray Wood, the United goalkeeper, came out to collect the bouncing ball. There was a sickening collision between them and both players crashed to the ground hurt. Wood came off much the worse: his injury was diagnosed later as a fractured jaw. He was also suffering from concussion and obviously could not continue. So, with substitutes not allowed, Jackie Blanchflower, having borrowed a photographer's cap, went in goal and made a memorably good job of it. Heroically, the dazed Wood came back on later to play on the wing, but he departed again before returning for a second time to take back the goalkeeper's jersey from Blanchflower for the last few minutes.

McParland, more solidly built than Wood, soon recovered from the collision and went on to score twice in the second half. To add insult to injury for United, the controversial Irishman was clearly in an offside position when he scored his second goal in the 72nd minute. According to Eamon Dunphy, Jackie Blanchflower told him that McParland, one of his Northern Ireland team-mates and 'a naive lad', had been instructed by Villa to test Wood by 'getting into him' as soon as possible. Whatever McParland's motives or intentions were, the villain of the piece succeeded in bringing United's season of immense promise and no little achievement to a frustratingly anti-climactic end. Tommy Taylor scored a consolation goal in a late rally by United, but not even Duncan Edwards, who had been forced to replace Blanchflower at centre-half for most of the match, could rescue the team most of the nation had taken to their hearts, regardless of which club they supported. 'This sad climax to a glorious season,' wrote Dunphy, 'saddened the nation, the majority of whom, though not *au fait* with soccer, had been enthralled by the blaze of youthful colour Busby's "Red Devils" had ingrained in England's image of itself. Fate as much as Peter McParland had struck down the young heroes. It was the way of the world, courage fated to lose even when triumph seemed inevitable. More than a Cup was lost in many hearts that day.'

Given the helping hand he offered fate, it was not a good day for the referee, Frank Coultas. McParland would have been sent off today for charging into Wood's face shoulder-first, as he did. Instead, he was allowed to continue and win the match for Villa. Coultas did not even realise a foul had been committed, according to Ken Aston, who was one of the linesmen that day and who was patrolling the side of the pitch where the incident occurred. Many years later, Aston told me he had had to wave his flag furiously to attract the referee's attention.

As for Ray Wood, he was one of nine FA Cup final victims of what, between 1952 and 1965, came to be called the Wembley Hoodoo. Walley Barnes (Arsenal 0 Newcastle 1, 1952), Eric Bell (Bolton 3 Blackpool 4, 1953), Jimmy Meadows (Manchester City 1 Newcastle 3, 1955), Bert Trautmann (Manchester City 3 Birmingham City 1, 1956), Roy Dwight (Nottingham Forest 2 Luton Town 1, 1959), Dave Whelan (Blackburn 0 Wolverhampton Wanderers 3, 1960), Len Chalmers (Leicester City 0 Tottenham Hotspur 2, 1961) and Gerry Byrne (Liverpool 2 Leeds United 1, 1965) all suffered injuries serious enough to affect the outcome of their finals – though not all did – and to force the authorities to address the issue of substitutes. At their AGM four weeks after Liverpool left-back Byrne had played all but the first three minutes of the two-hour 1965 final with a broken collarbone, the Football League approved the use of one substitute in the event of injury; this was ratified a few days later by the FA. But it was later still when substitutions were permitted for any reason, and it was not until 1986/87 that two substitutes were first allowed. That became three when the Premier League got under way in 1992/93, although one of them had to be a goalkeeper and only two could be used. The Football League followed suit a year later; then, in 1995/96, they joined with the Premier League in standardising the rule at three for any reason.

Few players were more familiar with the substitution rules than Wayne Rooney. In 2002/03, the season during which he made his grand entrance on the Premiership stage, the juvenile lead had come off the bench more times (nineteen) than he had started games (fourteen). In addition, he had begun only two of the six England internationals in which he had played. Now, with his stock and value soaring and the 2003/04 season approaching, the time had come to begin appearing regularly for club and country.

Having finished seventh in the Premiership, their highest position for seven years, in 2002/03, Everton were expected to push on from there and really begin to challenge the dominance neighbours Liverpool had enjoyed over them for longer than anyone in blue cared to remember. Everton manager David Moyes had predicted a shift in the balance of power in advance of the Merseyside derby at Goodison Park in April 2003, when both clubs were chasing a Champions League place. 'This may be an important game,' he said, 'but, believe me, there are going to be bigger ones than this. We have progressed this season, but this is just the start. At the start of the season, Liverpool were in a different league to us [metaphorically speaking, he meant], but not now. We are really ready to compete with them now.' But it did not work out quite like that – not immediately, anyway. Liverpool won the derby 2–1 and finished fifth, five points ahead of Everton. It meant they qualified for the UEFA Cup and the European football Everton longed to be part of again; the European football, moreover, they had been denied almost continuously since 1985, partly because of the lethal rioting by Liverpool fans at Brussels' Heysel Stadium that led to English clubs being banned from Europe for five years.

Howard Kendall's fine Everton side were champions of England and winners of the old European Cup Winners' Cup in 1984/85. They were fully primed to take over Liverpool's pre-eminent position at home and abroad when the door to the European Cup was suddenly slammed shut in their faces through no fault of their own. It took Everton a long time to recover from that massive psychological and financial blow. Although Kendall's team won the First Division title again two seasons later, 1986/87, their fortunes began to decline steadily when their inspiring young manager, bored with having only domestic honours to aim for, left to manage the Basque club Athletic Bilbao in 1987. By 2001/02 Everton were still in the top division, but usually to be found in its bottom half and often fighting to avoid relegation. A succession of managers, including Kendall himself in two other, ill-advised spells back at Goodison, tried to pull this great old club out of its slough of despond, but to no avail.

To no avail, that is, until Moyes came along in March 2002 as the successor to dismissed fellow Scot Walter Smith. Like a lot of ex-footballers of no great merit, Moyes had found football management to be where he excelled. Having finished his playing career at Preston, he had worked his way up the ladder from team captain to assistant manager and finally manager. That was in 1998, when Preston were in the new Division Two of the Football League (the Third Division before the First Division broke away to form the Premier League in 1992). Two years later, Moyes steered North End into Division One and then made them contenders for promotion to the Premiership. On the strength of that promising record, he was asked to restore Everton to the prominent position they had enjoyed twenty years earlier as one of English football's so-called 'Big Five', along with Liverpool, Manchester United, Arsenal and Tottenham. Moyes' first task was to save them from relegation, which he did quite comfortably. Then, in his first full season, 2002/03, he nearly got them into Europe. Now the proud possessors of the finest young English footballer to emerge in years, there seemed no limit to what Everton could achieve in 2003/04.

Unfortunately, very little went right from the start. Playing in a pre-season friendly against Glasgow Rangers at Ibrox, Wayne Rooney was stretchered off with ankle ligament damage that threatened his chances of starting the season proper. The injury did not prove to be as serious as first thought, and Rooney was fit enough to be included among the substitutes for Everton's opening match, a 2–1 defeat by Arsenal at Highbury. It was the start of a miserable opening sequence of results in which only two of the first twelve fixtures were won and six were lost. This, too, despite the best efforts of Rooney, who played in all but two of those games and scored a superb late equaliser in a 2–2 draw with Charlton at The Valley.

By the end of November, far from challenging for a place in Europe again, Everton were in the bottom three. Rooney's frustration at having to endure such unfamiliar and unexpected ignominy bubbled to the surface in a 2–0 defeat at Bolton, where he reacted furiously to being substituted. It was after that he really started to play. Having scored the winner in a 2–1 victory at Portsmouth, Rooney roused Everton when they were in danger of losing at home to Leicester. At 2–1 down, his equaliser gave the Blues the momentum that brought them a winning goal by Tomasz Radzinski.

Those successive wins were a rare bright spot, though, in a season of pervading gloom. The 2–0 victory over Aston Villa on 28 February was their first win in ten matches. Rooney kept scoring – he finished as Everton's top marksman in the Premiership with nine goals – but his club's form improved only marginally. In fact, they ended up only one place away from relegation, although they did have six points to spare over the eighteenth club, Leicester.

Nor did the FA Cup or Carling Cup provide much light relief. Everton went only as far as the fourth round in the FA Cup, where they were knocked out by Fulham after a replay. They fared a little better in the Carling Cup, going out on penalties to Middlesbrough in the fifth round. All in all, though, it was not the sort of season calculated to persuade even an Evertonian as committed as Wayne Rooney that his beloved local club could match his ambitions in the game.

CHAPTER 6

TWO LIONS

DUNCAN Edwards' progress into the senior England team was nothing like as swift and straightforward as Wayne Rooney's. This was not so much a question of ability as of football politics and competition. Whereas autonomous England coach Sven-Goran Eriksson could pick whom he liked, and had nobody else like Rooney to choose, Edwards had to contend with some talented rivals and an antiquated, often partisan selection system. This was the era of the dreaded, all-powerful FA Senior International Committee, otherwise known as the selectors, which comprised the chairmen or directors of various Football League clubs guided by the secretary of the FA, then the influential, long-serving Sir Stanley Rous, and England's first manager, Walter Winterbottom, appointed in 1946. There was a natural reluctance in that group of mostly middle-aged or elderly men to give youth, however talented, its head too soon. In fairness to the selectors, it must be remembered that television was in its infancy then and players could not make the instant nationwide impact they can in today's technologically sophisticated age of wall-to-wall football. So, for a variety of reasons, Edwards had to serve his time, so to speak, lower down the international scale before being allowed a full cap.

In those days, there was plenty of scope for bringing through potential international footballers gradually. In addition to the England U-23 team (which did not change into the U-21s until 1976, when UEFA decided the lower age limit provided a more realistic stepping-stone between youth and senior international football), there was the England B team and the Football League's representative side.

The B team played nineteen matches between 1949 and 1957, and Duncan Edwards appeared in four of them. He also played six times for the U-23s, scoring the remarkable total of five goals. His first cap at the junior level came on 20 January 1954, when England met Italy in Bologna in their first fixture of that kind. Edwards also set a record by becoming the youngest Englishman, at seventeen years and 112 days, to play for the U-23s, but it was not a happy baptism. Duncan, never the most relaxed of air travellers, was among several of the England youngsters who suffered badly from airsickness on the flight out the day before the game. Not surprisingly, then, England lost 3–0, and that is when, it is thought, his subsequent dislike of flying really took root.

In terms of the result, the return against the Italians at Stamford Bridge a year later was a totally different matter. Fielding a much stronger side than in Bologna, England won 5–1. Although Duncan did not score, he did not fail to impress. '[Ron] Flowers and Edwards, restless and strong both in the air and in the tackle, were the masters of midfield,' wrote the football correspondent of *The Times*, the incomparable Geoffrey Green, who yielded to no man in his admiration for the young leviathan. 'Edwards, indeed – the master of the 40- or 50-yard pass – played like a tornado, attacking, defending, always wanting to be at the eye of the storm,' Green enthused in his classic history of the decade, *Soccer in the Fifties*. 'Many were the great goals he scored, too, as he pounded forward on a solo run like a runaway tank to release a shell from the edge of the penalty area that would have penetrated a steel wall ...'

Green also recalled one of Duncan's finest hours as a U-23 international. It was in a 1955 game against Scotland at Clyde's Shawfield Stadium that England won 6–0. Substitutes were permitted in this so-called friendly, so when centre-forward Bobby Ayre was injured, England sent on Stan Anderson to play at left-half and switched Edwards to centre-forward. Frank Blunstone and John Atyeo having given the visitors a 2–0 lead at the interval, Duncan went on a second-half rampage that brought him a hat-trick and added to the legend that was beginning to grow up around him. A goal by Johnny Haynes completed a display so dazzling that even the fiercely partisan Scottish fans are said to have stood and applauded.

Everyone had begun to realise by now that Manchester United and England were fortunate enough to have been blessed with a truly exceptional young footballer. At about the time of Duncan's hat-trick against Scotland, the *Manchester Evening Chronicle*'s Alf Clarke wrote:

> I have said before and I repeat it, that Duncan Edwards is certain to be England's future captain. Chief problem is where to play him. He is a brilliant wing half back, can also adapt himself to centre half, and now both United and England realise his possibilities in attack.
>
> That is where I think he should be played. That is why United did so well at Huddersfield last weekend, and that is why England U23 won so handsomely at Clyde ... We cannot escape from the fact that Duncan Edwards is the greatest young player of his age. I know we had our [Cliff] Bastins, [Raich] Carters, [Peter] Dohertys and others, but I rank Edwards as the best young player I have ever seen.

Jimmy Armfield, the long-serving Blackpool full-back who was in the England squad that won the World Cup in 1966, both played with and against Duncan Edwards. So his admiration for the man, which prompted him to name his son after him, carries special weight. Armfield, now a respected summariser for Radio Five Live, used to write a column for the *Daily Express*. In one of them he said the following about the U-23 international against Czechoslovakia in 1957 in which they both played: 'He [Edwards] was the difference between the two sides, and England won 2–0. He scored both goals with terrific left-foot shots from outside the box, and every time he had the ball the Czechs went into immediate panic. It seemed to me that they were physically afraid. Every time he strode forward not one defender would risk the challenge. And that's how he got both goals.'

That game in Bratislava was Edwards' last as a U-23 international. By then, though still only twenty, he had become an established senior international and had outgrown the junior side. His first full cap had arrived on 2 April 1955, when he was just eighteen years and 183 days old. That meant he was the youngest player to have played at senior level for England up to then, a record that stood until Michael Owen broke it by 124 days in 1998. Then, of course, Wayne Rooney came along five years later to lower the figure even further.

Although Duncan Edwards broke records for youthfulness in the early part of his career, nobody could say he had not paid his international dues by the time he was selected for England's senior side. After appearing three times for the U-23s, against Italy twice and Scotland, he was selected for the B team that beat West Germany 4–0 at Gelsenkirchen in the first post-war international between the two countries. But just when everyone was tipping him for a full cap, an uncharacteristically poor performance for United in a 3–1 defeat at Arsenal in March 1954 sent the selectors away unimpressed and scuppered whatever chance he might have had of being included in the England squad for that summer's World Cup finals in Switzerland.

For the time being, Duncan had to be satisfied with selection for the Young England team that met the senior England side at Highbury on the eve of the FA Cup final between West Bromwich Albion and Preston North End. He was in good company: club colleagues Roger Byrne and Tommy Taylor played alongside him, and the opposing forward line read Matthews, Mannion, Lawton, Shackleton and Langton. Edwards confessed afterwards that those great players had given his team the 'run-around', but he still recalled it as being 'the most enjoyable match of my career to date'.

His very inclusion in the Young England team, of course, proved that the selectors regarded him as a senior international of the future – and the not too distant future at that. When a series of commanding displays by Edwards for United in the early months of the 1954/55 season attracted the attention of England selector Harold Shentall twice in four days, it looked as though his time had come. But still he had to wait. The more experienced Ray Barlow, of West Brom, and Bill Slater, of Wolves, were preferred when replacements were required for that seemingly permanent fixture at left-half, Portsmouth's Jimmy

Dickinson, in England's autumn victories over Northern Ireland, Wales and West Germany. Finally, two months after he had scored that startling hat-trick for the U-23s against Scotland in Glasgow, the selectors could ignore Duncan no longer.

By now, incidentally, some slight progress had been made towards autonomy for the England manager. As a concession, the FA allowed Walter Winterbottom, the chairman of selectors and one other selector to pick the team before submitting it to the full International Committee for their approval. And, in the aftermath of the two shattering defeats by Hungary in November 1953 and May 1954, Winterbottom was anxious to rebuild the England team and their morale by bringing through the many promising players he had seen in the U-23s.

It is hard to convey now the deep sense of shock in the motherland of football caused by those two overwhelming Hungarian victories. The first of them was the first any foreign national side had managed to achieve on English soil (if you disregard the Republic of Ireland's 2–0 victory at Goodison Park in 1949, that is), and the second savagely underlined the fact that complacent, old-fashioned England, who snootily declined to compete in the first three World Cups, were no longer masters of the game they had given to the world. In his official biography of Billy Wright, *A Hero for All Seasons*, Norman Giller quoted the England captain as saying, 'There was a mist over Wembley that afternoon and I think we felt as if we were lost in a fog as the Hungarians completely outplayed us. It was not that England played badly. Hungary were just in a different class, and playing a style of football that was, well, foreign to us ... It was a defeat that started a revolution in our game. We knew from that day on that we needed to get into the modern world.'

Radical change did follow, albeit slowly. The need for properly organised coaching and training was gradually accepted at club level, tactical formations more imaginative than the standard WM were tried, and players' kit changed out of all recognition. The baggy shorts and heavy boots gave way to much lighter and more flexible equipment. In the short term, however, all Winterbottom could do was try to get Duncan Edwards into the senior England team as fast as he could.

Duncan did not make it easy for him, however. In early March 1955, clearly fretting about his chances of winning a first full cap for England, he gave a clumsy, lifeless performance for the Football League against the Scottish League that must have made the selection committee wonder whether they were doing the right thing. But, at the end of the month, there was his name in the senior side to play Scotland at Wembley. Edwards was one of three debutants that early April day, the others being Chelsea right-half Ken Armstrong and Manchester City full-back Jimmy Meadows (neither of whom, strangely, played for England again), and the home side humiliated the Scots by winning 7–2. Wolves' Dennis Wilshaw (four), Bolton's Nat Lofthouse (two) and Manchester City's Don Revie shared the goals in a victory that could not have made Duncan's introduction to top-level international football much easier.

'During the week leading up to the match,' Edwards recalled later, 'I never really gave it much thought. On the Friday, however, I was a little nervous, while on the Saturday not too bad. But by lunchtime on the Saturday, I really had "butterflies". Once I got to Wembley itself and into the dressing rooms, there were good luck telegrams to read and I began to feel better. All the players wished me luck before we went out and Billy Wright said that if anyone shouted at me just to take it with a pinch of salt.'

It is doubtful whether Duncan got any abuse from his team-mates. Although his debut was not sensational by any means, he played well enough to look thoroughly at home in this company. Helped by having his club captain, Roger Byrne, playing directly behind him, and well used by now to appearing in front of a big crowd at Wembley, Edwards made a good case for retention by the selectors. Billy Wright was certainly impressed. 'Two things stick in my memory from this match: the four goals from my clubmate Dennis Wilshaw, and the storming debut performance of young Duncan Edwards,' the England captain said in his autobiography.

Duncan was the most exciting prospect I had ever seen. He had immense strength in the tackle, and was dynamic on the ball. Duncan played with such assurance and confidence that you would have thought he was a veteran rather than a young man just starting out on his international career. Walter Winterbottom summed it up when he said quietly to me after the match, 'I think we've uncovered a gem.' As Duncan was born and raised in Dudley in the West Midlands, Stan Cullis kept scratching his head while trying to work out how he had let him escape from on his doorstep to Old Trafford.

Even the FA's selection committee could see that Duncan Edwards was a rare find. So Winterbottom had no difficulty in retaining him for England's next three internationals, all of which came during a close-season tour of the continent that could hardly be called a runaway success. It began with a 1–0 defeat by France in Paris; then England drew 1–1 with Spain in Madrid before losing 3–1 to Portugal in Oporto.

Duncan was a little unlucky in that this was an experimental England team he had joined. Encouraged by the success Manchester City had enjoyed using Don Revie in the sort of deep-lying centre-forward role Nandor Hidegkuti had exploited so damagingly for Hungary, Winterbottom tried to replicate the ploy in the England team. Unfortunately, Revie picked up an injury against France and, in the manager's words, 'was never afterwards quite as effective'. Worse still, from Duncan's point of view, one of his rare mistakes had been responsible for Spain's equaliser. In his defence, it ought to be pointed out that the England tour began only a fortnight after Edwards had helped Manchester United to win the FA Youth Cup for the third time in a row by beating West Bromwich Albion 7–1 on aggregate. That was in addition to having made a total of 36 league and FA Cup appearances for United in the 1954/55 season. So, as strong and enthusiastic as he was at eighteen, Duncan could be forgiven the odd error after shouldering a workload as heavy as that.

Edwards missed the next four internationals and did not play for England again until the annual game against Scotland in April 1956 (which finished 1–1). This was largely because he, like most other boys of his age, had to begin his two years' National Service in the summer of 1955. The severe bout of influenza he had in September, which kept him out of seven United fixtures, did not help either. Maybe the selectors, not famous for their patience, were also mindful of his unspectacular contribution to the disappointing close-season tour of France, Spain and Portugal. Whatever the reason, or reasons, Edwards lost his place at left-half to the eternal Jimmy Dickinson in the autumn games against Denmark, Wales, Northern Ireland and Spain, all but one of which were won handsomely.

When Duncan was recalled against Scotland, England were already two matches into a run of sixteen without defeat. Together with Edwards, other outstanding graduates from the U-23 side such as Fulham inside-forward Johnny Haynes and Blackburn right-half Ronnie Clayton were beginning to give the side a very promising new look. With United's Roger Byrne and Tommy Taylor also providing defensive soundness and attacking potency respectively, twelve of those sixteen matches were won. Three of them enabled England to qualify for the 1958 World Cup over a year before the finals in Sweden. So all looked set fair for England's third tilt at the big prize.

Along the way, Edwards acquired a nickname as well as a legion of new admirers. The soubriquet was bestowed on him by the West German media in response to an awesome performance he, fresh from winning the First Division title with Manchester United, gave against their country at Berlin's packed Olympic Stadium in the final match of England's close-season tour of Sweden, Finland and West Germany in 1956. 'Boom Boom Edwards' they called him after he had picked up a throw from goalkeeper Reg Matthews and run more than half the length of the field with the ball before battering it into the German net from 25 yards. It was Duncan's first goal for England and the first of three the team scored in a 3–1 victory over the world champions – for West Germany had confounded all expectations by beating Hungary, the overwhelming favourites, in the final of the 1954 World Cup. 'The name of Duncan Edwards was on the lips of everybody who saw this match,' recalled Billy Wright. 'He was phenomenal. There have been few individual performances to match what he produced in Germany that day. He tackled like a lion, attacked at every opportunity and topped it all off with a cracker of a goal. He was still only twenty [still nineteen, actually] and was already a world-class player. Many of the thousands of British soldiers [from the British-occupied zone of Berlin] in the crowd surrounded him at the final whistle and carried him off. It was fantastic to be part of it. We had beaten the world champions in their own back yard.'

Duncan missed a few internationals before returning in early December at inside-left, and not left-half, for England's first 1958 World Cup qualifier, against Denmark at Molineux. Here was a notable change, because the four British nations – England, Northern Ireland, Scotland and Wales – had qualified previously by playing each other in the Home International Championship. Now, with the qualifying process supposedly toughened up, England found themselves having to overcome only Denmark and the Republic of Ireland to reach the finals in Sweden the following year. They began promisingly enough. The Danes were thrashed 5–2, England's goals coming from Tommy Taylor, who bagged a hat-trick, and Duncan Edwards, scorer of the other two. With Roger Byrne outstanding in defence, there was a strong Manchester United influence on a result that got the World Cup qualifying campaign off to a flying start.

This was hardly surprising, given that Walter Winterbottom was beginning to draw heavily on the captivating Red Devils team that was on its way to a second successive championship. Doggedly fighting to modernise the antiquated selection process and seeking some continuity at long last, England's first manager persuaded the selectors to pick only from a squad of 30 players he had submitted to them at the start of the 1956/57 season. Logically enough, it included six from the best team in the land: Byrne, Taylor and Edwards, plus goalkeeper Ray Wood and wingers Johnny Berry and David Pegg. Winterbottom had also made a mental note of the progress being made by an exciting young forward called Bobby Charlton and was preparing to enlarge the United contingent by calling him into the fold.

Duncan scored again in England's next international, the annual end-of-season dust-up with Scotland. In fact, he won the game with a blistering 25-yard shot six minutes from the end that went in off a post and brought his side a 2–1 win at Wembley. Despite sizeable victories over the Republic of Ireland (5–1), Denmark (4–1) and Wales (4–0), though, Edwards' name was on the score-sheet only once more before his short, sensational international career was brought to an end by forces beyond his control. The last of his five senior international goals came in a 3–2 defeat: Northern Ireland's historic first victory over England at Wembley and only their second on English soil in 75 years of trying.

That 6 November 1957 milestone also marked the end of England's unbeaten run. But it hardly seemed to matter when, in their next match at Wembley three weeks later, they trounced France 4–0. Blackburn winger Bryan Douglas was in scintillating form, three of the four goals coming from his crosses. The goals themselves were shared evenly between Tommy Taylor and a certain Bobby Robson, who was playing at inside-right and making his England debut. Walter Winterbottom was so excited by the performance that, at the after-match banquet, he confided to Billy Wright, 'Bill, I think we have a team that could make a really telling challenge for the World Cup.' That team, in the 2–3–5 listing of the time, read as follows: Eddie Hopkinson (Bolton Wanderers); Don Howe (West Bromwich Albion), Roger Byrne (Manchester United); Ronnie Clayton (Blackburn Rovers), Billy Wright, capt. (Wolverhampton Wanderers), Duncan Edwards (Manchester United); Bryan Douglas (Blackburn Rovers), Bobby Robson (West Bromwich Albion), Tommy Taylor (Manchester United), Johnny Haynes (Fulham), Tom Finney (Preston North End). It was, as Winterbottom believed, a well-balanced side of enormous promise; but it had no future. The runaway victory over France was the last match Edwards, Byrne and Taylor played for England. Three months later, the Munich air disaster tore the heart out of the national team as well as Manchester United.

Even so, England continued their winning streak as they approached the finals of the World Cup. With Wolves' Bill Slater replacing Edwards, United survivor Bobby Charlton coming in for Robson, Fulham's Jim Langley taking over from Byrne and West

Brom's Derek Kevan standing in for Taylor, Scotland were beaten 4–0 at Hampden Park and Portugal 2–1 at Wembley. In fact, it was not until the bandwagon rolled on to Belgrade in May 1958, a month before the finals, that the wheels began to come off. In a heatwave that brought several of the England players close to exhaustion, they were hammered 5–0 by Yugoslavia. 'This was the match when it really dawned on us just how much we had gone back since the Munich air crash,' Billy Wright was quoted as saying in *A Hero for All Seasons.* 'We were disjointed and totally lacking any sort of team pattern. If anything, the final scoreline flattered us. It did severe damage to our confidence with the World Cup finals so close. Poor Jim Langley was run off his feet by his winger, and he was never selected for England again. We were very subdued in the dressing room afterwards, and all Walter Winterbottom could bring himself to say was, "Well, at least we've got the bad game out of our system. Now let's focus on doing much, much better in the World Cup."'

It was not focus England needed so much as the missing Edwards, Byrne and Taylor. David Pegg and Eddie Colman, two of the other victims of Munich, would probably have made the squad as well. That was no certainty, though, because the selectors unaccountably picked only twenty players, when 22 were permitted. They compounded their mistake, many felt, by leaving behind illustrious veterans Stanley Matthews, still sprightly at 43, and Nat Lofthouse, 33. Not only that, they also ignored up-and-coming sharpshooters like eighteen-year-old Jimmy Greaves, Chelsea's new scoring sensation, and Brian Clough, 23, who had just completed a 40-goal season at Middlesbrough. Worse still, the whole operation was planned so badly that England arrived in Sweden only two days before the finals started and then discovered they did not have a proper training ground on which to prepare.

Changes were inevitable after the debacle in Belgrade, and Langley was not the only one to pay for that 5–0 thrashing. Bobby Charlton, Ronnie Clayton and Eddie Hopkinson were also dropped for England's last warm-up game before the finals. Their places were taken by Bobby Robson, Eddie Clamp and Colin McDonald respectively, while Tommy Banks came in for Langley. Bizarrely, England prepared for their first game of the tournament, against the USSR, by playing the same opponents in Moscow three weeks in advance of the real thing. They did quite well, too, a Kevan goal giving them an honourable draw in a game they might easily have won had that prince of goalkeepers Lev Yashin not been in such inspired form.

England drew (2–2) with the USSR in the finals as well. In fact, they drew with all their opponents in Pool IV – that was the trouble. The game against eventual winners Brazil was goalless, while the one against Austria finished 2–2. England and the USSR collected three points each with identical scoring records, so they had to play off for the second qualifying place behind Brazil. This is where England finally came unstuck. Changes were made again, Clayton returning at right-half and Chelsea's Peter Brabrook replacing the injured Douglas at outside-right. But few could understand why the Wolves playmaker Peter Broadbent was preferred to Charlton as the replacement for Robson at inside-forward. In the event, England went very close to winning. Brabrook hit a post and had a goal disallowed before Ilyin scored the goal that put the USSR through to the quarter-finals and England on the plane home. The sadness of the return was captured vividly and revealingly by Billy Wright in *A Hero for All Seasons*:

> That defeat by the Russians was one of my lowest moments in football. I knew in my heart this would be my last World Cup, and we had let ourselves down.
>
> When we arrived back in England, Walter Winterbottom was met at the airport by his young son, Alan, who asked the question on the lips of thousands of football fans: 'Daddy, why didn't you play Bobby Charlton?' I know that Walter had wanted to, but he was outvoted by the selectors who thought Bobby [then twenty] was too young. They should have watched what the Brazilians did. They introduced a seventeen-year-old youngster called Pele, and his presence turned them from a good side into a great one.

Don Howe believes England could have undergone the same kind of metamorphosis. 'We did OK in 1958,' he said, 'but with people like Duncan in the team we could have done so much better. Most international games are won across midfield, and I think Duncan would have scared people to death. Not because of his size, but because of his reputation. It was a bit like the situation before this [2006] World Cup, with everybody asking, "How good is Rooney? What's he going to do in the World Cup?" and other nations saying of England, "They've got a good squad now. That fellow Rooney is the problem – what a good player he is!" The same thing would have happened with Duncan, believe me.

'The final was between Brazil and Sweden, and the Swedes had a good team. But, no disrespect, we were as good as Sweden. So you tend to think that if they could have got to the final, so could we. We'd certainly got over the important hurdle, which was Brazil. There's no doubt about it, Brazil were very respectful towards us in that goalless draw. They wouldn't put Pele into the match, you know. They thought he was too young to play against an England team. They said we were too physical, although we weren't. They put Altafini up front instead. He'd been in Italy as well as Brazil and knew all about the game.'

Which brings us neatly enough to Wayne Rooney. Reassured by his young debutant's remarkable physical strength, Sven-Goran Eriksson had no hesitation in plunging Rooney, at seventeen years and 111 days, straight into senior international football. When Eriksson sent him on as part of the wholesale changes he made, controversially, to the team in the second half of a friendly against Australia at Upton Park in February 2003, Rooney became the youngest player ever to have appeared for England at that level. 'Wayne's only seventeen, but Pele was seventeen when he won the World Cup in 1958 in Sweden and he scored twice in the final,' the Swede had said when announcing his squad. 'Everyone that I've talked to says he's a special talent, so why not look at him in a friendly game? I'm not afraid of the age of seventeen. It's more important to see whether he's ready and whether he's good enough. My hunch is that he is.'

The freedom for Eriksson to back his hunch had been won for him by Sir Alf Ramsey when he took over as England manager from Walter Winterbottom following the failure to get beyond the quarter-finals of the 1962 World Cup in Chile. Interviewed by the FA for the job, Ramsey insisted on total control of playing affairs and, being a strong, stubborn creature, he was not prepared to accept anything less. In the end, the five-man International Committee had to agree to his terms, however reluctant they were to relinquish their right to select players and have a say in the adoption of tactics. A series of World Cup failures abroad and, most particularly, the fear of another at home in 1966 were probably the deciding factors. 'The selection committee, as such, is finished,' was FA chairman Graham Doggart's tart interpretation of a historic turning-point. Of course, Sir Alf justified his autonomy famously by winning the 1966 World Cup for England. So there was little chance of any diehards at the FA trying to put the clock back when Don Revie, another firm believer in managerial autonomy, succeeded Ramsey in 1974. England's football team, or rather its administrators, had been dragged kicking and screaming into the modern era, and there – or thereabouts – it has stayed ever since.

The process was driven partly by another profound change in the professional game over the last 50 years: the significant increase in the power and importance of the football manager that now elevates them, in many cases, above their teams. Herbert Chapman may have begun the cult of the manager before the war at Huddersfield and then Arsenal, but it was Ramsey, along with Matt Busby at Manchester United, Stan Cullis at Wolves, Bill Nicholson at Spurs, Bill Shankly and Bob Paisley at Liverpool, Brian Clough at Derby and Nottingham Forest, Don Revie at Leeds and Sir Alex Ferguson at Manchester United, who completed the process subsequently.

All of this meant little to Wayne Rooney, of course, when Eriksson exercised the hard-won privilege to name him in the 27-man squad to face Australia; the player himself was just trying to get over the shock. All the newspaper speculation had led everyone to believe the Everton discovery would be included in the England U-21 squad destined for a training camp in Italy. In fact, Rooney thought a mistake had been made and his name had ended up in the wrong group. When Everton manager David Moyes broke the good news to him, the youngster asked when the U-21s had to report. 'He just laughed,' reported Wayne, 'shook his head and said, "No, the full squad." I couldn't believe it. To have the chance to be around senior internationals is going to be a great experience and I can't wait.'

It is a striking measure of Rooney's outstanding talent and unusual physical maturity that he jumped straight from international youth football into England's senior side without once having played for the U-21s. Like Duncan Edwards, he was built like a man, and a very strong man at that, while still a teenager; unlike Edwards, he did not have to pay his dues at the intermediate stage of international development because the mechanism was in place for rapid advancement and times had changed with regard to the promotion of young players. It is not without relevance, either, that Wayne Rooney is considered by good judges to be one of the finest attacking players the game of football has ever seen.

On 12 February 2003, however, Rooney was just one of many youngsters called up by Eriksson in an ill-fated attempt both to experiment with new players and to placate the managers of several of the Premiership's leading clubs. By the beginning of the twenty-first century, the vexed club v. country issue had become a major headache for the manager of England. When Duncan Edwards was playing, there was only one European tournament – the European Cup – and just two domestic competitions – the Football League and the FA Cup. The European Cup was in its infancy then, too, and exclusively for national champions. But as Wayne Rooney prepared to make his England debut, the 45-year-old UEFA Cup had joined the European Cup, now misleadingly called the Champions League, in the crowded football calendar (the European Cup Winners' Cup was discontinued in 1999 to accommodate the expansion of the European Cup to include teams other than the champions of countries affiliated to UEFA, the governing body of European football). The League Cup, too, had long been added to the domestic workload. Understandably, therefore, the managers of the clubs at the top of the league – the main suppliers of players to the England team – had become more reluctant than ever to release their players for the extra wear and tear of international friendly matches. So, under pressure from the likes of Manchester United's Sir Alex Ferguson, Arsenal's Arsène Wenger and Liverpool's Gérard Houllier (then in charge at Anfield), Eriksson opted to play two completely different teams against Australia: one in the first half, the other in the second. It may have sounded fine in theory, but it proved a lot less successful in practice.

Blessed with several good players, most of whom plied their trade in Europe's best leagues, Australia fielded a side that was both talented and strongly motivated. The sporting rivalry between England and its former colony is familiar enough not to need any explanation; and these Australians knew that their country had never beaten the motherland at football in five previous attempts. This, too, was their first invitation to play England in England. To say they were really up for it, then, is to put it mildly.

The first-choice England side Eriksson sent out for the first 45 minutes were not half so gung-ho. Their lacklustre performance was typified by the erratic finishing of that normally reliable goalscorer Michael Owen, who had been going through a lean spell with Liverpool, his club at that time. While the little England striker missed a hat-trick of chances, Crystal Palace defender Tony Popovic and winger Harry Kewell, still with Leeds then, gave Australia a 2–0 lead at the interval.

Since England's so-called first eleven had been booed off at half-time with a disgusted chant of 'Are you West Ham in disguise?' ringing in their ears, the news that Eriksson still intended to field a completely new young side in the second half was greeted by the loudest cheer of the night. So it was that Wayne Rooney temporarily became the youngest player to play for England in a side that read as follows: Paul Robinson; Danny Mills, Wes Brown, Ledley King, Paul Konchesky; Owen Hargreaves, Danny Murphy, Jermaine Jenas; Darius Vassell, Francis Jeffers, Wayne Rooney. The 4–3–3 formation suggested attacking intent, and Rooney soon announced himself with a majestic cross-field pass that presented Vassell with an unconverted scoring chance at the far post. Then, in the 70th minute, the boy wonder combined with Jenas, one of the few other England successes on the night, and he provided the centre from which Jeffers headed what was to prove their team's consolation goal. Cue an outburst of pride at those Liverpool schools Our Lady and St Swithin's Primary and De La Salle, which had educated both Rooney and Jeffers and now saw them playing alongside each other for their country's senior professional side.

Another Australian goal, by Brett Emerton, now at Blackburn but then with Dutch club Feyenoord, put paid to any hopes of an equaliser, and Rooney's debut, in truth, was overshadowed by the implications for England of a 3–1 defeat at home by opponents who had not played together properly since losing a World Cup qualifier to Uruguay fifteen months earlier. Controversy raged, too, over Eriksson's decision to play two different teams at Upton Park. Some saw it as a good opportunity to look at promising young players, but the majority chose to regard it as further evidence of weakness and uncertainty on the part of England's Swedish manager.

The very fact that the Football Association had decided to appoint Eriksson as Kevin Keegan's successor in 2001, of course, was the clearest possible indication of a profound change in English football's view of itself. Once so convinced of England's natural superiority that invitations to take part in the new-fangled World Cup were arrogantly declined before the Second World War, the FA now conceded there was so much to learn from abroad that they were prepared to appoint the first foreign manager in the history of the mother country's national team.

Breaking down the domestic game's innate xenophobia had been a long and tortuous process. Despite mounting evidence that other countries were reinventing and refining the game all the time, it was only comparatively recently that the appointment of foreign managers was even contemplated. Rochdale, then in the old Fourth Division, were the first English club to broaden their horizons when they appointed the Uruguayan Danny Bergara for the 1988/89 season.

Aston Villa flirted briefly with the Czech Dr Jozef Venglos in 1990/91, but it was not until the late nineties that England's major clubs were really ready to take a chance on a foreigner. In effect, the FA were following the successful lead given by Chelsea, with Ruud Gullit and Gianluca Vialli; Arsenal, with Arsène Wenger; and Liverpool, with Gérard Houllier.

English or not, no manager could have failed to spot the star quality in Wayne Rooney. Eriksson certainly did not, as was proved by his inclusion of the youngster in the squad of 25 for the back-to-back qualifying games against Liechtenstein and Turkey in March and April 2003 that would go a long way towards deciding whether England reached the finals of the 2004 European Championship.

Turkey, England's main rivals for the one automatic qualifying spot in Group Seven, had stolen a march on Eriksson's men by playing, and beating, Slovakia before England had even started their qualifying programme. And when England did get under way, an unconvincing victory in Slovakia and an embarrassing draw at home with Macedonia left them trailing a long way behind the Turks, who had beaten Macedonia and Liechtenstein as well. Thus, there was enormous pressure on Eriksson and England to win both of the approaching matches. And for that reason, Rooney's call-up for competitive international football did not please everyone. David Moyes, his manager at Everton, was particularly outspoken in his belief that it was too much, too soon for the lad. Nor did he take kindly to Eriksson's plea for him to play Rooney more often in the Premiership so that he could prove his worth at that level. 'I can't do anything about that,' retorted Moyes sharply. 'If England are relying on a boy who has just turned seventeen, they have problems to mend. I do what is right for Everton. I don't think anybody has influenced me how we play Wayne and how we use him ... Wayne has done a tremendous job coming off the bench. He has played in every Premiership game except one this season, and for a boy that's fantastic. I have not shown any reservations about Wayne and England. If they think Wayne is good enough at his age then he should be picked. That's it. They have to decide if they want to play him – it's their shout. I would never hold Wayne back from being an international player – never. As a footballer he is ready. Mentally, I am not sure he is ready to go on to that level of spotlight.'

And so the game of verbal shuttlecock went on, Moyes desperately trying to protect his most valuable asset from burn-out and Eriksson anxious to get his hands on the most talented English footballer for a generation. At the same time, it has to be said, the England manager was well aware of the dangers of asking players to play too many games. In fact, at a press conference in advance of the friendly against Australia, he had chosen to ride one of his favourite hobby-horses and complain publicly about the heavy physical burden imposed on English footballers by the weight of the programme facing the top clubs by the early years of the twenty-first century. 'I talked before and after the [2002] World Cup about too many games in this country,' he said, 'and I would like to mention it once again. I am not talking only on behalf of the national team, I am trying to defend the clubs as well. There is only one English team playing in Europe before the end of March and I don't think that is because we don't have good clubs. It is because we play too much football and we pay very heavily. We play more football than any other country and we don't have any breaks at all.

'I am sorry to say it once again, but things will not change in the future if we don't change the number of games. I say it with my heart and I believe it strongly. How do we change that? That is the big, big question, which I cannot answer, although I have some of my own suggestions. The people who govern English football have to sit down and think about it, because it is not fair for the clubs and it is not fair for the national team at the end of the season. I talk to the people at the FA about it every time I see them, and they think I am awful, I guess.

'Every time I say something I will be criticised, but it is bad for the players, bad for the clubs and bad for the fans – and it is bad for me as well. Take Arsenal as an example, although I am here to defend them. But if you talk to a sports doctor about the fact they played Valencia on Wednesday, face Everton on Sunday and Chelsea on Tuesday, then they will tell you that to play three games in six days physically it is not possible. It is incredible. We don't give the players a fair chance. Italy and Spain both have three teams left in the Champions League and we have one, and I don't think we are worse than Italy or Spain.'

Eriksson's stance on this contentious issue was undermined somewhat by Liverpool's success, only two years later, in actually winning the Champions League by beating AC Milan on penalties after coming back from 3–0 down at half-time in the most dramatic final anyone could remember. Significantly, Liverpool also beat another English club, Chelsea, in the semi-final. The argument that English football is self-defeating because it imposes too great a workload on its players does not look too sound when challenged by the Champions League achievements of Liverpool and Chelsea in 2004/05, and Arsenal in 2005/06.

What Eriksson failed to take into account is the greater size and quality of first-team squads at England's leading clubs these days. Thanks to the almost unimaginable wealth of owner Roman Abramovich and the shrewd cherry-picking of former manager Claudio Ranieri and present manager Jose Mourinho, Chelsea, for instance, are quite capable of fielding two teams of similar merit. So they, and others, have the resources to rest players by 'rotating' their team selection.

Yet Eriksson had a point. There can be no question that the frequency, intensity and extreme physicality of matches at the highest level of the modern English game do not leave the England players in the best of condition for international tournaments at the end of a season, especially if they have to travel long distances to take part in them. Where the Premiership differs from most of Europe's other elite leagues is not so much in terms of size or a winter break, it is in the sustained competitiveness of the football. In other words, there are none of the comparatively easy matches to be found on the continent.

That, of course, is the reason David Moyes was so determined to introduce Wayne Rooney gradually to first-team football at Everton and so reluctant to see him rushed into England's senior side. Given, too, the tetchiness of Moyes' response to Eriksson's plea for the boy to play more in the Premiership, it was something of a surprise when Rooney was picked to start the game against Arsenal at Highbury on 23 March 2003. Partly because of the ban imposed on him for his sending-off at Birmingham, he had made only four appearances as a substitute in the previous three months. But now, with the England manager watching before finalising his squad for the games against Liechtenstein and Turkey, Rooney was back in the Everton team.

Maybe it was just a coincidence that Moyes felt then, after four run-outs as a substitute, the youngster was ready to return; maybe not. Whatever the reason for Rooney's inclusion in the Everton team on that particular day and in those particular circumstances, he shone again, scored his side's goal in a 2–1 defeat and was promptly ushered into the England squad for a second successive time. He was preferred to Alan Smith, then still a striker with Leeds, who was suspended for the first of the two approaching qualifiers.

After the game at Arsenal, Moyes was still chuntering on about the importance of bringing Rooney along gradually. He continued along the same lines, too, when the squad was announced and it was put to him by the press that Rooney's selection again for the seniors was better for his confidence than dropping down into the U-21s, as had been widely expected. 'I don't think that would damage his confidence,' countered the Everton manager, 'but it's a difficult one to answer. It was good that he got recognised for the last squad, but he's just got a lot more development to do. We're just trying to bring him on in the correct manner. He's got some fabulous pieces to his game, but he still has a lot of parts to be worked on. You've got to say, what's he going to be like when he's 25 or 26, the same age as Thierry Henry? Sometimes, because it feels like he's been in the Premier League so long – but it's only a year – everyone thinks that he's ready. But there are too many players who were raved about when they came into the game, but then fell away. I'm just trying to do the right thing for him.'

With less invested in the boy, Arsenal manager Arsène Wenger could afford to be more objective and enthusiastic. 'He is a special talent,' declared Wenger at the post-match press conference. 'We said that after he scored the winner against us at Everton earlier this season and he has made a step forward since then. You can see he's more of a man now. He looks much more mature than when he came on against us in October last year. This boy is international class. Is he good enough to be in front of other players in the England squad? That's down to Sven to decide, but he will certainly one day be a regular international. What he makes of his career will be down to the mental aspect, as the talent is clearly there.'

Whatever else Eriksson might be, he is no fool. While not as anxious as Moyes to nurse Rooney through the early stages of his career, the England manager was well aware that he had to be introduced gradually to senior international football. To that end, he announced well in advance of the qualifier against Liechtenstein that Rooney would not start the game in Vaduz. Refusing to say whether the youngster would come on as a substitute, Eriksson pointed out that the experience alone of being with the squad would be to his benefit.

In the event, the England manager waited until the last ten minutes of a disappointing team performance to bring on the boy wonder for Emile Heskey, then of Liverpool. It was just an attempt to give him experience because the match had already been won with goals from Michael Owen and David Beckham. Even though he failed to take a couple of chances, Rooney still enlivened England's play sufficiently to stake a claim for a place against Turkey the following Wednesday at Sunderland's Stadium of Light.

But nobody really thought that Eriksson, a manager famed for his caution, would take the gamble of starting the boy in a game of such importance. Even though Heskey was still troubled by the knee injury that had necessitated his substitution in Vaduz, it seemed extremely unlikely Rooney could expect anything other than a place on the bench again. Eriksson certainly did everything in his power to play down the possibility of a place for him in the starting eleven. During the build-up to the game, he hinted that he might turn to Darius

Vassell or Francis Jeffers as a replacement for Heskey, if required, or even move Paul Scholes forward from midfield. The England manager even went so far as to express the hope that Heskey would recover from his injury in time to play against the Turks; and he also spelt out why it would be wrong to start Rooney in his place. 'I think Wayne Rooney is ready, but only part-time,' he said following the game in Liechtenstein. 'I don't think we should expect him to come in and resolve a game against Turkey ... It could happen, who knows, if he comes on, as he's physically strong, good on the ball, quick and he scores goals ... Let me think about it, but maybe starting him isn't fair on him.'

It was all a smokescreen designed to protect Rooney from the media pressure building up around the game. Whether they were part of the subterfuge or not, other members of the England squad helped obscure Eriksson's intentions at the regular press conferences in the days leading up to the match. Central defender Sol Campbell, for instance, called Rooney 'a fantastic prospect', but pleaded for everyone to give the boy time to find his feet in international football. Striker Michael Owen, whom Rooney had just supplanted as the youngest player to play for England, predicted he could go on to be 'an unbelievable player', but harked back to his own teenage years and the times when he was rested at Liverpool. He had hated that, he said, but admitted now that the manager was right to have done it. Owen also pointed out that he had played a few more games for Liverpool and England before being given his big chance.

As the debate gathered pace, former England managers/coaches came down on opposite sides of the fence. Glenn Hoddle, for example, was definitely in the 'No' camp when it came to saying whether or not Rooney should play against Turkey. 'I think Sven should resist calls to play him from the start,' opined Hoddle. 'He is used to coming on as a substitute and he is still finding his feet as a Premiership player. He has turned games from the bench and could do the same for England. But Sven knows that to play him from the start would put too much pressure on him. He will cope with that pressure eventually, but he doesn't need that pressure right now.' Sir Bobby

Robson, on the other hand, urged Eriksson not to think twice about playing Rooney against Turkey. In his *Mail on Sunday* column, the former England manager had this to say:

> Sven-Goran Eriksson is truly blessed by the emergence of the wonderfully talented Wayne Rooney. Now Sven must be brave enough to begin reaping the benefit immediately. England need Rooney on the pitch from the very start of the vital European Championship qualifier ... His is a phenomenal talent that must not be denied or restricted. Age is merely a number – whether it's seventeen or, as in my case, seventy ...
>
> I have watched the boy play on several occasions. He takes my breath away – he is sensational. He can do things which are way out of reach of any other player. And already he has the confidence to do them ... Paul Gascoigne was twenty three in 1990 when I, as England manager, had no hesitation in determining that I had a very special talent at my disposal ... Sven urgently needs to inject a spark to discover fresh impetus, to lift the mood and raise the optimism. He needs a great player, and Rooney, even if he is only seventeen, is already a great player.

Sir Bobby's upbeat view was echoed by one of Turkey's leading players, Yildiray Basturk. 'We know Wayne Rooney will be a big threat if he plays,' admitted the midfielder. 'I am not saying Owen and Heskey are not top strikers, but Rooney would give the crowd a lift and maybe give England that spark they have been missing recently. I watch the English league every week and have seen the goals he scores. He is incredibly quick and his finishing is excellent. It is unbelievable to think he is just seventeen. If he plays we know our defence and midfield could have problems.'

As Basturk suggested, Eriksson was having to make a difficult choice between his loyalty to Heskey, now fit again, and the immense promise of Rooney. Like Heskey's Liverpool and England team-mates, the Swede appreciated the pressure the big striker's hard work took off attacking colleagues. But he was equally aware that Heskey, for all his selflessness and greater experience at club and international level, was not a prolific scorer. Rooney, on the other hand, offered goals, and a lot more besides.

Even Eriksson's coaching staff were divided on the issue when he consulted them. What may have made up the England coach's mind was a magical moment in training. Having beaten two men, Rooney calmly lifted the ball over the advancing goalkeeper before trotting back to the centre-circle as though nothing out of the ordinary had happened. Reportedly, it was not the first time seasoned England internationals had stopped in the middle of a practice match to applaud the outrageously talented whippersnapper who had come among them.

In the end, as we all know now, Eriksson decided to gamble on the kid. Although the *Sun* had mounted a typically vigorous campaign on behalf of Rooney – 83 per cent of that populist newspaper's respondents voted for him to start against Turkey – the England coach insisted he had not been swayed by such things. 'I will never think of public opinion when picking my team,' he told the BBC. 'I have to be convinced that it is the right thing, whether it is naming a squad or a side. If I am convinced, I do it. But I couldn't listen to public opinion before making my decision.' Even David Moyes accepted the decision with good grace. The Everton manager said he was delighted for Rooney and called his selection 'a great honour'. Protective to the last, however, he did appeal to the media and the public not to expect too much of the boy.

As it turned out, there was little danger of their being disappointed. It may have taken Rooney half an hour to get into the game, but when he did he started to open up the Turkish defence with his willingness to take on opponents and the quality and imagination of his passing. The pressure he stimulated finally produced results fifteen minutes from the end. Rustu, Turkey's goalkeeper, kept out a volley by Rio Ferdinand, but Darius Vassell, who had come on for the injured Owen after 57 minutes, snapped up the rebound. Rooney had played so well that, with two minutes remaining, Eriksson paid him the compliment of substituting him so that he could be given a standing ovation by the England supporters. His replacement, the fleet-footed Kieron Dyer, was promptly brought down in the penalty area by Ergun. So up stepped captain David Beckham to convert the spot-kick and make it a 2–0 victory for England.

It was a result, at the halfway stage of the qualifying process for Euro 2004, that lifted England above Turkey to the top of Group Seven. As such, it gave them every chance of qualifying automatically for the finals provided they could win their next three matches, against Slovakia (home), Macedonia (away) and Liechtenstein (home), and avoid losing to Turkey in Istanbul in the teams' last qualifier.

And with Rooney in the team, everything now seemed possible. His electrifying effect on England was front-page news in the national newspapers, and the realisation that English football had produced a young maestro of unquestionable world class prompted a sudden surge of optimism throughout that part of the nation to whom the game mattered. 'He's a great talent, we knew that before,' said Eriksson after the victory over Turkey. 'But now we know he's ready for the big matches. I can't see any reason why I should leave him out if he plays like that.' Both Eriksson and goalkeeper David James marvelled at the boy's almost unnatural maturity and coolness in a high-pressure football context. 'When I told him he was playing,' the England coach recalled, 'you could see that he was focused and not that nervous. He is very mature to only be seventeen.' James, who is a lot brighter than your average goalkeeper, had an obvious touch of awe in his voice as he said of Rooney, 'You look in his eyes and he is seventeen. But then you watch him play and it is as if he is 32. I was watching him on the bus heading to the match and he didn't seem to have any nerves at all. He was just having a laugh with Rio Ferdinand and, if I hadn't known better, I would have sworn he was just one of the experienced players.'

While others marvelled at Rooney's sang-froid, it was possible to detect in the teenager's own version of the build-up to the game a degree of the nervousness and apprehension you would expect in one so young. 'Most of the players were quiet in the dressing room before the game, but I spoke to the captain [David Beckham] and he helped me along,' said Rooney. 'He just told me to keep focused and go out there and play my normal game. Most importantly, he told me to enjoy myself. All I was thinking about on the pitch was winning the game for England. It was a massive qualifier, and I wanted to make sure I performed to the best of my ability, not only for myself but for club and country. The England players are all good lads and have made me feel welcome whenever I join up with the squad. I keep in touch with [Liverpool's] Steven Gerrard off the field and that helps when England get together as it is good to have a familiar face around.'

Unfortunately for Rooney, he had now made himself as indispensable for England as he was for Everton. Consequently, he soon became the prize in a fierce tug-of-war between Eriksson and Moyes as the perennial club v. country issue threatened to sour relations between his two bosses. The friction was caused by a friendly match the FA had arranged against South Africa in Durban for 22 May. They had done so for a variety of reasons, among them money, prestige and football politics. The ruling body of English football wanted not only to boost income with their £1 million fee, but to curry favour with the African nations, to which end they also planned to meet Nelson Mandela. Eriksson also had a valid reason for wanting the match. Since the final European Championship qualifier of the season, against Slovakia at Middlesbrough, had been scheduled for the ridiculously late date of 11 June, he had to keep his players match fit during the month between the end of the Premiership season and the important game at the Riverside. His plan was to play South Africa in Durban on 22 May, then take the squad to the La Manga sports resort in Spain for a week's rest, relaxation and light training before completing the preparations with another friendly, against Serbia & Montenegro (one half of the former Yugoslavia), at Leicester on 3 June.

Moyes, however, felt that Rooney had done more than enough for an eighteen-year-old already during the 2002/03 season, what with Everton's attempt to clinch a UEFA Cup place, and was determined the youngster would not be taken on a 12,000-mile round trip to play in a friendly in South Africa. 'People forget how young he is,' said the Everton manager. 'He has been involved in every Premier League game this season, bar the four when he was suspended. He has had an injury and it has been a hell of a long season for a boy. People have to appreciate that.'

Eriksson thought he had sorted out the club v. country problem in a series of meetings with eleven Premiership managers, among them David Moyes. In return for a promise that they would not stand in the way of their players playing for England, Eriksson agreed to limit the number of friendly matches and get-togethers during the season and guaranteed that, after 2004, no friendlies would be arranged for April. Moyes, however, was angered by what he saw as Eriksson's failure to honour a mutual agreement between them not to talk about Rooney following the 'summit' meeting involving them both. 'Why should he not go to South Africa?' the England coach had said in response to media questioning about the player. 'I haven't picked the squad yet. It is too early. But if he is picked, he will play. Why not?'

The upshot of it all was a call from Everton informing Eriksson that Rooney had sustained a knee ligament injury in his club's final Premiership game of the season, a 2–1 defeat by Manchester United, and would not be fit for the trip to South Africa. Moyes added that the player was probably doubtful for the games against Serbia & Montenegro and Slovakia as well, and had a scan of his knee to prove it. Knowing that Rooney had completed the 90 minutes against United and taken part in Everton's end-of-season lap of honour after-wards, Eriksson had good reason to question this information. He included the Everton starlet in his squad of 25 for the three end-of-season games and demanded that he report for duty with the rest of the players at a Heathrow hotel.

This Rooney duly did; but he was not alone. With him down to London went not only Moyes and the Everton physiotherapist, Mick Rathbone, but his agent, Paul Stretford. Clearly suspecting he was having the wool pulled over his eyes, Eriksson had insisted on

Everton's scan being sent to England's head doctor, Leif Sward, for closer examination. When it came to it, though, the FA's medical staff had to agree that Rooney would be better off returning to Everton for treatment than making the gruelling journey to South Africa. The only scrap of good news for the England coach was that Everton were prepared to let the player join up with the rest of the party at La Manga, should he respond to treatment. Rathbone, however, thought he had a better chance of being fit for the game against Slovakia than the one against Serbia & Montenegro.

As for Moyes, he mounted a fierce and peevish defence of his unyielding position on the issue. 'We told the FA on the Sunday, straight after Wayne was injured against Manchester United, that he was struggling, and on the Monday we sent the scans to their specialist,' he explained. 'They knew then that he couldn't possibly play, and yet somehow it seemed to get overlooked that he was injured, and they appeared to be even suggesting he could go to South Africa. The results of the scans were clear, and they knew exactly the extent of the injury.

'And yet I felt that our integrity was being brought into question. I felt that they did not believe what we were saying, even though we gave them clear evidence. Maybe it was because I said he shouldn't go to South Africa and a lot of people were probably thinking, "Here's a manager pulling a fast one" – which wasn't the case.

'I get on with Sven fine. But my position has not changed on the South Africa issue. A lot has been said in English football in recent years about the dangers of overplaying young players. We are supposed to be far more careful about how much we play them, and here was a young player going halfway round the world when he's tired after a long season. We need help to protect Rooney. Suddenly, he's found out that everyone wants a piece of him. Everywhere he goes, they want something from him.'

The spat between Eriksson and Moyes over Rooney was more than just another manifestation of the vexed club v. country argument. It was the clearest possible indication of the immense value and importance the boy had suddenly acquired as a footballer. Moyes, incidentally, was furious the FA had obliged Rooney to undergo a medical, while Nicky Butt's ankle injury was taken at face value and the midfielder, then still with Manchester United, was allowed to return home for a summer's rest. But Butt is not the sort of player who can win you silverware almost single-handed. Eriksson put it in a nutshell when he said, 'Rooney is the best seventeen-year-old I've had. I had Roberto Baggio [at Fiorentina] when he was young, and he was brilliant, but Wayne Rooney is exceptional. David Moyes has a diamond on his hands.' The Everton manager was well aware of that. 'He's got everything – movement, pace, power and an unbeliev-able football intelligence,' Moyes had said excitedly of Rooney when the boy was still only sixteen. 'He's as good as any player I've ever trained, easily the best for his age.'

Needless to say, then, Eriksson was relieved and delighted when Rooney did turn up at La Manga almost fully fit and ready for six days of R&R. The England coach resisted the temptation to plunge him straight back into the team against Serbia & Montenegro at the Walkers Stadium and waited until the second half to bring him on as a replacement for Michael Owen, one of five substitutions this serial substituter made that night. Rooney's introduction unsettled the Serbian defence, but it was Joe Cole who won the game 2–1 for England. He did so with a stunning 25-yard free-kick in the 83rd minute, Steven Gerrard's first-half goal having been cancelled out by Nenad Jestrovic.

Although there was some speculation as to whether Eriksson would renew his loyalty to Emile Heskey, who had begun the friendly against Serbia & Montenegro as Owen's partner, it hardly came as a surprise when Rooney for Heskey turned out to be the only change from that starting line-up for the qualifier against Slovakia. For once, though, the young prince did not have things all his own way in a poor performance by the standards he had set for himself against Turkey. For the first time that season, only a year after the teenager had been concentrating on the final of the FA Youth Cup, Rooney finally began to show signs of the tiredness the Everton manager had predicted and feared. Sensing this, Eriksson substituted him after 58 minutes and Moyes gave him an extra week off before reporting back for pre-season training.

To their credit, England beat Slovakia 2–1 without Rooney at his best. It was not a dazzling display by any means, but Owen secured the team's fifth straight win with two second-half goals that kept England a point ahead of Turkey at the top of the group. Pleased with the outcome, Eriksson urged everyone to put Rooney's disappointing contribution to the victory in perspective. 'I am happy with what he did,' said the England coach before going off on holiday. 'It is dangerous for me, the crowd and the critics to expect him to be the best player on the pitch every time he plays for England. That is absolutely not fair ... He is one of the biggest talents I have worked with and he will go on getting better and better and will stay in the England side, for sure. I am so happy he is English.'

Rooney missed the first international of the 2003/04 season, a 3–1 victory over Croatia in a friendly at Ipswich, but was back for the next one, a 2–1 European Championship qualifying win against Macedonia in Skopje on 6 September. In fact, he and David Beckham scored the goals. He got another one, too, when England beat Liechtenstein 2–0 at Old Trafford four days later – a record eighth successive victory that kept them a point ahead of Turkey as the five-country Group Seven headed for a showdown between the top two in Istanbul the following month.

All England needed to stay ahead of the Turks and claim the one automatic qualifying place for the finals in Portugal the following summer was a draw – no easy task in front of a crowd as intimidating as those in Turkey can be. With the fans creating an infernal din and the Turkish players not too fussy about how they tackled the opposition, the match proved to be every bit as challenging as expected. England, however, hung on to draw 0–0. They could have won, but Beckham, uncharacteristically, ballooned a penalty kick over the bar as he slipped on some loose turf in the act of kicking the ball.

When the draw was made for the finals, England found themselves in a group with France, the reigning European champions, Croatia and Switzerland. The following June they began the tournament well enough, Frank Lampard giving them a 1–0 lead against France. But a free-kick conceded by substitute Emile Heskey and a penalty caused by Steve Gerrard's suicidal back-pass enabled Zinedine Zidane to snatch victory for the French in the dying minutes.

It was then that Wayne Rooney imposed himself on the tournament. In the next match, the England striker scored twice as Switzerland were beaten 3–0. Four days later, in Lisbon's Stadium of Light, Rooney scored two of the goals with which England beat Croatia 4–2 and qualified for the quarter-finals. It was not just his eye for goal that attracted attention, either. Rooney's pace, trickery, ability to run at defences and general awareness had defenders worried to death about playing against him.

England were on a roll now and, given that Rooney was beginning to emerge as one of the finest attacking players in Europe, it hardly seemed to matter that the next opponents were the hosts, Portugal. Confidence grew, too, when Michael Owen opened the scoring after only three minutes. But then, not much more than twenty minutes later, came the beginning of the end when a challenging Portuguese defender accidentally trod on Rooney's right foot and broke it. With Darius Vassell on in place of their wounded talisman, England held on to their lead until late in the game. Dropping deeper and deeper all the time, though, they invited Portugal on to them; so there was a degree of inevitability about the equaliser when substitute Helder Postiga scored seven minutes from the end. Frank Lampard replied to Rui Costa's goal in extra time, but there was to be no happy ending. Taken to penalties once more in a major tournament, England lost again – 6–5 this time.

So England's failure to win a major trophy since 1966 continued. No blame could be attached to Wayne Rooney, though, whose capacity for meeting each new challenge with further proof of his outstanding ability was beginning to mark him out as one of the finest players English football had ever produced.

CHAPTER 7

ALWAYS A BLUE?

WHEN, after scoring the opening goal of the 2002 FA Youth Cup final, Wayne Rooney whipped off his Everton shirt to reveal a T-shirt carrying the scribbled pledge 'Once a Blue, Always a Blue', he made a rod for his own back. At the time, that demonstration of his devotion to the club was seen quite properly as just youthful enthusiasm, a simple act of faith by a boy who came from a family of Evertonians and had supported Everton ever since he could tell the difference between Goodison and Anfield. It was also, of course, a reaffirmation of his decision to choose Everton in preference to Liverpool. So the Everton diehards loved him for it.

With the benefit of hindsight, however, it might have been better for him if he had kept his shirt on. For the moment that pledge of loyalty was displayed proudly to the Everton fans, Rooney offered himself as a hostage to fortune. From then on, the man on what used to be the terraces, intoxicated by the thought of watching such an outstanding young footballer transform Everton's fortunes, confidently expected him to stay for quite some time. And, to be fair, everything the lad said encouraged the belief that, unlike his recent predecessor as boy wonder at Goodison, Francis Jeffers, he would not be off to a richer or more successful club at the first opportunity. Jeffers' transfer request, and subsequent move to Arsenal, had sickened the Everton faithful. They were delighted, therefore, to hear Rooney seemingly entrust his future to the club when he signed his first professional contract with them in January 2003. 'If people asked me "Real Madrid, Inter Milan or Everton?",' he told a packed press conference, 'it would be Everton every time.' Such certainty, such commitment calmed the fears of supporters alarmed by newspaper speculation that some of

Europe's most glamorous clubs were beginning to give Rooney the eye at a time when it was well known Everton were hard up.

What changed the situation is not as straightforward as it may seem. Lack of money, you may be surprised to learn, did not come into the equation; but, with Rooney giving compelling performances for England in the finals of the 2004 European Championship, success as an international footballer did. The burly, confident youngster terrified opposing defences with his strength, speed and abnormal maturity as England progressed to that quarter-final tie with Portugal, the host nation. Rooney broke his foot for the first time in that highly charged game, of course; still, he came away from the tournament knowing he had graduated with honours as an international footballer. Every big club in Europe knew it, too, and the race was on to prise him away from Everton.

The Merseysiders did not look to be in a strong position to resist because the financial pressures on them had intensified. With the club estimated to be £40 million in debt, there must have been times when chairman Bill Kenwright wondered what he had got himself into. There was even talk of his relinquishing control of the club he loved, the club he had battled long and hard to buy from the previous, unpopular chairman, Peter Johnson, in 1999.

Formerly a popular *Coronation Street* actor, Kenwright had forged another career as an extremely successful theatre impresario and producer in the West End and elsewhere in Britain. Liverpool born and bred and an Evertonian to his fingertips, he had become saddened and frustrated by Johnson's inability to reverse the decline in Everton's fortunes. So, with three other businessmen, he formed the True Blue group to buy control of the club for £23 million.

It was not an easy process, and life did not become any more comfortable for Kenwright and his associates once they had taken over. By July 2004 they had fallen out. Kenwright and one of the other directors, Paul Gregg, clashed over the substantial investment from an outside source everyone knew was needed urgently. Gregg said he could arrange such a transfusion, but it would involve Kenwright stepping down – something the chairman was determined not to do.

The disagreement became so counter-productive that Trevor Birch, the chief executive, resigned in frustration only six weeks after being appointed. Birch, a respected insolvency expert, had facilitated the Roman Abramovich takeover at Chelsea and had somehow kept Leeds United, with debts of £100 million-plus, out of administration. Significantly, Birch had been strongly in favour of two draconian measures to improve Everton's fiscal problems that were under discussion. One was a move from historic but antiquated Goodison Park to a new stadium big enough to generate the sort of match-day income that would enable the Merseyside club to compete financially with the likes of Manchester United and their 70,000-capacity Old Trafford. At the time, Everton were considering either helping to fund a new stadium as part of the redevelopment of Liverpool's docks or, whisper it quietly, sharing Liverpool FC's proposed new ground in Stanley Park, the green space that separates the city neighbours and rivals topographically.

For fairly obvious reasons we will not go into here, neither of those ideas came to fruition. But the other drastic step favoured by Birch did: to get as much money as possible for Wayne Rooney. Selling the club's best player was not the former chief executive's idea, as such; Everton had been forced to think the unthinkable for several months before taking the step that must have broken Bill Kenwright's heart and the heart of every other true blue. After all, it was Kenwright who, when Rooney had finally signed his first professional contract with Everton in January 2003, said wryly, 'It's just a pity a seventeen-year-old can only sign for three and a half years. We did try for thirty-three and a half, we really did.'

But here was the boy, only one year and a half into that much-trumpeted contract, wanting to leave. Although Rooney did not submit his transfer request until 27 August 2004, it had been common knowledge within the club for some time that, contrary to what 'Once a Blue, Always a Blue' had implied, he had become unhappy at Goodison. There was more than one reason for his change of mood. As revealed belatedly in his autobiography, he did not get on with David Moyes. It had been suggested to me much earlier that Rooney did not enjoy working for a manager as flinty and humourless as Moyes can be; but the player himself seems to have objected more to what he saw as his dour Scottish boss' controlling nature and jealousy over his growing fame. In any case, they were barely on speaking terms towards the end. A second reason for Rooney's itchy feet was the realisation that his abundant natural gifts could make him a truly great player – a thought process doubtless prompted by his rapid promotion to the full England team and marked success on the international stage. Coupled with that realisation was the evidence, provided by their dreadful 2003/04 Premiership season, that Everton were unlikely to be able to match his own upgraded ambitions. And, as everyone knows and every manager fears, being picked to play for England means joining a squad in which salaries and conditions at other players' clubs are discussed and even direct approaches to move made.

Everton, though, did not just stand back and let things happen. Led by Kenwright, they fought tooth and nail to keep Rooney at Goodison Park, regardless of by how much his sale could have reduced their overdraft. Early in July, they made the youngster, now a household name after his exploits the previous month at Euro 2004, a record offer to stay. The £40,000-a-week contract they promised would have made him the highest-paid player in the club's history, and Moyes appealed to him to accept the deal to 'repay' the club he had supported as a boy. Even £40,000, however, was chicken-feed by comparison with what could be earned at wealthier clubs.

Another factor entered the equation on 27 July, when Rooney discovered for the first time that being famous in Britain entails having any dirt in your private life dug up by the tabloids. Newspaper reports that the player had visited a seedy Liverpool brothel caused him no little embarrassment, especially as previous stories had made great play of the fact that he was engaged to be married to his pretty childhood sweetheart, Coleen McLoughlin. All of a sudden, getting out of town must have seemed an attractive option.

The situation took an unexpected turn on 24 August. A couple of days after Rooney had finally resumed training with Everton following his recovery from the foot injury he had sustained at Euro 2004, Newcastle had a £20 million bid for him turned down. Manchester United matched it a couple of days later, only to see Newcastle increase theirs to £23.5 million. The following day, saying it was 'the right time to move on', Rooney submitted his transfer request. A day later, United put in what was believed to be an increased bid of £25 million, prompting the Everton fans to show what they thought of Rooney and the, by now, inevitable transfer by jeering his name during a 2–1 win against West Bromwich Albion at Goodison Park.

The final element in Rooney's wish to leave Everton was, almost certainly, his agent, Paul Stretford. While there is no hard evidence to suggest that Stretford was instrumental in persuading the player to submit a transfer request, he is hardly likely to have discouraged him from doing so. In any case, once it became apparent that the boy was unhappy at Goodison, it was Stretford's duty to facilitate the best possible transfer he could for his client. In the process, of course, the agent stood to make an awful lot of money. Just how much can be imagined from the size of the final fee – £27 million – Manchester United agreed to pay Everton for Rooney just before the transfer window closed on 31 August. No imagination is required, actually, because United, admirably, are one of the few clubs now in the habit of revealing exactly what slice of the transfer cake goes to agents. Thus, chief executive David Gill made it clear that Proactive Sports Management Limited, as Stretford's agency is known, could receive as much as £1.5 million as their share of the deal.

Like the £27 million fee, Proactive's £1.5 million cut was to be paid in stages. Guaranteed £1 million of it, they would receive £500,000 immediately with the balance payable in equal instalments over the following five years. The additional £500,000 was dependent upon Rooney's remaining registered to Manchester United until 30 June 2007, a conditional date also factored into the transfer details agreed between the two clubs. That deal guaranteed Everton *only* £20 million, half payable at once and the other half on 1 August 2005; another £4 million was dependent on United's success, or lack of it, the renewal of Rooney's contract and his appearances at international level.

As Kenwright had promised the fans, all the money Everton received was passed on to Moyes to buy players. The records will show that the manager spent more than £25 million in the calendar year between January 2005 and January 2006. Yet the mistaken belief persists among Everton fans that the club sold Wayne Rooney simply because they were hard up and needed the money to pay off their debts. Perhaps that is the only way some supporters could handle the betrayal of trust represented by Rooney's departure so soon after he pledged himself to them and the club. 'Bill Kenwright got hammered because the fans thought he'd sold Rooney just to raise cash,' said Ian Ross, Everton's head of communications, 'but that was the complete opposite of what was going on. Even until the last week before Wayne went, we were still making him what was, by the club's standards, a fantastic offer. We were that desperate for him to stay. But he'd made up his mind months before that he wanted out and was going to go. There was nothing we could do. We had to sell him primarily because he didn't want to stay. He wasn't going to play, he wasn't happy, so Bill just thought long and hard and got the best available deal for him that he could. I know he gave Manchester United hell that day. He pushed them and pushed them, and was a pain in the arse until he'd virtually got everything he'd looked for. But Rooney was always going to leave.'

A wry postscript to Rooney's move from one end of the East Lancashire Road to the other, and an indication of how long United had coveted the boy, was provided by Everton's academy manager Ray Hall. 'We had a game at U-15 level and Wayne, for once, played in his own age group,' he said. 'We were beaten 5–1, I think, but a friend of mine who works for Manchester United said he went straight out of the ground, drove to their manager's house and told him, "There's a player playing for Everton – we need to get him!" And it took them four years.'

The reaction of the Everton fans to the transfer ranged from the disgusted to the deranged. But an email to the *Manchester Evening News* website from 'BlueBoy, "Moyeseyside"' spoke rationally, if bitterly, for all of them:

Rooney has shown his only loyalty is to money. He could have left Everton earlier in the transfer window, giving them a chance to sign players before the deadline, but he instead chose to move at the last possible moment. I wish him luck in his career, but hope that one day he comes to appreciate why Everton fans feel so betrayed.

Everton fans never expected him to stay for ever, but if he'd stayed just a couple more years and at least tried, then he could have left the club with happy memories, and a welcome back any time. Instead, he leaves the fans with an overwhelming sense of betrayal, disappointment and anger. If he ever had been a 'true blue' he would never have left the club in that manner, and for him to even claim that he's still an Evertonian is an insult to all real fans. Good luck Wayne, and thanks for everything: thanks for nothing. Wayne Rooney: 'Once a Blue, always Man U'.

Not all the Everton fans kept their emotions as tightly controlled as that. Proactive Sports Management complained that the Cheshire-based Stretford and his family had been subjected to 'unpleasant' threats, details of which had been passed on to the police. And, as soon as the transfer had been completed, Proactive went out of their way to heap praise on him. In a formal statement, the company said:

Negotiations were carried out on behalf of our client (Wayne Rooney) by one of the company's directors Paul Stretford and his team. The board would like to place on record its thanks to Paul Stretford and his team for the manner in which they have conducted themselves during what has been a difficult period.

Wayne Rooney has been the subject of a great deal of speculation surrounding the transfer and much has been inaccurate and sometimes malicious in its contents. Partly as a result of this, Paul Stretford and his family have recently received a number of threats from misguided people purporting to be football fans, details of which have been passed on to the police. We will naturally co-operate fully with any investigation which subsequently may take place.

Long before the transfer to United, Stretford had made enemies on Merseyside. He had stirred up a hornets' nest, in fact, when he 'poached' Rooney from his original agent, Peter McIntosh, in September 2002. Complaints were made that Proactive, allegedly, had lured the player away from McIntosh and his company with offers of a £250,000 house for his parents, £150,000 in cash and promises of a new, £13,000-a-week contract with Everton. Whatever the truth of those allegations, it is a fact that Rooney's parents and brothers no longer live in downmarket Croxteth. They moved to a much swankier home in Sandfield Park, an exclusive development just round the corner from Everton's Bellefield training ground, while Rooney was still with the Liverpool club. No one seems quite sure who paid for the house. Some say Rooney himself, others believe the money came from Proactive. It hardly matters who was responsible: Stretford's aggressive business methods caused a bitter resentment on Merseyside that festers to this day.

Some Scousers, especially those with Everton leanings, took more exception than others to Stretford, an interloper from the hated Manchester area, muscling his way in on the club's great young discovery. A little over a month after the player joined United, three men went on trial at Warrington Crown Court charged with blackmailing Stretford. They were John Hyland and brothers Christopher and Anthony Bacon, all of them from Merseyside. The prosecution alleged that the trio had threatened Stretford with violence if he did not sign a contract forcing him to hand over half of Rooney's earnings for the next ten years. It was claimed they had done so after bursting into a meeting at a Cheshire hotel between Stretford and Dave Lockwood, a business associate of Peter McIntosh, Rooney's original agent. It was not entirely without significance, then, that Hyland, a Liverpool boxing promoter, was also a business associate of McIntosh's and, like him, a devoted Everton fan.

Since the scene was videoed secretly, it looked like an open and shut case until new evidence indicated that Stretford had misled the court. Documents were produced to prove that Rooney's current agent had poached him from McIntosh in September 2002, and not December of that year, as he had claimed. Therefore, he had been representing the young striker while he was still under contract to McIntosh. Confronted with this proof of the unreliability of their main witness, the prosecution declared their intention not to offer any further evidence against the accused and the judge passed not guilty verdicts on Hyland and the Bacon brothers.

It was a case that opened a real can of worms. Not only did Stretford walk away from the court in disgrace for not telling the truth, but some of the questionable business practices of football agents had been revealed for all to see. During the case, Stretford admitted to Lord Carlile QC, Hyland's barrister, that he had received an arrangement fee from Manchester United for the Rooney transfer. And when Lord Carlile suggested that, as Rooney was his client and not United, this constituted a conflict of interest, Stretford replied, 'I don't see it as a conflict of interest. It's the normal course of the business.' Clearly astonished by Stretford's response, Hyland's barrister persisted. 'You know perfectly well,' he said, 'that if this sort of arrangement, making money from two clients, happened in any other business, subject to guidelines, it would be unacceptable.' To which Stretford, completely unabashed, replied, 'I can't speak for other businesses, but it's the normal business structure in our industry.'

So normal, in fact, that the Football Association were powerless to act against Stretford on those grounds. However, the ruling body of the English game did charge him, on the evidence presented in court, with three breaches of the FIFA Players' Agents Regulations over his acquisition of the right to represent Wayne Rooney in 2002/03. They also charged him, under their own rules, with bringing the game into disrepute by allegedly making false and/or misleading witness statements to the police and giving false and/or misleading testimony to Warrington Crown Court.

But if the FA thought Stretford would be cowed into submission by having the book thrown at him, they were wrong. Backed unreservedly by the Formation Group, the parent company of Proactive Sports Management, Rooney's agent declared his intention to take the ruling body to the High Court. Claiming the disciplinary proceedings brought against him were a breach of natural justice and the European Convention on Human Rights, Stretford denied he had breached any of the regulations cited by the FA and revealed he had entered a formal plea of not guilty.

Knowing that, should the FA find otherwise, he stood to lose his agent's licence and his livelihood, he was concerned he might not get a fair hearing at Soho Square. 'Given that the tribunal empowered to hear the case is entirely appointed by the FA, and consists mainly of FA councillors and officials,' said a Proactive statement on his behalf, 'it is Mr Stretford's contention that it cannot be of an independent and impartial nature and thus is clearly in breach of Article 6 of the Convention [on Human Rights]. Effectively such a tribunal would mean that the FA, as the professional governing body, would be able to act as prosecutor, judge and jury in a hearing which could prejudice the livelihood of Mr Stretford.' The agent, the statement added, had been fully prepared to co-operate with the FA provided they were willing to appoint an independent and impartial tribunal. Since the FA would not agree to his request, he had no alternative but to take them to the High Court. Roused to indignation by this, the governing body responded with a statement of their own. 'The FA,' it said, 'totally refutes these claims put forward with regard to the FA's disciplinary procedures. We will robustly defend our procedures and are confident that they are fully compliant with all applicable laws.' That was issued in September 2005, and the case came to court in February 2006. Although Stretford claimed victory, the FA insisted the judge had ruled in their favour and, at the time of writing, the situation remained unresolved.

If Duncan Edwards were alive today, he would probably be bewildered by all this fuss over football agents and goggle-eyed at the huge amounts of money in which they were dealing. Nobody, perhaps, illustrates more starkly the difference between the two eras than the now ubiquitous football agent. In Edwards' day, such people were virtually unknown. Film stars and famous music hall acts had agents, but not humble footballers. Bobby Charlton, who survived Munich and went on to have a long and successful career that stretched into the early seventies, did not have an agent at any time. That is not quite true: in the latter part of his career, Charlton did employ an agent to handle his commercial activities off the field, but he always negotiated his own contracts with Manchester United.

Not that there was much negotiating to be done, or money to be made. Even after the abolition of the maximum wage in 1961 and George Eastham's successful challenge to the pernicious retain and transfer system a couple of years later, most clubs continued to operate their own private maximum wage and make it difficult for players to change clubs without their consent. Very few, certainly, received anything like the £100 a week Fulham chairman Tommy Trinder famously paid Johnny Haynes.

The only substantial way Edwards and Charlton had of supplementing their modest weekly wage – never more than a basic £20 in Edwards' case – was by letting their name be used to advertise some product or other in newspapers and magazines. Duncan did it with Dextrosol Glucose Tablets ('A natural source of energy which you could rely on any time, anywhere'), but that venture into commercialism hardly brought in enough to make him a rich man. Basically, there were no football agents as such in the fifties because footballers did not earn enough to make it worth an agent's while to take them on as clients.

Yet the seed was still sown in that austere post-war decade. Today's army of agents owe their existence partly to the sharp instincts of a chap called Bagenal Harvey. When he spotted the commercial potential of famous cricketer/footballer Denis Compton, a talented, good-looking sportsman with enormous popular appeal, a new profession was born. It all started when Middlesex and England batsman Compton gave Harvey a lift in his car and the passenger noticed the back seat was overflowing with correspondence. When he enquired as to the reason, Compton explained that they were letters he had not had the time or inclination to answer. Harvey volunteered to take on the job for him, and it all grew from there.

'In those days,' said Geoffrey Irvine, Harvey's assistant for many years, 'Bagenal was working for a magazine publisher in and around Fleet Street – particularly the *Eagle* comic. I think he got Denis to do something for the *Eagle*, got this lift in the car and said, "I'll take this lot away!" That's how it started in the late forties or early fifties. Then one or two others – [Kent and England wicketkeeper] Godfrey Evans and people like that – came along and asked him to look after their stuff. Suddenly he had to decide whether he was in magazines or agency work.

'Agents these days are involved in all the transfer deals, whereas in those days players were employed by their football clubs on a PAYE basis and agents were not permitted to interfere in any club matters. So what Bagenal was doing was the fringe stuff – advertising, newspaper pieces and that sort of thing. [Who, of a certain age, can possibly forget those Brylcreem ads Harvey negotiated for Compton?] He was directly involved in Jimmy Greaves' move to Italy, though. He worked with Gigi Peronace, the famous Italian agent of the time [who arranged Greaves' transfer from Chelsea to AC Milan for £80,000 in 1961]. We also represented Bobby Charlton for a long time, but never, ever had anything to do with his Manchester United situation.

'Jimmy Hill was always around the scene, too. When he was battling for the abolition of the maximum wage, he was sitting in the next-door office to Bagenal. That resulted in [Football League Secretary] Alan Hardaker making some rather indiscreet remarks about Bagenal. He didn't name him, but it was pretty obvious who he was referring to as "an evil influence on the game". Bagenal sued Hardaker, won the case and gave the money to charity. Hardaker was absolutely opposed to Bagenal: he hated him.'

Although he recognises that today's football agents can make more from one deal than Bagenal Harvey's company ever dreamt of making in a year, Irvine is not sorry they did not become involved in this dog-eat-dog business. 'I don't think Bagenal would have been very comfortable dealing with the world of football today,' he reflected. 'I don't think he would have fitted in very comfortably. There are some nice people: I like Jon Holmes [the chairman and chief executive officer of the SFX Sports Group] and people like that. They are fine, but there seem to be far too many people I wouldn't want to do business with.'

If Bagenal Harvey was the British pioneer in the sports agency business, his American counterpart was Mark McCormack, Jon Holmes' inspiration. Starting with iconic golfer Arnold Palmer, McCormack built up a powerful and lucrative empire, IMG, in the well-heeled worlds of golf and tennis. 'Unlike McCormack, Bagenal was not prepared to spend half his life on an aeroplane,' said Irvine. 'And that's what he would have had to do if we had gone into the profitable areas like golf and tennis.'

These were the people who beat a path for others through the tangled world of sport. Today, there are more than 2,500 football agents licensed by FIFA around the world. At the last count, 284 of them came from England, 40 from Scotland and four from the Republic of Ireland. This is one area of sporting activity in which England leads the world, because only Spain, with 276 agents, comes close to the English total. After that, you are down to Brazil's paltry 107. There is also an unknown number of unlicensed agents.

For all the criticism of Paul Stretford, it is pretty obvious he gets on well with Rooney and his family. Nor can there be much doubt that the former vacuum cleaner salesman has helped to make the player a very rich man with the six-year contract he negotiated for him at Manchester United. Although, because of his age, Wayne's basic salary is thought to be as *low* as £50,000 a week, image rights and the like probably take it nearer £100,000. Stretford, as is evident from television commercials and newspaper stories daily, has negotiated lucrative endorsement deals for Rooney with blue chip companies like Nike and Coca-Cola, not to mention a £5 million book deal with Random House. Coleen has proved no slouch at making money, either. Her earnings from fitness videos, fashion shoots and the like in 2005/06 were rumoured to be £5 million, giving them a joint fortune – according to *The Sunday Times Rich List* – of £20 million.

It is self-evident, too, that the player is likelier to realise his dreams of winning things with United than he was with Everton. He said as much at the media conference called to confirm his move to Old Trafford. 'It was a tough decision to leave Everton, the club I've supported and played for all my life,' he admitted, 'but I'm excited to be joining a club as big as Manchester United. I feel this can only improve my career, playing with top players in top competitions like the Champions League, and I can't wait to meet up with the team.' United manager Sir Alex Ferguson, too, was excited. 'I think we have got the best young player this country has seen in the past 30 years,' he said, valuing Rooney even more highly than Paul Gascoigne. 'Everyone is delighted by this signing.'

Well, everyone who supported United, that is. Another email to that *Manchester Evening News* website radiated the pleasure their fans were feeling and patronised their Everton counterparts in the process. 'I think the transfer is the best thing English football has seen for a long time,' wrote Mike Hallam, of Manchester. 'But that's coming from a Red. However, I can understand why Everton fans are so disappointed, but they should try to understand, Rooney wants more money and to be at a more successful club. That's the bottom line. Any player would have made the same decision, and I back him 100%. Real football fans will appreciate his decision and his reasons for doing so.'

The youngster could not have made a more sensational start to his career with United. Held back until he was fully recovered from his broken foot, Rooney scored a breathtaking hat-trick as Turkish champions Fenerbahce were given a 6–2 thrashing in Group D of the Champions League at Old Trafford on 28 September 2004. It was a startlingly emphatic victory considering Fenerbahce boasted several members of Turkey's national team, plus a sprinkling of Brazilians and the maverick Dutch striker Pierre van Hooijdonk.

It was something of a false dawn for Everton's expensive acquisition, however. For the most part he was overshadowed in the

European fixtures by his more experienced strike partner, Ruud van Nistelrooy. The Holland international had scored both of United's goals in the 2–2 draw at Lyon which had preceded the slaughter of Fenerbahce, and he also claimed one of the six put past the Turkish side. Then, against Sparta Prague at home, Van Nistelrooy scored all of United's goals in another handsome win, 4–0, breaking Denis Law's European scoring record for United of 34 goals in the process. Finally, at home to French champions Lyon, the prolific Dutchman provided the winner in a 2–1 victory, giving him a total of eight goals in six games and, remarkably, 36 in 37 European matches overall.

That last win was not enough, however, for United to top the group. That honour went to Lyon, who finished two points ahead. Coming second, of course, meant that Rooney and his new team-mates had to prepare themselves for a tough tie against one of the other group winners in the knockout stage of the tournament. And they do not come much tougher than AC Milan, the talented and seasoned Italian side United were unlucky enough to draw. At home in the first leg, Rooney and company lost 1–0 to a fine goal by Hernan Crespo, the Argentina striker on loan from Chelsea. Then, in the away leg, Crespo did it again in another 1–0 win.

Out of the tournament at the last sixteen stage, United could only watch with envy as Liverpool, who had finished fourth – fifteen points behind them – in the Premiership the previous season and had scraped through the group stage with a last-gasp victory over Olympiakos, went all the way to the final and won it in the most dramatic fashion imaginable. Liverpool's unexpected and unlikely triumph was given real merit first by their victories over Juventus and Chelsea in the quarter-final and semi-final, although Chelsea maintain to this day that Luis Garcia's winning goal did not cross the line. Then, in a Champions League final staged in Istanbul for the first time, Liverpool excelled themselves against United's conquerors, AC Milan. Outplayed to an embarrassing extent in the first half and trailing 3–0 at the interval, they somehow came back at the Italians to level the scores and win Europe's premier club trophy for the fifth time in a history that was in sore need of being brought up to date. After a heart-stopping 30 minutes of extra-time had failed to separate the sides, Liverpool became the new champions of Europe by virtue of winning the penalty shoot-out 3–2.

Watching back home, Wayne Rooney said he had hated every minute – bar the first half – of a spectacle most observers dubbed the greatest final of the competition ever, perhaps even the greatest football final, full stop. But what else could he have said, given his Everton origins and new allegiance to Manchester United, Liverpool's fiercest rivals? By then, 25 May 2005, Rooney had had a bellyful of frustration anyway. Only four days earlier, at Cardiff's Millennium Stadium, United had lost the FA Cup final to Arsenal 5–4 on penalties after completely outplaying the surprisingly unadventurous London club, yet drawing 0–0 with them. Rooney, the game's outstanding performer, scored the fourth of United's five penalties, but the damage had been done earlier, when Arsenal goalkeeper Jens Lehmann saved Paul Scholes' kick. So the Gunners completed a double of sorts over United, having finished six points ahead of them in the Premiership's second automatic Champions League place.

But both of these clubs, hitherto the dominant forces in the domestic game, were well adrift of the new champions and new powerhouses of English football, Chelsea. Arsenal, who were finishing in the top two for the eighth consecutive season and had won the title three times during that golden period, trailed home a full twelve points behind their west London rivals. The previous season, the positions had been reversed, Arsenal finishing eleven points clear of Chelsea. But now the affable, eccentric 'Tinkerman', Claudio Ranieri, had departed and been replaced as manager at Stamford Bridge by the brooding, self-anointed 'Special One', Jose Mourinho. A bombastic and egocentric title, certainly, but seldom has anyone been more appropriately named. Making full use of the many outstanding players Ranieri had brought to the club with the seemingly limitless funds of new Russian billionaire owner Roman Abramovich, and adding a few of his own, Mourinho had pulled off the extraordinary feat of winning the Premiership with a nascent team in his first season. This, too, after leaving Porto as champions of Europe for the first time in their history.

It must have crossed Rooney's mind at some point, then, that he might have joined the wrong club if he wanted to win things. Perhaps that fleeting thought had occurred to him as early as 26 January, when Chelsea, who had also been interested in buying the boy wonder from Everton at one point, knocked United out of the Carling Cup at the semi-final stage. They did it in the grand manner, too, winning 2–1 at Old Trafford following a goalless draw at Stamford Bridge in the first leg.

So Wayne did not have a lot to show for his first season with United: no Champions League triumph, no Premiership title, no FA Cup, no Carling Cup, no automatic qualifying place for the following season's Champions League. It cannot have helped that Everton, whom he had decided could not match his own ambitions, had flourished following his departure. Relieved of their reliance on their outstanding young star, strengthened by new signings and playing more as a team again, the Merseyside club succeeded in claiming fourth place in the Premiership – their highest position in the top division of English football since 1987/88. It meant they finished one place above city rivals Liverpool and qualified for the Champions League for the first time.

All Rooney had to console him for manifold disappointments was a scoring record in all competitions that totalled seventeen goals and made him United's leading marksman, one ahead of the specialist in that discipline, Van Nistelrooy. In other words, he had almost doubled the number of goals he had amassed as Everton's joint leading scorer the previous season, and from five fewer appearances. All of which suggested he was thriving on being in a better team and playing with better players. As Sir Alex Ferguson struggled to rebuild United on the remains of the Beckham–Giggs–Scholes–Nevilles generation and what was left of Roy Keane's waning powers in midfield, the one area of the team he did not have to worry about was the sharp end.

Rooney and Van Nistelrooy hit it off as a partnership right away. They proved that by scoring a goal apiece in the tempestuous 2–0 victory over Arsenal at Old Trafford on 24 October, Rooney's nine-teenth birthday, that ended the London club's record-breaking 49-game unbeaten run and led to the throwing, allegedly, by an Arsenal player, or players, of pizza and soup at the Manchester United manager in a farcical scene outside the dressing rooms afterwards. The Gunners were never the same all-conquering outfit again after being bullied to defeat in that match, a fact that offered United a crumb of comfort after finishing just below them in the Premiership and losing to them in the FA Cup final.

Another notable victory was recorded at Anfield on 15 January. When Ferguson was appointed manager of United in 1986, he came to Old Trafford with the express purpose of knocking Liverpool off the top perch of the domestic game they had occupied for the best part of ten years. As a result of his success in doing that, and the dislike the neighbouring Lancashire cities have always had for each other, matches between the two clubs have become probably the fiercest contests in English football. And this one was no exception.

Having scored what proved to be the only goal of the game after 21 minutes, Rooney celebrated instinctively in front of Liverpool's famous Kop, the denizens of which had not hesitated to remind him impolitely of his Everton past. Needless to say, the Kop did not respond kindly to such taunting, and Rooney was lucky not to be seriously hurt by a mobile phone thrown at him by one enraged and, presumably, well-off Liverpool fan. But, for Wayne, scoring that winning goal must have been one of the few satisfying moments of a largely frustrating season for player and club.

If Rooney did have any doubts about whether he had joined the right club, they would have multiplied during the summer of 2005. That was the time when Manchester United and their supporters were plunged into turmoil, civil war even, by the unwanted £790 million takeover of the club by American tycoon Malcolm Glazer. The United board had resisted Glazer's overtures for as long as they could, but resistance was useless once the American had obtained a controlling interest by buying the key shareholding of John Magnier and J. P. McManus, the Irish racehorse owners and breeders. Significantly,

Sir Alex Ferguson had fallen out with his former Irish friends previously over the stud fees for the successful horse Rock of Gibraltar, part ownership of which they had given him as a gift.

Since Glazer had borrowed most of the money for his takeover bid, United were transformed overnight from the soundest and most profitable football club in the world financially into one with £650 million of debt – six times more than the millstone that had dragged Leeds United down a few years earlier. While some United fans fretted about the implications of indebtedness on such a mammoth scale, others feared for the soul of the club. Most, in fact, were scandalised that the United board had sold out to someone who, as an American and owner of the NFL club Tampa Bay Buccaneers, could not possibly understand our game of football or the traditions of a great club like United.

A sizeable minority not only staged a protest march at Old Trafford but resolved never to darken its doors again. An independent club, FC United, was set up by the disaffected fans, many of whom now support the breakaway team on a regular and exclusive basis in the North West Counties League, where they have enjoyed immediate success. In the 2005/06 season, for instance, they were promoted to its top division. Those who remained loyal to the Old Trafford outfit did not hide their displeasure at what had happened, either. They voiced their feelings at matches as the 2005/06 season got under way, and one of their number actually berated Ferguson in person for not resigning in protest at the takeover as United and their fans arrived together at Budapest airport in late August to play the Hungarian side Debrecen.

That game was the second leg of a Champions League qualifying tie United were obliged to undertake as a consequence of their failure to finish in one of the top two places in the Premiership the previous season. They won it by the same score as the home leg, 3–0, and progressed comfortably into the group stage of the competition proper.

That, though, is where their troubles began. Their opening fixture in Group D, a goalless draw away to the underrated Spanish side Villareal, saw Wayne Rooney sent off for unwisely taunting the Danish referee Kim Milton Nielsen, who had become notorious in England as the official who dismissed David Beckham for the most innocuous of offences during the England v. Argentina game at the 1998 World Cup. Things picked up a bit for United when they beat Portugal's Benfica 2–1 at home in their next Champions League game, but it was another false dawn. Having been held to a goalless draw at home by Lille, United then lost to the French side 1–0 in the return. Worse still, Paul Scholes was sent off in the game at Old Trafford. Rooney tried desperately to improve matters with what the *Manchester Evening News* described as a 'barnstorming' performance when Villareal came to Old Trafford in November, but again the contest finished goalless. That made it four times in five Champions League matches that United, always famed for their attacking prowess, had failed to score. Sir Matt Busby must have been spinning in his grave at the news.

The bottom line here was that Sir Alex's misfiring, transitional team had to win their final game, away to Benfica in December, to qualify for the knockout stage of the competition. They actually managed to score this time, Scholes giving them an early lead, but their Portuguese opponents hit back to win 2–1 and dump them ignominiously out of European football for the season. Finishing bottom of the group meant United could not have even the consolation of a place in the UEFA Cup, the safety net in the new year for the clubs coming third.

It was a sign of the changing times, perhaps, that this was the first time for ten years United had failed to reach the later stages of Europe's most prestigious club competition, annual participation in which they have come to regard as their birthright. Not since they were pipped to the Premier League title by Blackburn in 1994/95, and therefore did not qualify for the following season's tournament, had it happened. Added to Chelsea's increasing domination of the Premiership, United's disastrous Champions League campaign indicated very strongly that their thirteen-year domination of English football was under serious threat.

Whatever he might have been thinking in private, Wayne Rooney was still insisting he had not made a mistake by moving to Old Trafford. 'I've no regrets whatsoever about joining United,' he told the *Daily Mirror* on 17 February 2006. 'I love the club, I love the fans. And even if I could go back in time, I'd make the same decision ten out of ten times. I think the move to United has really improved me as a player. This has been a difficult season watching Chelsea do so well, but I believe there's a great future ahead at United. That's what you play for, to win trophies. We've a chance of winning the Carling Cup and the FA Cup this season, and we want both.'

Unfortunately for Wayne and his ailing club, United were down to just the Carling Cup a day later after being knocked out of the FA Cup by Liverpool at Anfield in the fifth round. It was one of the most feeble performances anyone could remember from a team managed by Sir Alex Ferguson, and Rooney was almost anonymous in a nebulous right-wing role that was part of a weird and thoroughly ineffective 4–3–3 formation. There were discordant echoes here of the early part of the season, when the most potent support striker in the country was asked to play wide right or left in a new and unpopular system allegedly devised by Carlos Queiroz, Ferguson's Portuguese right-hand man.

United's real problem was in midfield, where Ferguson had failed to make up for the loss of Keane's drive, technical excellence and leadership following the ageing Irishman's abrupt decision midway through the season to end his career at Old Trafford and move to Celtic. Against arch rivals Liverpool, in a cup-tie that was bound to be intensely physical, Ferguson and/or Queiroz asked Ryan Giggs, a slightly built, flying winger, to play the anchorman in midfield. Too late did they call the combative Alan Smith off the bench to do his enthusiastic but imperfect impersonation of Keane. Sadly, the converted striker then suffered the freakish injury of a dislocated ankle and broken leg blocking a piledriver from John Arne Riise.

Smith's long-term injury was the last thing United needed in a season that had seen the departure of Keane and the loss of another key midfielder, Paul Scholes, because of a serious eye problem. All of a sudden, the earlier decisions to let Nicky Butt and Phil Neville move on seemed foolhardy. It was not as though United lacked the money to buy reinforcements, however. By permitting Ferguson to spend more than £20 million on three new players, goalkeeper Edwin van der Sar and defenders Nemanja Vidic and Patrice Evra, new owner Malcolm Glazer had allayed supporters' fears about the size of the transfer fund he would allow the manager.

Having gone out of the Champions League and the FA Cup and trailing so far behind Chelsea that the Premiership title was virtually out of reach by the season's halfway point, all United had left to play for in 2005/06 was second place and the Carling Cup. They had reached the final of the latter by a fairly undemanding route, beating Barnet, West Bromwich Albion and Birmingham City comfortably before they overcame Mark Hughes' revitalised Blackburn narrowly over two legs in the semi-finals. Their winner in a 2–1 (3–2 aggregate) second-leg victory at Old Trafford was scored by Louis Saha, the France international striker who had struggled with injuries for most of the two years since his transfer to United from Fulham for £12.85 million. As a result of these problems, Saha had fallen well behind Van Nistelrooy in the pecking order to partner Rooney up front in the first team. So much so that, when the Frenchman did recover full fitness Sir Alex Ferguson played him in the Carling Cup to give him match practice and, it seemed, allow leading scorer Van Nistelrooy a well-earned rest.

Fielding reserves in the lesser of England's two major knockout competitions has long been common practice for the leading Premiership clubs, of course. And there is little doubt this tournament had again been at the bottom of United's list of priorities at the start of the season. But beggars cannot be choosers, so Ferguson and his players concentrated all their energies on winning what had once been cruelly dubbed the 'Worthless Cup' (a play on a previous incarnation, the Worthington Cup) to avoid ending a second successive season without any silverware – a nightmarish prospect for a club of their standing and, thanks to the Glazer takeover, indebtedness.

Three of the reclusive American tycoon's sons were present at Cardiff's Millennium Stadium at the end of February 2006 to see a full-strength United romp to a 4–0 victory over Wigan. Rooney scored two of the goals and also hit the bar in what Henry Winter, the *Daily Telegraph*'s football correspondent, called 'a master class of attacking play'. The other goals came from Cristiano Ronaldo, the flamboyant young Portugal international, and Saha, who had been preferred to Van Nistelrooy, Ferguson said, because he deserved to play after scoring five goals in the run to the final. Sceptics, however, preferred to believe demotion was the Holland international's punishment for being strangely lethargic in the FA Cup defeat at Liverpool eight days earlier. They also detected the first signs of a rift between the manager and his senior striker.

As easy on the eye as Rooney's display, and United's, might have been, the general feeling among the pundits was that this counted as a fairly hollow triumph. For all their astonishing success in climbing into the top half of the table on their Premiership debut, Wigan were still a team of only moderate talents. They certainly did not have enough gifted individuals to take United on in an open game of football, as they tried to do in Cardiff. So while Paul Jewell, Wigan's impressive young manager, should be commended for doing the honourable thing and not resorting to smothering tactics for a showpiece match, he hardly made life difficult for United on this occasion.

Not that any of these misgivings seemed to bother anyone in the jubilant United camp. Wearing 'For You Smudge' T-shirts donned in honour of horribly injured team-mate Alan Smith, the players jumped up and down with the cup on the victors' podium as though they had won the Premiership title, the FA Cup and the Champions League rolled into one. More delighted than anyone could recall for some time, Sir Alex made a point of lifting the trophy with oft-criticised coach Queiroz. Relieved, no doubt, to have shown the Glazers he had not lost his winning touch, he predicted the victory could be the start of another fruitful period for the club, just as it had been after they had last won the tournament, in 1992, when it was known as the Rumbelows League Cup.

While most people took such confidence with a pinch of salt, it was impossible to overlook the fact that this was the seventeenth major trophy Ferguson, at 64, had won in his twenty-year career at United, and the 27th collected during his 32 years as a manager in Scottish and English football. It is a staggering record, and one that makes him easily the most successful British club manager in the history of the game. Even so, Sir Alex cannot have been any more pleased in Cardiff than Wayne Rooney, for whom winning the Carling Cup was clearly the biggest thrill to date in his short career as a footballer.

Astonishingly, considering he is the possessor of gifts that make him one of the finest players in the world, Rooney had not won a thing, not a sausage, since he was a thirteen-year-old playing for Copplehouse in Liverpool junior football. Even when he was terrorising defences in the FA Youth Cup with Everton, they lost in the final to Aston Villa. So this was his first winners' medal, and it was completely unnecessary to ask him how he felt about it. His often surly or angry face beamed with a smile so bright and open that it lit up his whole being and told of a softer side to an outwardly aggressive personality.

Rooney had other reasons to be happy. Before his brace of goals in the Carling Cup final, this regular scorer had failed to find the net for two months. In fact, his form as a whole had tailed off to such an extent in the Premiership and the FA Cup that United supporters were beginning to wonder aloud why he seemed to play so much better for England than he did for his club. Acknowledging that there was some truth in the assertion, Kevin McCarra, football correspondent of the *Guardian*, came up with an interesting theory as to why that might be the case:

> Rooney hits the heights when he has the invitation to rise to the great occasion. The United side has usually not been good enough to bestow such opportunities on him since he signed in 2004. Even England are not sure to stir his talent all the time; he did not score at all in the World Cup qualifiers ... This trait of Rooney's merits celebration rather than a whine about

inconsistency. How lucky English football is to have a footballer who taps his talents to their deepest extent in the most
riveting dramas. No stage fright for him ... His first encounter
with each new level of the sport galvanises him ... Presented
with an FA Cup final, he dominated in Cardiff last season.
Arsenal were very lucky winners of a shoot-out, having spent
most of the two hours in defence. Rooney put them there, and
if he neglected to score then it was an omission he put right on
his return to the Millennium Stadium.

Not for the first time, either, Ferguson's knowledge of his team
and of the game was proved to be spot-on. United's Carling Cup win
proved to be such a catalyst that they promptly went on a run of nine
successive Premiership victories that turned them into Chelsea's
most dangerous challengers. Bizarrely, a goalless draw at home with
Sunderland, bottom of the Premiership and doomed for most of the
season to relegation, ruined their chances of catching Chelsea; but
there was little doubt that United, with Giggs and John O'Shea form-
ing an unexpectedly resilient and inventive pairing in central midfield and Saha proving a more effective attacking partner than Van
Nistelrooy for the often outstanding Rooney, were on the mend.

Then, on Saturday, 29 April 2006, came a fateful trip to play Chelsea
at Stamford Bridge. Trailing the league leaders by as many as eighteen points at the beginning of March, United had cut the gap by half
with their revitalised form during the intervening two months. With
just three Premiership games each remaining, and Chelsea still nine
points ahead, this was United's last chance of staying in the title race.
To take it, they had no option but to win at a ground where Chelsea
had not lost a single game since Jose Mourinho took over as manager
in June 2004.

In the event, the challenge proved beyond them. All Chelsea
needed to retain the title was a draw; but, as if responding to the
widespread criticism of their play as being little more than ruthlessly
efficient, they turned on the style to such an extent that United were
not only outplayed, but outclassed. An early opportunist goal by

William Gallas, an absolute gem by Joe Cole and a late flourish by Ricardo Carvalho brought the London club a 3–0 victory that was never in any doubt. Wayne Rooney, the only United player to challenge Chelsea's superiority, did have a rare chance to make it 1–1, but he screwed his shot wide.

Unfortunately, the frustration Rooney feels when his team is being outplayed engulfed him early. A dangerous tackle on John Terry left the Chelsea captain with a gash in his ankle that needed ten stitches. Then, in the closing stages, Rooney elected to chase a pass down the left. United were three goals behind by then and it was a lost cause, really; but, true to form, the tough young Scouser was not prepared to throw in the towel until the final whistle went. As he ran, however, Rooney was checked with a sliding tackle by Paulo Ferreira, Chelsea's Portuguese right-back. Ferreira took the ball with his right foot, but did serious damage with his left knee as it came down accidentally on the heel of Rooney's vertical right foot and trapped it against the turf. It would be an exaggeration to say the nation held its breath as the United and England striker went down and stayed down, but millions of England fans must have sworn under their breath when the agonised look on Rooney's televised face warned them of the dreaded news to come. Even the normally unemotional and imperturbable Sven-Goran Eriksson was moved to curse. 'Shit!' he admitted to having said at that fraught moment.

Sure enough, it was soon confirmed that Rooney had again broken his right foot, this time in two places. 'As soon as my foot came up off the floor I felt something pop in my foot and I probably knew straight away that I'd broken it,' he said a few days later as the England manager, players and supporters tried to come to terms with the fact that the country's best player could be out of the 2006 World Cup finals, only six weeks away.

CHAPTER 8

CRUEL, CRUEL FATE

FOR Duncan Edwards, the summer of 1957 brought with it a new sense of freedom and purpose. On 6 June, 23145376 Lance Corporal Edwards was demobbed from the army and could now concentrate fully on being a professional footballer – not an encouraging thought for opponents who had witnessed how formidable he could be dividing his time between the professional game and the British Army XI. His status in English football by then can be judged by the special 'Photo News' feature in the *Daily Express* that greeted his release. Headed 'A Soldier Ends Double Life', it said of Edwards, 'at 2 o'clock yesterday, he stopped being a 9/- [nine shilling, or, in today's money, 45p] a day "Lance Jack" and became once again the full time soccer star said to be worth £50,000 in the Common Market – Soccer Branch'.

For the record, it is estimated that during Duncan's two years of National Service he played more than 180 matches in all, or over 90 matches a season for club, country and army. Such overplaying by a teenager would be frowned upon today, when much more is known about sports science; but the fact that it did not seem to have any deleterious effects on Edwards between the ages of eighteen and twenty is testament to the strength of his remarkable physique and lifelong dedication to physical fitness.

The big, amiable Black Country lad was also engaged to be married. There are conflicting versions of how he came to meet his fiancée, but in 23-year-old Molly Leach he had found the good-looking girl he wanted to marry. According to Gordon Clayton, the boyhood friend who was signed by Manchester United at the same time as Duncan and who used to socialise with him, they met at a Manchester skating rink called the Derby Street Ice House. But Clayton's memory might just have been playing tricks on him because Molly herself recalled that the crucial, romantic meeting with Duncan had taken place at Manchester's Ringway Airport, where he had gone for a cup of coffee with a friend.

Edwards' engagement must have come as quite a shock to his team-mates because he had never seemed comfortable with the opposite sex. 'He never really enjoyed a big group,' Gordon Clayton told Eamon Dunphy. 'He'd go to the Locarno [Dance Hall], but he wouldn't dance. He wasn't one for the "birds". He had a dabble here and there like the rest of us, but he was very shy with girls. At the Locarno Duncan would be on the edge, just standing there looking.' Wilf McGuinness supports that assessment of Edwards with a recollection of his own. 'Duncan,' he said, 'wasn't a lad about town, let's say, but he would come into town. I always remember when we won the FA Youth Cup and we were seventeen and eighteen years of age. Eddie Colman was with us and, to celebrate, we went into a pub for the first time – something we shouldn't have done, really. It was a pub in town called Willoughby's, and it just shows we weren't that into the nightlife because it was a gay bar! It was quite amusing when we found out. "Oh," said Duncan. "Oh, dear!" He wasn't in the dance halls and that, like some of us were, but he was smashing.'

Perhaps the difference was that Duncan was actually introduced to Molly, so he didn't have to pluck up the courage to go and ask her for a dance. Not that the giant of the football field was totally tongue-tied in such situations, as McGuinness recalled. 'When I signed for United, Jimmy Murphy took me and Duncan to Ireland as a treat. I think it was because Duncan had captained England Schoolboys the year before I did, and then we'd both gone to United. Anyway, Jimmy had to go to Bray on club business and he took us with him. We stayed at the International Bray Hotel and there was the Arcadia Dance Hall next door. Duncan and I had a look in and we did walk a couple of girls home. In fact, it was about a seven-mile walk home, and we didn't even get to kiss them goodnight!'

With Molly, though, it was obviously the real thing. 'She was his first love,' said Gordon Clayton. 'He was a strong character, and as soon as he set eyes on her you knew that was it. Molly was a nice girl, very nice, a bit up-market for us. Not what you might call a footballer's girl.' Duncan rarely talked to her about football and certainly never bragged about his exploits. In fact, she reported, he longed to get away from the hero-worship and the limelight. 'He hated being recognised,' Molly revealed in a *Daily Express* interview. 'He would do anything to avoid fuss. In fact we never planned to be engaged. We were just going to get married and no one would have known until afterwards.'

Frank Taylor recalled an amusing incident that backed up all Molly had said. On arrival in West Germany for a game after Duncan had become famous there as 'Boom-Boom' Edwards, he was so alarmed by the media clamour for photographs and interviews that he tried to persuade the short, portly football writer to pretend to be him!

Duncan's liking for a low profile would not have surprised his Aunt Marjorie. 'He was a quiet boy who was brought up properly,' she said. 'Although he was an only child, he was never spoilt. He'd got no airs and graces, and nothing went to his head. For all he was good at football, he never boasted. I know he was a footballer, but he was a gentle chap inside. He was as famous as Beckham at one time. It was Duncan Edwards this, Duncan Edwards that. Now Rooney's taken over from Beckham.'

Duncan and Molly lived the quiet life. They occasionally went to the cinema or the theatre, but seldom to the dance hall. More often than not, they spent their evenings playing cards with friends. Games of tennis in the summer were about as exuberant and exciting as it got. The relationship did cause Edwards to fall foul of the law, however. One night, he was riding back to his digs on Molly's bicycle without lights when he was stopped by a policeman and fined ten shillings – quite a lot then, but the equivalent of about 50p today. In other words, it would be hard to imagine anything more unlike the lives of today's king and queen of football, self-publicity and excess, David and Victoria Beckham.

The strength of the relationship between Duncan and Molly could be judged by the risks he was prepared to take on her behalf. The bicycle incident, it seems, was not the only time he trod a fine line in order to get home. In *Red Voices – United from the Terraces*, a compilation of Manchester United supporters' views and recollections by Stephen F. Kelly, trade union leader Lord Stan Orme recalled catching Edwards in another tricky situation:

> I was chairman of my trade union branch, the AEU, in Broadheath and we used to meet every fortnight on a Friday night. I used to catch the all-night bus coming back at about twenty to twelve from Broadheath, and I remember getting on one particular night and Duncan Edwards was sat there in the corner seat and the conductor was talking to him. Edwards was courting a girl in Timperley and he'd just taken her home. And you know Busby had them all in digs in Trafford with a landlady to look after them. I said to Edwards, 'Big game tomorrow.' And he said, 'Don't let anybody, especially the boss, know I'm on this bloody bus at quarter to midnight. He'll go mad!'

Apart from minor indiscretions like that, Duncan's behaviour off the field was exemplary. This, too, at a time when the austerity and social rigidity of the immediate post-war years was beginning to be challenged by the increasing prosperity and youthful rebelliousness that gave birth to the so-called Swinging Sixties. In the late fifties, Teddy Boys were smashing up dance halls and cinemas to the revolutionary music of Bill Haley and Elvis Presley as rock 'n' roll began to carry all before it, including such previous behavioural norms as respect for your elders and deference to your supposed social superiors. But for Duncan Edwards, all that mattered was his football. 'His youth was well behaved most of the time because he was in digs in the Trafford area,' said Wilf McGuinness. 'He didn't get a car early on, or anything like that. He would use his bike or walk for the exercise. He was very conscious of keeping fit, and drinking wasn't part of that. He wasn't what you called a drinker.'

Bobby Charlton reckons his and Duncan's abstemiousness was a matter of simple economics as much as anything else. 'Like everybody else, we went to the pictures in our spare time. That was about it, really. We considered we were lucky because we were earning £14 to £16 a week [when the average weekly wage was £12]. But if you were young and you were going and buying clothes, there wasn't a lot left for anything else. I certainly never went out drinking with Duncan, and he was never a nightclub man or anything like that. As I've said, he was a fitness fanatic.'

Not all the Busby Babes found it difficult to raise the price of a drink or two, though. Tommy Taylor and Jackie Blanchflower, for instance, are said to have had a regular Saturday-night routine. The two close friends, who were also among the older members of the team, would start at the greyhound track, continue with a Chinese meal and finish at one or two of Manchester's nightclubs, plentiful even then. Eddie Colman, one of Duncan's closest friends, and David Pegg liked the nightlife, too; so the temptation to follow suit was there if he had felt so inclined. But, as every witness has insisted, football was the only thing that mattered to him.

He would have been delighted, then, when United began the 1957/58 season by winning five of their opening six fixtures and drawing the other. It was just the sort of start a team hoping to chalk up a hat-trick of league championships would have wanted to make. Edwards was outstanding, too, as United beat Everton 3–0, Manchester City 4–1 and Leeds United 5–0 at home, and Leicester City 3–0 and Blackpool 4–1 away. Only an injury to Blanchflower stopped them winning at Everton, where they had led 2–0 at half-time before drawing 3–3.

But then came a sudden dip in form. They lost three of their next four First Division games, the last of them 3–1 away to their great rivals of the time, Wolves, who replaced them at the top of the table. The first of those three defeats was inflicted at Bolton, where Duncan came up against his second cousin and former Dudley Schools team-mate Dennis Stevens. 'Came up against' is putting it mildly. Edwards, usually hard but fair, appears to have kicked lumps off his relative as Bolton romped to a shock 4–0 victory. Reports of the game, a typically fierce Lancastrian derby, suggest that Duncan twice 'did' Dennis with heavy, hurtful challenges. Carried off on a stretcher after the first one, and left limping on the wing as a result, the older of the two cousins was then flattened by an Edwards showing his wounded relative no mercy. Not surprisingly, Stevens took exception to this kind of rough treatment and a slanging match between them ensued. Stevens laughs about it now. 'We got on very well, really,' he said, 'although we used to have battles when United played Bolton. He crocked me one time – he went over the ball – and I had a go at him; but it was all in fun, really. What a wonderful player he was, though. He could play anywhere. He was big and strong, yet so nimble on his feet. I think he was one of the greatest: there's no question about that. A nice lad, too.'

All was not gloom and despondency during that early fallow period. Three days before losing to Wolves at Molineux, United had got their latest European Cup campaign off to a flying start by thrashing Shamrock Rovers, the best club side in Irish history according to Eamon Dunphy, 6–0 at Dalymount Park in the first leg of their preliminary round tie. With a lead like that, it must have been difficult for United to get themselves up for the return a week later, but all credit to Rovers for losing only 3–2 at Old Trafford. The Babes negotiated the first round pretty comfortably, too. A 3–0 win at home against Dukla Prague, of Czechoslovakia, provided plenty of insurance for the second leg, which Dukla won 1–0. Edwards' performance in the first leg was so good that he had the scribes in the press box delving deeper and deeper into their store of compliments. 'For United, the real hero was once again Duncan Edwards,' wrote the man from *The Times*. 'From the first minute to the last, he was wonderful. There was no other word for him. He was an express train in full cry, always under control, always influencing affairs, always a danger whenever in possession.'

Domestically, however, United's form continued to be as erratic as one might expect from such a young side. Busby's answer to the problem, after successive defeats at Old Trafford by Tottenham and Chelsea at the end of November and beginning of December, was to go out and buy the Northern Ireland international Harry Gregg from Second Division Doncaster Rovers for £23,500, then a world-record fee for a goalkeeper.

At 25, Gregg was older than most of United's team and more experienced than many when they had come into the side. Before joining Doncaster, he had played for three Irish clubs, Dundalk, Linfield and Coleraine. Crucially, so far as Busby was concerned, he was a goalkeeper capable of commanding his area, something for which expert shot-stopper Ray Wood was not noted. In fact, Gregg was so keen to come off his line and even out of his area that his own defenders had to be careful this big, brave, red-headed Irishman did not mow them down. As Ivan Ponting said in his loving and exhaustive catalogue *Manchester United – Player by Player*, 'If there could be such a thing as an attacking goalkeeper then this vociferous acrobat was definitely it.'

Secretly, I think, Gregg would have preferred to be an outfield player. It certainly seemed so from a story Noel Cantwell, the elegant former United and Republic of Ireland left-back, once told me. Apparently, Harry liked nothing more in practice matches than to play at centre-forward; and, on this particular occasion, he was waving for a cross as Shay Brennan set off on a run down the wing. Ignoring Gregg, Brennan beat one man, then another. Harry, in space and waving like mad for Brennan to cross the ball to him, was now apoplectic. So when the full-back tried to beat a third opponent and lost possession, Gregg snapped. Sprinting out to the wing, he did no more than attack Brennan physically. And before the other players could drag the incandescent goalkeeper-cum-centre-forward completely off his startled team-mate, he sank his teeth into Brennan's backside. 'You could have heard the screams all over Manchester,' said Cantwell with a grin.

The recruitment of this fiery Irishman to play in goal was but one step Busby took to remedy United's inconsistency. Ray Wood was not the only first-teamer to get the chop: Johnny Berry, David Pegg and Billy Whelan joined him in the reserves, as the manager set about removing any complacency from the squad. The dropped trio of outfield players were replaced respectively by Kenny Morgans, an eighteen-year-old right-winger from the side that had won the FA Youth Cup for a fifth successive time the previous season, Albert Scanlon and Bobby Charlton.

The shake-up worked, too. United won four of their next seven games and drew the other three, scoring 24 goals in the process. Nearly a third of them came in a 7–2 trouncing of Bolton at Old Trafford on 18 January 1958. Dennis Stevens got his own back on Duncan to some extent by dispossessing him and setting up Bolton's equaliser after United had taken an early lead; but the visitors were overwhelmed from then on by the sheer quality of their opponents' play. Charlton scored his first hat-trick for the club, and Edwards added his name to a mounting score-sheet by banging home his team's seventh goal from the penalty spot.

Progress was also made in the FA Cup, Workington presenting few problems in the third round. The Third Division (North) side did have the pleasure of taking the lead against their distinguished opponents, but a Dennis Viollet hat-trick did the trick. Ten days later, United were confronted by a rather more rigorous challenge in the form of the famous Yugoslavian side Red Star Belgrade, their opponents in the quarter-finals of the European Cup.

It is worth stopping here to consider the fact that United were in the last eight of Europe's most prestigious club competition after only two rounds, or four matches. Liverpool, when they won the modern version of the tournament, the Champions League, so unexpectedly in 2005, had played a total of ten matches on their way to the quarter-finals via a qualifying round, group stage and knockout stage. The Champions League is a much larger competition than the old European Cup, of course. There were just 24 starters in 1957/58, when only the champions of their respective countries were allowed to take part. Now, with up to four clubs permitted from Europe's stronger leagues, and with the fragmentation of the Soviet bloc creating many more leagues than before, 56 clubs have to battle through up to three qualifying rounds for sixteen of them to mix it with the sixteen top seeds at the group stage. Statistically, in other words, the Champions

League now is much more difficult to win than the European Cup was then. Everything is relative, though, and the fact is that United were having to take on the continent's other true champion clubs on a straight knockout basis. No provision for group-stage second chances then, or for the next 33 years, come to that. They could do no more than beat what was put in front of them, and now it was Yugoslavia's most popular and successful club.

Red Star had been founded only thirteen years earlier, at the end of the Second World War, by students at Belgrade University. They had made a name for themselves by winning their domestic title four times between 1951 and 1957. Like United, in fact, they went into the European Cup in 1957/58 with two successive league titles under their belts. Like United, too, they had reached the semi-finals of the tournament the previous year and were eager to improve on that. Their team had formed the basis of the Yugoslav national side that reached the quarter-finals of the 1954 World Cup before losing 2–0 to West Germany, the eventual winners of the tournament. The acrobatic goalkeeper, Vladimir Beara, the formidable midfielders Dragoslav Sekularac and Rajko Mitic, and the lethally left-footed winger Bora Kostic collected a total of 180 caps between them. So, United had their work cut out to win this one.

They made a reasonable start by winning the first leg, in front of 63,000 at Old Trafford on 14 January, 2–1 with goals by Charlton and Colman. But the ability of the seasoned Red Star players to mix muscularity with skill made life difficult for United. Even someone as sturdily built as Edwards found the going hard. Rugby League fans would have taken exception to the punishment he received on his forward runs, reported one newspaper at the time. Nevertheless, Duncan kept ploughing his way through Red Star's packed defence with such success that Beara had to make three fine saves from him. Edwards also helped create Charlton's goal. But it was questionable whether a one-goal lead would be insurance enough for the second leg three weeks later.

During the long gap between the two legs of the European Cup quarter-final, United could concentrate on making progress in the

First Division and the FA Cup. Although the European tournament was enormously important to Busby, given his pioneering role on behalf of English football, he made no secret of the fact that his most cherished ambition at that point was to win three championships in a row, just as Huddersfield and Arsenal had done before the war thanks principally to the brilliantly inventive and innovative management of Herbert Chapman. So that 7–2 victory over Bolton on 18 January must have lifted the United manager's spirits appreciably.

A week later, his rejigged team beat Ipswich 2–0 in the fourth round of the FA Cup. Then, a week after that, came United's last First Division fixture before the European Cup second leg against Red Star. It was against Arsenal at Highbury, and it will go down in the annals of English football as one of the most enthralling games ever played. Leading 3–0 at the interval, Edwards having opened the scoring, United looked to have the match in their pockets. But the Gunners hit back so hard in the second half that they made it 3–3. Recovering from the shock and taking control again, United went 5–3 up only for Arsenal to claw back another goal and go looking in vain for an equaliser. Not surprisingly – at least, not in those more innocent days – the teams left the field arm in arm to a standing ovation.

Writing in the *Sun* in 1983, Jack Kelsey, the Arsenal goalkeeper, recalled what it had been like to take part in the Babes' farewell to English football. 'It was the finest match I ever played in,' said the Wales international unequivocally. 'United won 5–4 but it was so full of incident that the result could easily have been 9–7. Duncan Edwards had all the promise in the world. Even in the conditions of that day, which were awful, his strength stood out. He was a colossus. Even today it hurts me to think about that final game at Highbury. But if there is any satisfaction to be had 25 years later, it is that I played against the Babes when they were at their peak. That's something I'll never forget.'

Eamon Dunphy summed it up this way: 'The final score was 5–4, the match a classic, Busby's team living up to its reputation for brilliance and a daring that bordered on recklessness.' Others were less admiring and less charitable, however. Jack Peart, of the *Sunday Pictorial*, for instance, accused the United players of being 'far too cocky and casual' and claimed that Duncan Edwards, whom he blamed for Arsenal's fourth goal, was the worst offender. Nor was Peart alone among the press corps in beginning to wonder whether United were in danger of becoming victims of their own success.

The sceptics were offered further ammunition by that European Cup quarter-final second leg against Red Star in Belgrade on 5 February. At first, it looked all too easy for United to go through to the semi-finals. Totally outplaying the Yugoslavs, they took a 3–0 lead by half-time with an early goal by Viollet and two from Charlton. Once more in the second half, though, they gave ground to suddenly inspired opponents. Two goals by Kostic and a penalty by Tasic cut United's aggregate lead to 5–4 and condemned them to a harrowing last few minutes. But they dug in and held on for a narrow victory.

What happened next is documented only too well. After what used to be, in those more leisurely days, the customary post-match banquet and overnight stay on the Wednesday, United set off for home in their chartered, twin-engined Elizabethan aircraft the following morning. The flight plan was to refuel at Munich en route to Manchester. Unfortunately, it was snowing quite heavily when the plane landed at the West German city's Reim Airport. As a result, the pilots, Captains James Thain and Ken Rayment, had difficulty taking off once the refuelling had been completed. The first attempt was abandoned, as was a second, in order to check why the aircraft's engines were experiencing a potentially disastrous fluctuation of boost pressures.

Back in 1958, commercial airliners had few of the technical aids available today, so flying became a good deal more hazardous in bad weather. In fact, arranging midweek flights to and from central European destinations in the depths of winter was a real problem then for club secretaries because the Football League, who had never wanted their clubs to take part in the new-fangled European Cup in the first place, were only too ready to impose heavy fines on those who failed to fulfil their domestic commitments. Conscious of that threat, and remembering they had nearly been stranded in Prague by fog in the previous round of the competition, United were anxious to get home. It was not just a question of keeping the Football League sweet, or of reacquainting themselves with home comforts: United needed time to prepare for what promised to be a pivotal match in their battle with Wolves for the First Division title. Having gone seven league games without defeat and having closed to within four points of their great rivals, they were looking forward to cutting that lead in half when the Midlands club came to Old Trafford in two days' time.

After the second aborted take-off, though, the players assumed there would be an overnight stay in Munich. Duncan even went so far as to send a telegram to his new landlady, Mrs Dorman, telling her, 'All flights cancelled – flying tomorrow.' So everyone was surprised when the party was asked to board the Elizabethan once more. No faults had been found in the engines of Zulu Uniform, as it was code-named, so the pilots made a third attempt to take off at approximately three p.m.

Once again, however, the airliner refused to become airborne. This time, unfortunately, the point of no return had been passed before Thain and Rayment tried desperately and in vain to apply the brakes. So, travelling at virtually full speed down the runway, the plane smashed through the perimeter fence and collided first with a house, then with a wooden hut on a concrete base. The port wing was torn off by the first collision and the rear part of the fuselage was ripped away by the impact with the wooden hut. Frank Taylor, the only one of the nine accompanying journalists to survive the crash, subsequently wrote a dramatic and deeply moving account of the disaster, *The Day a Team Died*. I leave it to him to describe what followed.

By now, what was left of the undercarriage had been torn away, and this left the front of the airliner, still with that starboard wing attached to the fuselage, slithering and screeching along on its belly, the wing carving great chunks out of the trees in its path like a giant scythe. This part of the wreckage, in which I was strapped, was spinning around helplessly in circles.

As it did so, a number of passengers, including some of the team, were thrown out into the snow. What was once a sleek aeroplane was now a smouldering ruin, leaving a trail of death and destruction in its wake. Less than a minute previously I had been sitting in the company of the Young Kings of British Soccer, laughing and joking in the full flush of their athletic prowess. Now they lay dead ... or dying ... or brutally injured and dumbly shocked by the tragedy which had hit them.

With them in the snow was their manager Matt Busby – still, like Bobby Charlton, strapped in his seat. They, like me, were among the lucky ones.

So, too, was Harry Gregg, the big, strong, fiery goalkeeper who would bite team-mates' bums if they crossed him and not the ball. Now, though, he was the hero who ignored Captain Thain's orders to get as far away as possible from the aircraft and its combustible fuel tanks. Bravely, Gregg and *Daily Mail* photographer Peter Howard led a frantic bid to rescue as many people as possible from the wreckage before it went up in flames. Among those Gregg personally conveyed to safety were Mrs Vera Lukic, wife of the Yugoslavian air attaché in London, and her twenty-month-old baby daughter. Both had been allowed to travel back from Belgrade with United. Those beyond saving included seven players – Roger Byrne, Eddie Colman, Tommy Taylor, David Pegg, Billy Whelan, Mark Jones and Geoff Bent – coaches Tom Curry and Bert Whalley, and club secretary Walter Crickmer. Suffering from injuries that ranged from the life-threatening to the relatively minor were manager Matt Busby and players Duncan Edwards, Johnny Berry, Albert Scanlon, Bobby Charlton, Dennis Viollet, Ray Wood, Jackie Blanchflower and Ken Morgans.

As the dead were counted and the injured rushed to Munich's Rechts der Isar Hospital, news of the tragedy began to filter through to Manchester and the rest of Britain. People wept openly in the streets when they heard that such a wonderful young football team had been cut down in its prime. It may be hard to believe now, when relations between the two sets of supporters – and some players – are so rancorous, but I cannot have been the only Liverpool fan who shed tears for United that tragic day. The Busby Babes were so thrillingly successful that they had become everyone's second favourite team and carried all of English football's hopes of a glittering future. Nobody described the effect of the news on Manchester more movingly or perceptively than Arthur Hopcraft in his classic study of the game *The Football Man.*

> Anyone who was in Manchester in February 1958, particularly if he lived there, as I did, will remember for ever the stunning impact on the city of the air crash at Munich airport which killed eight of Manchester United's players. The shock was followed, just as it is in particularly closely tied families after a death, by a lingering communal desolation. No other tragedy in sport has been as brutal or as affecting as this one.
>
> It was not simply that very popular athletes had been killed and a brilliantly promising team destroyed. There was a general youthfulness about this particular Manchester United team which was new to the game. Manchester relished this fact. The old, often gloomy city had a shining exuberance to acclaim. These young players were going to take the country, and probably Europe too, by storm. To identify with this precociousness, to watch people in other towns marvelling and conceding defeat, gave a surge to the spirit. Suddenly, most of the team was dead.

Like Matt Busby, Duncan Edwards was seriously injured in the crash. He had sustained a smashed right thigh, broken ribs and severe shock. Worst of all, though, were the internal injuries he had suffered. In fact, he was in such bad shape that the initial casualty list described him as 'mortally injured'. However, drawing on his remarkable fitness and natural strength, and being the fighter he was,

Duncan lingered for fifteen days before finally being overwhelmed by the complications caused by kidney damage.

It was an agonising time for his family, for United and their fans, and for everyone else willing this fine young footballer to pull through. The daily bulletins on Edwards and Busby were devoured eagerly back home as Professor Georg Maurer, chief surgeon at the Rechts der Isar Hospital, and his staff fought to keep them alive. One day, it would look as though Duncan was on the mend; the next, he would have a relapse. And so it went on for more than a fortnight before we heard the news everyone dreaded.

He was not unconscious all this time: he had moments of semi-lucidity. Famously, he asked assistant manager Jimmy Murphy during one of them what time the kick-off was for United's crucial match against Wolves the following Saturday. Poignantly, he said he was desperate not to miss it. Murphy, who had not gone on the trip to Belgrade because he had been wearing his other hat as manager of the Wales national team, had flown straight out to Munich on hearing of the crash. Now, fighting back the tears and knowing the boy's career was almost certainly over anyway, he told Edwards gently not to worry: United had decided to rest him for that match.

Bobby Charlton also spoke to Duncan before he died. Bobby, who suffered a head injury and shock after being thrown 70 yards from the plane still strapped in his seat, had been treated on the floor below the intensive care unit up to which Duncan, Busby, Johnny Berry, pilot Ken Rayment and journalist Frank Taylor were rushed. So, when he was fit enough to leave hospital, Charlton went to say goodbye to his old mate and heard echoes of the agitated greeting he had got from Duncan on arrival at Nesscliffe to do his National Service. 'I went in to see him as I was coming away, and he gave me a bollocking!' Bobby recalled. '"Where have you been?" he demanded. "I've been downstairs," I told him. And then he rambled ...' At this point, Bobby became too upset to continue the reminiscence. When he had recovered his composure, he added, 'Duncan was as strong as an ox, so his injuries must have been very serious. But I imagine it must have driven him mad lying still and not doing anything, because that was the right opposite of what he was. Yes, he was marvellous, and yes, it was a great shame.'

In *The Day a Team Died*, Frank Taylor remembered vividly the moment he and Jackie Blanchflower were told Duncan had lost the battle against his injuries. (He was mistaken about the date – Edwards died on 21 February; 26 February was the day of his burial – but allowances have to be made for post-traumatic shock.)

Doctor Graham Taylor, of British European Airways, looked rather more serious than usual when he walked in to see Jack Blanchflower and myself on the morning of February 26th, 1958. Normally, the Doc, a lithe, springy figure, came bounding in, cracking jokes and doing all he could to bring cheer into the place ...

But it was obvious something was on his mind. He walked quickly to the door and opened it, turned while still holding the handle and remarked as casually as he could: 'I'm afraid I have some bad news for you both. I know you'll understand, but Duncan couldn't quite make it. He died early this morning. I know you won't tell Matt Busby this sad news. He is too ill to be told yet.'

The news sank in numbly. Duncan Edwards, just twenty-one years of age, the greatest footballer of his generation, had died in the Rechts der Isar Hospital; just twenty-one days after he had played his last game of football in Belgrade. For the last twenty days, that powerful body had lain crushed, but the stupendous spirit kept Duncan Edwards going. The world had followed every communiqué of Duncan's twenty days' fight following the crash. But the Big Fellow who feared nothing on a football field had no chance. His injuries were too severe.

He fought with all the unforgettable fury of that unconquerable spirit. And when he died a great sigh went round the sports fields. It was as though a young Colossus had been taken from our midst.

Yet, when the tears were dried, one of Duncan's nearest and dearest friends told me: 'Maybe it was better this way. The doctors said, had he lived, he might have had to spend the rest of his life in a wheelchair. Duncan couldn't have stood that. Now I can remember him as he was – the greatest thing that has happened in British football for years.'

Fighting for his own life at the time, Busby was unaware of the enormity of the tragedy unfolding around him. 'In some of my rare moments of consciousness,' the United manager recalled in *Soccer at the Top*, 'I heard the sounds of suffering. It was Duncan. Then one day, in another moment of awareness, I heard a clergyman in the hospital say: "Duncan is dead." The clergyman was given a telling off for saying such a thing anywhere near me, but that was when I first began to be really aware that something awful had happened. I was afraid to ask, but I asked.'

Duncan Edwards died on 21 February, the day before the first league fixture United played after Munich. He passed away peacefully in his sleep in the early hours after finally losing his battle against the effects of a damaged kidney. The problem was an excess of nitrogen in the blood so great that at one point the level was six times higher than normal. An artificial kidney was rushed to the Rechts der Isar Hospital to reduce the amount of nitrogen, but the machine also reduced the ability of Edwards' blood to clot and he began haemorrhaging internally. Blood transfusions were administered, but this desperate, self-defeating circle of treatment sapped his strength to such an extent that not even he could cope with it in the end.

Duncan's parents, Gladstone and Sarah Ann, and his fiancée, Molly, had dashed out to Munich to be with him during his fight for life; but it looks as though his death took them by surprise, because they were at their hotel when they were informed that he had died. It is not difficult to imagine how distraught they must have been, because the news came like a thunderclap to people back home who did not even know the boy. 'His mother and father never got over it,' said his aunt, Marjorie Perry, of Duncan's death. 'My sister went and saw him in hospital and he wanted to come home. But he'd got all tubes and things in him.' It prompted 'if only' thoughts, too. 'My brother-in-law was a scout for West Bromwich Albion,' said his cousin, Betty Cooksey, 'and I think he went to see my Uncle Glad about signing Duncan, but Duncan didn't want to go to the Albion. We did say recently that if he had played for West Brom this wouldn't have happened. The family were disappointed when he didn't join one of the local clubs, but he always wanted to go to Manchester United, and you can't foresee all these things.'

Of those in the intensive care unit, Rayment also became one of the crash's 23 fatalities, but Busby, Berry and Frank Taylor pulled through. In Busby's case, it was very much a question of beating the odds. Although not old at the time, the 49-year-old United manager had not been in the best of health at the start of the trip to Belgrade. A few days before departure he had entered hospital for an operation on veins in his leg and it had sapped his strength. Frank Taylor remembers him looking 'grey-faced and tired' when he boarded the plane in Manchester. Now, Busby had much more to contend with in the unwelcome form of a crushed chest, lung damage and a broken foot. Not expected to live, he was given the last rites by a Catholic priest. But the tough Scot was also a fighter; and, as a former professional footballer himself, he still had some physical strength and fitness in reserve. Three days after being taken into intensive care, Busby and Taylor were removed from the critical list. That, though, was just the start of a long period of recovery for the United manager and several of the players who had survived the crash.

Some did not recover fully. Johnny Berry and Jackie Blanchflower, for instance, never played again. But even those who eventually got over the physical and psychological damage were not immediately available to play. Which meant that Jimmy Murphy, to whom the stricken Busby had whispered 'Keep the flag flying, Jimmy, until I get back', had a colossal task on his hands to find a team strong enough to fulfil United's remaining fixtures. The Football League and the FA did what they could to help: the League allowed United to postpone that once so-important First Division fixture against Wolves until later in the season, and the FA permitted them to delay their fifth-round FA Cup tie against Sheffield Wednesday, scheduled for 15 February, by four days.

Even so, it was a close-run thing. For the cup tie against Wednesday at Old Trafford, Murphy got a team together so late that there was a blank space in the programme where the United XI should have been. In the end, the names had to be announced over the Tannoy. They were, in the 2–3–5 formation of the day: Gregg; Foulkes, Greaves; Goodwin, Cope, Crowther; Webster, Taylor, Dawson, Pearson, Brennan. In other words, only two of the survivors of the Munich air disaster, Harry Gregg and Bill Foulkes, were fit enough to play. The rest of the side comprised United reserves and kids promoted from the youth and A teams bolstered by the experience of two hurried signings. The first was Ernie Taylor, the clever little inside-right who had been a major, unsung influence behind Blackpool's victory over Bolton in the epic 'Matthews Final' of 1953. Taylor, then 33 and a one-cap England international, cost £8,000. He was followed to Old Trafford, somewhat reluctantly, by the tough Aston Villa wing-half Stan Crowther, for £23,000. Crowther was not keen on the move, but Murphy talked him round only hours before the game and the FA agreed to overlook the fact that he was cup-tied, having played for Villa in the third round.

Murphy revealed later that Liverpool and Nottingham Forest were the only clubs who had come forward to see if any of their reserves could help United. He also revealed he had seriously contemplated signing Ferenc Puskas, the great Hungarian inside-forward, who later became part of the wonderful Real Madrid side that dominated the early years of the European Cup. Puskas, then a refugee following the 1956 uprising in Hungary, was available; but United's assistant manager decided he would be betraying the principles of the club if he did recruit him. 'Importing a Continental, on reflection,' he said in a signed article for the *People*, 'seemed a negation of all that Matt and I had tried to build – a team of all the talents found mostly by our own scouts. We had to buy British players to help United over the hill.' (Now where have we come across that sort of subject before, I wonder?)

Before the gates were closed that night, nearly 60,000 people crowded into Old Trafford. Thousands stood silently outside as those inside gave vent to their emotions through tears or wails of anguish. The atmosphere was so highly charged, the Sheffield Wednesday players could not cope with it. Having lost only 2–1 to the Babes in a league game at Old Trafford three months earlier, the strong Yorkshire side surrendered surprisingly meekly to two goals from Shay Brennan, converted from wing-half to outside-left on the night, and one from centre-forward Alex Dawson.

And so it continued, as United rode a rising tide of emotion through the rest of the rounds to Wembley. Most of the country was willing them to win the FA Cup as a tribute to those who had died at Munich; but Bolton, their opponents in the final, were not prepared to roll over to order and United's makeshift team was running out of emotional steam. Although Bobby Charlton and Dennis Viollet were back in action by then, two goals by Nat Lofthouse, the second of which would have been disallowed today for a foul on Gregg, finally shattered the illusion that Murphy and Busby, who returned to Old Trafford a week before the final, had somehow conjured up a team capable of replacing the Babes.

One Bolton player for whom that May day brought decidedly mixed feelings was Dennis Stevens. Nothing would have delighted him more than to have renewed at Wembley the rivalry that had developed between him and his second cousin, Duncan Edwards. But, like the rest of the nation, he had been left deeply saddened by what had happened at Munich. 'I was so upset about that,' he said. 'I never left the wireless because I didn't want to miss any of the news about the crash. At first, Duncan was "getting better"; then it was "he's not doing so bad". Finally, all of a sudden, he'd gone. It was so tragic. Everyone in the country wanted United to win the final because of the disaster, but it wasn't as difficult for us as you might think. I mean, you go out to win, don't you? You forget what's happened. We did very well really. We were not a footballing side, but everybody gave 100 per cent effort and there was a good team spirit within the camp.'

United fared no better in the European Cup. Five days after losing to Bolton at Wembley, they beat AC Milan 2–1 at Old Trafford in the first leg of the semi-final their defeat of Red Star Belgrade had entitled them to; but it was far from enough. Although Kenny Morgans was also back in the side by now, Milan, with players of the stature of Nils Liedholm and Juan Schiaffino, won easily, the Uruguayan Schiaffino scoring twice and the Swede Liedholm once in a 4–0 victory. United might have done better had they been able to include Charlton in the team. But the FA insisted he play in a World Cup warm-up match against Portugal on the night of the first leg, then took him away for the friendlies in Yugoslavia and the USSR that England played before going to the 1958 finals in Sweden.

Charlton himself has no doubt at all that United at full strength would have won the European Cup that year, Real Madrid or no Real Madrid. 'Everything was just right,' he said, eyes gleaming behind the spectacles he now wears. 'We were getting better and gaining more nous with every game we played in Europe. The one thing about the English game is that it is built for stamina. We always thought we could go the full 90 minutes and the continentals couldn't. They like playing nice and soft, with time on the ball, but you don't get that in the English game. I think if we'd won it that year, we'd have won it a lot more. Not United particularly, but English clubs.'

At the end of a season in which United were entitled to think in terms of a league championship–FA Cup–European Cup treble, the First Division offered no solace, either. A team as flimsy as the one Murphy was obliged to put out simply could not cope with the burden of fighting on three fronts, and their league form suffered accordingly. At one point, in March, they lost four games in a row, and of the fourteen fixtures remaining after Munich they won only one. Wolves, the eventual champions, won that postponed game at Old Trafford 4–0, and United could finish no higher than ninth.

The game the day after Edwards' death, watched by a crowd of 66,124 made more sombre than ever by the sad news from Munich, was against Nottingham Forest at Old Trafford. It was drawn 1–1, as if that mattered. The Dean of Manchester conducted an inter-denominational memorial service for all the Munich victims on the pitch before the kick-off. At much the same time, Duncan's body was being loaded on to a plane at Munich for transportation back to London. From there, it was driven up to Dudley for the funeral four days later.

Thousands of people lined the streets of his home town as the cortege took him from his parents' home to St Francis' Church on the Priory Estate, the estate where he had grown up and played so much of his early football. Two of Duncan's United team-mates, Gordon Clayton and Bobby English, were scheduled to join four of his international colleagues, Billy Wright of Wolves, Ray Barlow and Don Howe of West Bromwich Albion, and Ronnie Clayton of Blackburn Rovers, in carrying the coffin into the church, but snow delayed them on their journey from Manchester and their places as pall-bearers had to be taken by two players from Aston Villa, Peter McParland and Pat Sayward. 'It was a very sad occasion,' recalled Howe. 'I've never seen anything like it. We were walking down the aisle with the coffin on our shoulders and everybody was standing up. All the seats were taken, and anywhere you wanted to stand you couldn't get in. It was absolutely jam packed. It was the same outside: there were people everywhere. Following the hearse through the crowds afterwards, it really was awesome. Everybody had their heads down and it was all very respectful. He was a hero in a place like Dudley, of course.'

The service was conducted by the vicar, the Rev. A. Dawson Catterall, a keen football fan. In a moving sermon he said, 'The mark of sacrifice and genius is deeply imprinted on this young Priory community. We are proud that the great Duncan Edwards was one of our sons. His history gives us an honoured place in the world. His football record needs no praise within these walls, for it was known throughout the world; and this great game was something England had given to the world. He goes to join the immortal company of Steve Bloomer and Alex James. Talent, and even genius, we shall see again, but there will be only one Duncan Edwards.'

Some 3,000 people, it was estimated, were waiting in the bitter cold to pay their respects at Queen's Cross Cemetery, where Duncan was to be buried. According to the *Birmingham Post & Gazette*, as the newspaper was called then, wreaths made a carpet of colour 30 yards around the grave. There were about three hundred of them, from all over England and parts of the continent, and they had completely covered the front garden of Duncan's old home at 31 Elm Road before the funeral. They came from a wide cross-section of sources whose very variety reflected just how many lives Duncan had brightened during his relatively brief existence. Manchester United and most of the other First Division clubs sent a wreath, as did the Football Association and the Football League. The newspaper industry, which had chronicled Edwards' career with growing awe and had suffered grievously itself at Munich, also paid its respects in this way. So, too, did the army. Local clubs like Woodside Wanderers and Dudley Town were also represented, as were Duncan's old schools, Priory Junior and Wolverhampton Street. On a more individual level, there was one wreath with the simple message 'From four supporters of Manchester United', and a bunch of flowers from 'Judith aged 9'.

Eight months later, another well-attended ceremony saw Matt Busby, now fully recovered from his injuries, unveil a special memorial on Duncan's grave. A crowd of 2,000 watched as the Manchester United manager pulled back a red and white covering to reveal a tall headstone in black and grey Swedish granite. At the top of the headstone is an engraving of Duncan taking a throw-in. Below, the simple, unsentimental inscription reads:

In Loving Memory of
Our dear son
DUNCAN EDWARDS
Who died February 21st 1958
from injuries received

In an Air Crash at Munich
Aged 21 years

At the foot of the grave there is another inscription that denotes
that Duncan is buried with his younger sister, Carol Anne, who died
as a baby. On the grave itself there are three flower vases, one of them
shaped like a football. This is always filled with fresh flowers, usually red and white, by either family members or visiting United fans
coming to pay their respects to a legend of the past. At one time they
could talk to Duncan's father, Gladstone, who took a job as a gar-
dener at the cemetery so he could be near his son. The day I made the
pilgrimage, a red United bobble-hat had been laid reverently on the
grave and a foreign football fan had tied a scarf around the flower
vase. It was disturbing, though, to be told that vandals had knocked
over the headstone in the recent past, necessitating its repair. Is nothing sacred any more?

However inexcusable that display of flagrant disrespect by one
or two of Dudley's citizens may be, it is more than outweighed
by the substantial efforts the Black Country town has made to
honour the memory of one of its most famous sons – perhaps
even *the* most famous. In St Francis' Church, for instance, there
are two beautiful stained-glass windows commemorating his life
and career. One shows him in Manchester United red, the other
in England white, and the inscription reads, 'Thanking God for
the life of Duncan Edwards, died at Munich, February 1958'. The
windows, unveiled by Matt Busby and dedicated by the Bishop of
Worcester at a special service in 1961, cost £300 – the equivalent
of £4,500 today. The mystifying thing about them is that the coats
of arms of Brentford and Crystal Palace can be seen alongside
those of Manchester United and the city of Munich. Apparently,
both London clubs contributed to the cost of the windows, but
nobody seems to know why. Neither Duncan's family nor the two
clubs themselves were able to offer an explanation for the unlikely
link. More understandable was the financial help provided by the
local Wren's Nest Bowling Club, acknowledged by the picture at

the bottom of the windows of a tiny wren with her nest. Again, Duncan Edwards' popularity seems to have crossed all sporting boundaries and rivalries.

Nor was he quickly forgotten. Twenty-two years later, Wolverhampton's *Express & Star* newspaper ran a story about the response there had been to an appeal for the restoration of the rotting woodwork around the stained-glass windows. 'A member of the Parochial Church Council wrote to Manchester United, who put the letter in a match programme,' wrote their reporter. 'He received 60 letters enclosing a total of £412.00 in reply. Duncan Edwards is still remembered by United fans all over the country and is obviously still held in tremendous esteem. A boy of 10 sent a 10p donation and said that his father was always talking about the great player.'

Today, Dudley offers other enduring reminders of Duncan's greatness. In the foyer of the town's Leisure and Recreation Centre, for instance, there is a comprehensive display of the many shirts, caps, trophies and photographs he collected from schools and professional football between 1951 and 1957. In one showcase there is also a rare copy of *Tackle Soccer This Way*, the book written secretly by Duncan before his death and published posthumously.

The most imposing memorial of all, though, is to be found more centrally. Go to Dudley Market Place and you will find a statue of the town's favourite son dominating its busy hub. It was unveiled in 1999 by the mayor, Duncan's mother and, by then, Sir Bobby Charlton. Depicted in an England strip and in the act of kicking a ball, Edwards stands on a plinth that extols his virtues and reminds us of his career records. Above the facts and figures, a heartfelt assessment by Jimmy Murphy, Matt Busby's assistant manager, catches the eye and fires the imagination. 'He was the most complete player I have ever seen,' Murphy is quoted as saying, with a touch of awe almost tangible still.

'These memorials,' Arthur Hopcraft wrote in *The Football Man*, 'commemorate not only Duncan Edwards' football but also the simple decency of the man. He represented thousands in their wish for courage, acclaim and rare talent, and he had all three without swagger. The hero is the creature other people would like to be. Edwards was such a man, and he enabled people to respect themselves more.' Both Hopcraft and Eamon Dunphy added beautifully to the eulogies. 'News of Duncan Edwards' death,' wrote Dunphy, 'deepened the sense of loss at Old Trafford. He more than anyone had been the symbol of indestructible youth, the most awesomely vigorous of the "Red Devils".' Hopcraft was even more poetic. 'It was the death of Duncan Edwards which gave the deepest, most lasting pain,' he wrote. 'This was not because he was liked personally any more than the others, but because there was a special appeal to people's ideals about him. Walter Winterbottom, the England manager at the time, called him "the spirit of British football". He meant the football that exists in children's daydreams and good men's hopes: honest, brilliant, and irresistibly strong.'

We can only speculate as to what Duncan might have gone on to achieve in football had he lived beyond 21; but it is quite likely he would be mentioned automatically now in the same breath as Pele, Diego Maradona and Alfredo di Stefano when football men discuss the greatest players the game has ever seen. As it is, he is remembered still as one of the finest footballers to have graced the English and European game.

His premature death, and that of the seven other young players who died at Munich in 1958, undoubtedly had a devastating effect on Manchester United, both practically and psychologically. As we have heard, Bobby Charlton reckons that but for Munich, United would have won the European Cup that year, broken Real Madrid's stranglehold on the tournament and encouraged other English clubs to follow suit. Yet, thanks to the fortitude of Matt Busby and his and Jimmy Murphy's team-building skills, United recovered so strongly from the disaster that, only ten years later, they became the first English club to win the European Cup. It took another nine years after that, though, before another of England's leading clubs, Liverpool, won the first of their five European Cups and sparked an English domination of the trophy between 1977 and 1984. Perhaps the process would have taken place many years earlier had that Elizabethan airliner not made an ill-fated third attempt to take off through the slush on the runway of Munich airport, which was identified eventually as the cause of the disaster.

England were hit as hard as United by the loss of so many outstanding young players. Duncan, Roger Byrne and Tommy Taylor would have been certainties for the 1958 World Cup squad, while Eddie Colman and David Pegg must have had a very good chance of joining them and Bobby Charlton in Sweden. Interviewed by the *Express & Star* in 1983, former England captain Billy Wright said, 'Some people believe we would have won the World Cup in 1958 if the crash had not happened. The great Brazilian side had just emerged and we drew with them 0–0 in the final stages in Sweden. What a contest we would have seen had Duncan been able to play against the young Pele, who had just come into the Brazilian side.'

Walter Winterbottom, to his eternal credit, refused to bleat about the damage Munich had done to his team and its hopes of winning the 1958 World Cup. Don Howe, a member of that squad and later an outstanding coach who served as assistant to three England managers, said he could not remember Winterbottom referring to the tragedy, other than to express sympathy for the families of those who had died. In his knowledgeable and insightful history of England's attempts to win the World Cup, *Jules Rimet Still Gleaming?*, Ken Jones quotes right-back Howe as saying of Winterbottom, 'He'd lost some terrific players, not only Duncan Edwards, Roger Byrne and Tommy Taylor, but also David Pegg and Eddie Colman ... From being in a position to win the World Cup, he had to think again. But it wasn't in Walter's nature to complain. He kept his thoughts to himself and got on with the job.' Jones also quotes Bill Nicholson, who assisted Winterbottom in Sweden. 'Duncan had it all,' said the former Tottenham Hotspur manager. 'The range of his ability was exceptional and ... he had tremendous enthusiasm for the game. I think if Edwards had lived, Byrne and Taylor, too, because they were both outstanding in their positions, England would have gone close in Sweden. It was a hell of a job [replacing them] because there were not that many international-class players around, and one or two who looked up to it weren't ready.'

Bill Slater of Wolves was the player handed the unenviable task of replacing Duncan at left-half in the England team. He was more than ready for it, being 31 at the time and having won a couple of consecutive caps before Edwards arrived so irresistibly on the scene. 'I suppose there was an element of disappointment in having to drop out of the team,' said Slater of being displaced by United's boy wonder in the first instance. 'But whether I would have gone on in the team, I don't know. I mean, I was getting on a bit. I didn't really start playing as a professional until I was 27. I stayed as an amateur with the Wolves for a couple of years, and I think I must have been past 30 in 1958. So it wasn't as though I was a young player coming in, and here was another young player who was certainly more talented than I was. I was quite a bit older; so, in that sense, we were not really rivals or competing. But I wasn't in his class: he was something special.

'I don't know what to say about him that hasn't been said before. In possession of the ball he was so strong. He could ride tackles and still come out with the ball. Defending and hard tackling weren't the only things to his game, either. He was a good user of the ball as well, and he could score goals. I don't know what his goalscoring record was, but it must have been quite high for a wing-half. In short, he was a very strong, attacking wing-half, and it was a great tragedy that we weren't to see more of him. He was a great loss to United and to the England team as well.'

Slater's career is, in itself, an example of how radically English professional football has changed during the past half-century. As a 24-year-old amateur studying for a physical education degree, he found himself deputising for the Scottish international Alan Brown at inside-left in the Blackpool team that lost 2–0 to Newcastle in the 1951 FA Cup final. Then, when he got a teaching post in London and was released by Blackpool, Slater was taken on by Brentford, where he made up a half-back line with Ron Greenwood and Jimmy Hill. Finally, a move to the Midlands as a lecturer led him to Wolves. Reluctant at first to sign him, manager Stan Cullis relented when he saw in a trial match what Slater could do. The fearsome master of Molineux must have been impressed because he even allowed the new recruit to play as a part-timer when he decided to turn professional. Slater responded by gaining international recognition and by captaining Wolves to victory over Blackburn Rovers in the 1960 FA Cup final.

But just try to imagine the following taking place now in the modern, money-driven game: in order to play in the World Cup finals of 1958, Slater had to take unpaid leave of absence from his job at Birmingham University. The £50 match fee, he said, meant he just about broke even. 'My head of department at the university was very good about it,' said Slater about the whole business of being a part-time professional footballer. 'It would have been very difficult for him, and for me, if I was constantly going to ask for time off, to arrange lectures and that sort of thing. So we had an agreement that if, for any reason at all, the university commitment crossed with a football commitment, the university commitment would be the one I should honour, as it were. I did occasionally miss matches, particularly midweek matches that were perhaps away at Newcastle or whatever; but, for the World Cup, I did take leave of absence for six months – the summer term and then on into the summer vacation – and that seemed to work quite well.'

Do not, however, be misled by Slater's academic background or his natural modesty. 'Bill was an exceptional player himself, there's no doubt about that,' insisted Bert Williams, the former Wolves goalkeeper, who played in Duncan Edwards' first four games for England. 'Bill, an exceptional person as well as an exceptional player, was one of the stars at Wolverhampton and fully deserved his international caps. He and Duncan were vastly different in style. Duncan was a strong, forceful player, dashing up and down, whereas Bill was studious. But I thought they were equally brilliant.'

Coincidentally, it was yet another Wolves player, Ron Flowers, who took over from Slater in the England team after the 1958 World Cup and made the left-half position his own until the next World Cup, in Chile, and beyond. Indeed, Bobby Moore had to settle for right-half until Alf Ramsey took over as England manager from Winterbottom in 1963. As good a player as Flowers was, though, it must be doubtful whether he would have enjoyed such a long international career had Duncan Edwards been around to contest the left-half spot.

Come to that, you have to think the unthinkable and wonder whether even the godlike Bobby Moore would have been capable of keeping him out of the side. After all, Edwards would have been only 29, and in his prime, in June 1966 and was, in the opinion of just about anyone who mattered, destined to captain his country. So it could quite easily have been Duncan, and not Bobby, in those photographs we see of the jubilant England captain hoisted on the shoulders of his team-mates and brandishing the World Cup in triumph 40 years ago. Moore was such a fine footballer himself, however, Ramsey would certainly have found a way of playing them both in the same England team.

The intriguing question here is this: which of the legendary Boys of '66 would have had to make way for him? 'For me,' said former Everton and England wing-half Colin Harvey forthrightly, 'Duncan would have developed into a dynamic second centre-back, and Bobby Moore would have had problems staying in the England side – if he'd ever got in. I think Duncan, and not Bobby, would have played alongside Jackie Charlton. It's sad, isn't it, that we never saw his full potential? From what I remember of him from the papers and the odd times I actually saw him play, he was fantastic. Occasionally, old footage of him comes on television and you see the range of passing and the strength and mobility of him. "Blinking heck," you think, "it would have been lovely to see it developed!"'

Wilf McGuinness, who vied with Slater and Flowers for the left-half position in the national team after Edwards had gone, thinks a player other than Moore might have had to make way for Duncan. 'I think Roger Byrne would have been the first to captain England after Billy Wright,' he says. 'He was a great leader and a proper captain. Duncan, who was seven or eight years younger than Roger, would have developed into our best player whether as captain or not. But I think he would definitely have been captain by 1966 – and Bobby Moore wouldn't have minded that, I'm sure.

'I don't know where we would have played everybody, though. I think Jack [Charlton] might have hit the deck somewhere along the line. But maybe not. It could have been Jack, it could have been Nobby [Stiles], it could have been anybody, because Duncan would certainly have been there. Oh yes, without a doubt!'

Don Howe doesn't think it would have been a question of someone dropping out of the '66 team because they would not have been there in the first place. 'Duncan would have been in the team from 1958 onwards,' he insisted, 'so his position would never have been in doubt. I think Walter Winterbottom knew what a great player he had coming along, and Alf Ramsey would have been the same. Duncan would have been a permanent choice. It would have been a case of, "England game? Duncan Edwards is playing." Just as now it's, "England game? Rooney's playing."

'I'm not sure, though, that having Duncan in midfield would have meant there was no need for Nobby Stiles. Nobby did a Makelele job; he was the one who sat in front of the defence and did all the screening. Alf was into that, and I think he would have gone for Nobby and Duncan in midfield. Duncan would have been bombing on, going forward, making runs, getting shots in and all that stuff, while Nobby would have been the fellow just keeping the balance right, the positional strength right.

'Bobby Charlton would have finished up like he did finish up, with freedom to move around, but principally playing off the centre-forward. Whether the centre-forward was Geoff Hurst or whoever, you can imagine Duncan coming up behind him with Bobby. So you would have had two people with fantastic shots coming from deep positions and letting fly from the edge of the D. I wouldn't have wanted to be the opposing goalkeeper!

'Roger Byrne was the one who was going to take over from Billy Wright as captain of England; but Roger was nearing 30 in 1958, so I think Duncan would definitely have been captain by 1962. Johnny Haynes was the captain in Chile, if I remember correctly, and a good captain, too. Duncan, though, would always have had this deciding factor in his favour: there are some players who, as soon as they walk on the pitch, cause the opposition concern. And the opposition take a different approach because they are worried and distracted.

Sometimes, just the presence of a truly great player can give his team an edge.'

The last word on the subject, appropriately, should be left to Sir Matt Busby. Writing in 1973, the Manchester United manager had this to say:

Duncan Edwards was ... and has always remained to me, incomparable. His death after the Munich crash in 1958 when he was only twenty-one, but with eighteen caps already, was as far as football is concerned the biggest single tragedy that has happened to England and to Manchester United. I believe he would have been playing for England still. He seemed indestructible.

He was a Colossus first among the boys and then among the men. In his early days Jimmy Murphy and I would go watch him with the juniors and try to find some fault with him. He seemed to be too good to be true. We could find nothing wrong with the lad. What could we work on? Nothing. Whatever was needed he had it. He was immensely powerful. He was prodigiously gifted in the arts and crafts of the game. His temperament was perfect.

Work-rate, which became fashionable much later, would never even have had to be mentioned to Duncan. He couldn't have enough matches. And he couldn't find enough work in any of them. He was utterly indefatigable ...

He was the most valuable member of one team I ever saw anywhere. He was worth two of most, and two good ones at that. We seldom lost a match, but if we did, most players, as most players will, tried to banish defeat from their minds. Not Duncan. It didn't finish there. He regarded defeat as a personal reflection on himself. 'What am I doing letting that lot beat us?' he would say.

Ignoring the bit about temperament, does it remind you of anyone by any chance?

CHAPTER 9

ENGLAND EXPECTS

BECAUSE of the broken foot he had sustained during the finals of Euro 2004, Wayne Rooney missed the first three England internationals of the 2004/05 season: a friendly against Ukraine and the 2006 World Cup qualifiers against Austria and Poland. In Portugal during the summer, Rooney had increased the attacking potency of the side to such an extent that playing, and winning, without him had become almost unthinkable. However, England managed quite nicely in the opening fixture, staged at Newcastle's St James's Park on 18 August. Goals from David Beckham, Michael Owen and, on his senior international debut, substitute Shaun Wright-Phillips saw off Ukraine with ease.

The first competitive match, away to Austria in Vienna on 4 September, was rather more difficult. Two goals up with less than half an hour to go, thanks to influential midfielders Frank Lampard and Steven Gerrard, England let Austria back into the game. In the space of three minutes, Kollmann scored with a curling free-kick and Ivanschitz equalised with a shot that went under David James' body and cost the Manchester City man his place as England's first-choice goalkeeper for the foreseeable future.

James was replaced by Tottenham's Paul Robinson four days later, by which time England had moved on to Chorzow to play Poland in another World Cup qualifier. A second change by Sven-Goran Eriksson brought in Robinson's clubmate, Jermain Defoe, for Manchester United striker Alan Smith, who had not impressed as Rooney's replacement against Ukraine or Austria. Both adjustments worked perfectly. Robinson was calm and assured in goal, while Defoe, who had hit a post after coming on as a substitute in Vienna, gave England a half-time lead against the Poles and looked dangerous throughout. Poland equalised early in the second half, but England continued to dominate and could have won by more than Glowacki's own goal. So, even without their new talisman, Wayne Rooney, Eriksson's team had begun the qualifying campaign for 2006 with an encouraging four points from two away games. The win in Chorzow was particularly important because Poland were regarded, quite rightly, as the opponents in the six-team Group Six most likely to deny England the one automatic qualifying spot at its top.

Rooney did not return to international action until 9 October, when England faced Wales at Old Trafford in their third qualifier. What had been expected to be a difficult game against British opponents who loved nothing more than to beat the English turned out to be a stroll. Fielding three strikers in Rooney, Owen and Defoe, England did pretty much as they liked. Only some heroic defensive resistance by Wales kept the score down to 2–0, the goals coming from Lampard and Beckham.

The fashion now for back-to-back qualifiers – so different from ten years ago, never mind 50 – saw England move on to Baku for their first full international against Azerbaijan, one of the many countries made independent by the break-up of the old Soviet Union. Eriksson persisted with his three-pronged attack, but his positive intentions were blunted to a large extent by the weather. On a night when the wind and rain were so bad that the game was nearly postponed, all England could manage against opponents ranked 107 places below them was a goal by the ever-reliable Owen. Fortunately, it proved to be enough.

With ten points from four games, England led the group by one point from Poland and looked set fair for qualification. But before the European qualifying process went into hibernation for the winter, England played one more friendly. It was against Spain in Madrid and it turned out to be a disturbing experience in more ways than one. Fielding a full-strength side, England were beaten 1–0 by a goal from future Chelsea full-back Asier Del Horno, and were completely outplayed. Worse still, England's black players were subjected to disgraceful racist chanting by the Spanish fans in Real Madrid's Bernabeu Stadium, Ashley Cole and Shaun Wright-Phillips coming in for the worst abuse.

Nor was that the end of it. As if the defeat, and the manner of it, were not worrying enough, Wayne Rooney's behaviour on the pitch was so out of control that Eriksson felt obliged to replace him with Alan Smith three minutes before the interval to save the boy wonder from being sent off. Before being substituted, Rooney had been guilty of wild challenges on Spain's Iker Casillas and Carlos Marchena and had been sniping at referee George Kasnaferis all the time. As he left the pitch, not at all happy about being hauled off so early, Rooney compounded his misdemeanours by taking off and throwing down the black armband the England players were wearing in memory of the late Emlyn Hughes. But, as this was the first time in eighteen England appearances Rooney had allowed occasional indiscipline at club level to spill over into his international career, the tantrum was put down to the youthful enthusiasm and immaturity of a boy who had not long turned nineteen. His talent was so great, certainly, that there was never any question of his being dropped from the team.

Rooney played in three of England's five remaining matches in the 2004/05 season without any further disciplinary problems. Those three games were a friendly against Holland at Villa Park and World Cup qualifiers against Northern Ireland and Azerbaijan at Old Trafford and St James's Park respectively. England drew 0–0 with the Dutch, but at the end of March beat Northern Ireland 4–0 and Azerbaijan 2–0 to keep themselves firmly in the driving seat in Group Six. Like a lot of other first-choice players who needed a rest, though, Rooney did not go on the FA's flag-waving, money-making trip to the United States in May, when they beat the USA 2–1 in Chicago and Colombia 3–2 in New York with virtual reserve teams.

The absentees returned, supposedly refreshed, for the friendly against Denmark in August that got 2005/06 off to the worst possible start. Early-season internationals have always been a problem for England, and this one was so early it took place only four days after the start of the Premier League campaign, brought forward by a week to give England more preparation time for the World Cup finals. Whatever the reason for England's poor display, they were thrashed 4–1 in Copenhagen, Rooney claiming their consolation goal.

Nor was that disappointing performance a one-off. When England resumed their World Cup qualifying campaign the following month, they struggled to beat Wales 1–0 in Cardiff and, to general disbelief, lost 1–0 to Northern Ireland in Belfast. At Windsor Park, too, Rooney's quick temper got the better of him again. Booked for a rash challenge on Keith Gillespie and nearly shown the yellow card for a second time soon afterwards, the snarling teenager responded with a volley of invective when his own captain, David Beckham, and clubmate Rio Ferdinand tried to calm him down. Equally ineffective was the rather pathetic attempt on the touchline of Eriksson's assistant, Steve McClaren, to get Rooney to smile.

Because of the unexpected defeat by Northern Ireland, England were now under more pressure to claim the one automatic qualifying place in Group Six than they had hoped to be. It meant that the two remaining qualifiers, home games in October against Austria and Poland, assumed much greater importance. Third-placed Austria were not really in with a chance of qualifying, but Poland had kept winning and sat two points ahead of England at the top of the group.

The question of whether to pick Rooney for the match against Austria was taken out of Eriksson's hands by the yellow card the player had picked up in Belfast. As it was his second of the tournament, he was automatically suspended for the following competitive fixture. Losing a player of Rooney's quality, of course, was exactly what England did not need at a stage where they knew they had to win their two remaining qualifiers to be sure of pipping Poland for the leadership of the group, which their rivals now held by five points thanks to a subsequent victory over Wales.

Out of the England team Rooney may have been, but not out of trouble or the nation's consciousness. A week after the debacle in

Belfast, he was sent off playing for Manchester United against Villareal in the Champions League. His offence was to clap the referee sarcastically after being handed a caution he did not think he merited. Unfortunately, the referee was the pernickety Dane Kim Milton Nielsen, who had sent off David Beckham for that little kick at Argentina's Diego Simeone during the 1998 World Cup. So there was no surprise when Nielsen promptly flourished the yellow card at Rooney for a second time, followed by the red.

It was then that the national debate about the prodigy's suspect temperament began in earnest. The argument had kicked off a week earlier, following the embarrassing defeat by Northern Ireland. Under a banner headline spread across two pages and reading 'Rooney Rage Shows Split at Camp David', Joe Lovejoy, the *Sunday Times'* forthright football correspondent, rightly excoriated the player for his behaviour and England coach Sven-Goran Eriksson for his handling of the team. Being the responsible and well-informed journalist he is, Lovejoy also examined the possible reasons for Rooney's outburst at Windsor Park. Arguing that Eriksson had indulged David Beckham by pushing Rooney out on to the left wing so that the England captain could fulfil his ambition of becoming a central midfielder, Lovejoy wrote:

> For a long time now Eriksson has allowed his celebrity captain to have an undue influence on just about everything, from where England stay to team selection and tactics. The unavoidable impression is that whatever Becks wants, Becks gets, and that the coach is too weak to gainsay him.
>
> According to well-placed sources within Camp David, this belief was at the root of Rooney's obnoxious behaviour on Wednesday night, when he told his captain and Rio Ferdinand to '**** off'. The red mist descended after 41 minutes, when Rooney was booked for recklessly leading with an arm in an aerial challenge on Keith Gillespie. He reacted to the yellow card with a stream of abuse at the referee, and when Beckham tried to calm him down, he was told where to go.

As the players left the pitch at half-time, Ferdinand asked his United team-mate what was wrong; he too was told to '**** off'. The row continued in the dressing room at the interval, when Beckham said Rooney had been 'out of order' and was told to 'get stuffed'. The two players squared up and had to be separated by Ferdinand and others before order was restored by Eriksson's assistant coach, Steve McClaren.

At his (McClaren's) insistence, Beckham and Rooney shook hands on the pitch at the start of the second half, in a public show of reconciliation, but Rooney 'lost it' again after the match, when he objected to a rebuke from McClaren. Witnesses present interpreted Rooney's attitude towards Beckham as, 'You're the reason I'm stuck out on the left wing', and a high-profile club manager, who was privy to the United striker's thoughts, said, 'He no more wanted to be out there than he wanted to be the man on the moon.'

Some will sympathise with Rooney's reluctance to play in a role he clearly does not enjoy. Others will not and will be appalled by his show of dissent. Old-timers would have given their right arm for an international cap, regardless of position, but those days are long gone. This is the era of 'player power', and more care must be taken to prevent it becoming power without responsibility. Too much is made of what top footballers earn, which is in no way disproportionate in the entertainment industry, but they do inhabit the most luxurious of comfort zones, and accountability is the price they must accept for all that mollycoddling ...

Some of the England players are exemplary professionals. Others, Rooney among them, need taking down a peg or two, and Eriksson is either not inclined to do it or is ill-equipped for the task, leaving it to McClaren to try.

Lovejoy's polemic was accompanied by a 'crime sheet' listing most of Rooney's misdemeanours on the pitch:

Dec 2002: sent off for the first time in his professional career with Everton against Birmingham.

Nov 2004: substituted at half-time during England's 1–0 defeat in Madrid to prevent him being sent off.

Dec 2004: caught on camera shoving Bolton defender Tal Ben Haim in the face in Old Trafford clash. Charged with violent conduct by the FA and banned for three matches.

Feb 2005: lucky not to be sent off after aiming a barrage of foul-mouthed abuse at referee Graham Poll in televised match between Manchester United and Arsenal at Highbury.

Mar 2005: booked after another tirade, this time aimed at referee Mark Clattenburg during Manchester United's goalless draw with Crystal Palace.

May 2005: English Schools FA drop him as a guest at a schools football match because 'he is not a good role model'.

Aug 2005: ahead of England's humiliating 4–1 defeat at the hands of Denmark, Rooney vows to keep his volatile temper in check. 'I have matured a lot, both on and off the field,' he says.

Sept 2005: clearly seen telling David Beckham and later Rio Ferdinand to '**** off' as it all goes pear-shaped in Belfast.

Unsurprisingly, given that the team ethic is the bedrock of success in football and many other sports, Rooney's team-mates rushed to his support. Rio Ferdinand, one of the England players who had got the rough edge of Rooney's tongue in Belfast, said, 'It's a cliché, but if you take that edge away from Wayne he would not be the same player. I'd rather have the Wayne Rooney we have now than any other player. He will learn from the positive and negative things that happen to him and this is one of those. In the long run it can become a very positive thing for him and United. All young players when they are growing up are going to have difficult situations in their career, and this is one of those situations with Wayne.' Alan Smith, also Rooney's team-mate at United and with England, added, 'That is how he plays – he plays on the edge. Sometimes he is going to step over the line and, unfortunately for us, he did that here. When you are a world-class player, there comes a lot of attention and focus. Up until now he has conducted himself in the right way. I think for a young man who could possibly be one of the best players in the world, we have simply got to put an arm around his shoulder and help him through the difficult times.'

Old pros, too, were sympathetic. Gary Lineker, the former Leicester, Everton, Barcelona and England striker, who now presents BBC TV's flagship football programme *Match of the Day*, wrote this in his *Sunday Telegraph* column:

> The behaviour that saw Wayne Rooney sent off in Manchester United's game at Villareal in midweek was totally unacceptable, so I am not going to attempt to condone it. But I would just like to put in a plea for us not to destroy him for another attack of the red mist.
>
> We have a tendency in this country to accentuate the negative, and I would just ask that we give Wayne some slack; to lay off him a little bit. I was blessed to be born without a temper, whereas Rooney clearly has a lot of anger and cannot help expressing it. We should not forget, however, that as a football player, his talent is way above his age and it is a shame that his behaviour is not.
>
> He is, though, a product of his generation, and we live in a world where teenage kids seem to go out and get drunk all the time and cause problems for everyone. Rooney grew up in a tough environment, but thanks to the disciplines of football, he behaves in a much more responsible manner than almost any other normal lad of 19 with his background.

Alan Smith, Lineker's former attacking partner at Leicester and with England, also tried to be understanding. But Smith, another ex-footballer who now earns his living in the media, also offered a vivid insight into one of the key changes in English football between the eras of Duncan Edwards and Wayne Rooney. Writing in his *Daily*

Telegraph column, Smith said this of Rooney's two egregious examples of misbehaviour:

> First the outburst in Belfast playing for England, now a red card for Manchester United in the Champions League. The teenager's tantrums seem to go on and on. Once again, following his dismissal against Villareal, the national debate resumes on England's best player.
>
> A reprehensible lout, way out of control, or an immensely talented youngster with a very short fuse? For what it's worth, I lean towards the latter, while admitting that there are problems that need to be addressed ... At the risk of sounding like an old bore, this kind of thing would never have happened in my day. In the years that preceded multi-millionaire footballers carrying a sense of immense power, cheeky miscreants would be put firmly in their place. A friendly hand on the throat would do it as a senior pro pinned the cocky upstart against the dressing-room wall. Failing that, a nice quiet word usually did the trick.
>
> Ferguson is one of the few managers in the game with the clout to exercise that method. Not in the physical sense, not at least these days, but by taking the player aside for a stern lecture; reminding him that such senseless indiscipline hurts both him and the team. Whether the penny will eventually drop, we must wait and see. Some players go through an entire career without growing up. Rooney could be one of them. The 'edge' that his team-mates talk about might never fade and we will just have to get used to the occasional lapse.
>
> Let's face it, the compensations aren't bad. For all the negative points, Rooney has been blessed with a rare ability to lift the mood of the people. It's only natural, in turn, that from time to time he needs lifting himself.

Patrick Collins, the *Mail on Sunday*'s award-winning columnist, was less forgiving.

The manager stood by the touchline, staring out at the pitch and trying to keep the contempt from his face. The player walked past on his way to the dressing room. He was seething with anger and self-pity, like a child ordered early to bed. Nothing was said, not a glance was exchanged. They behaved like total strangers.

It was a fleeting cameo, yet those images of Sir Alex Ferguson and Wayne Rooney in Spain the other evening told us a great deal about the current anarchic state of English football.

A week earlier, the Manchester United manager had put at hazard both his credibility and his self-respect by attempting to defend Rooney's conduct in England's game with Northern Ireland. You will recall that the young man had insulted a linesman, flung an elbow at an opponent, collected a yellow card and squared up to his own captain. 'I'd rather have a player who showed a bit of heart than one who didn't,' said Ferguson. 'Christ, do England want players who want to lose?' It was a foolish response, and one he must privately regret. After Rooney's latest pathetic outrage, he merely went through the defensive motions: 'He's just 19 years of age. He's a fiery competitor ... Wayne reacts to what he considers are injustices.'

It was feeble stuff and it served to demonstrate the ultimate impotence of the manager. Of course, we were told that Ferguson had dealt with the matter in private. There was talk of the so-called 'hairdryer' treatment, by which players have their shortcomings exposed in explosive detail and at perilously short range. Tosh and nonsense. The reality is that Rooney is far beyond Ferguson's control ...

The opinions of two former England managers fell somewhere between the extremes represented by Rio Ferdinand and Alan Smith on the one hand and Joe Lovejoy and Patrick Collins on the other. Sir Bobby Robson used his *Mail on Sunday* column to draw attention to what he saw, rather tenuously, as the likeness between another gifted *enfant terrible*, Paul Gascoigne, and Rooney in terms of their self-destructive behaviour on the pitch.

What Wayne must be aware of is that Gazza's self-destruction and occasional loss of control on the pitch did harm his football career, the thing that meant most to him. Wayne will turn 20 next month and the time where he will have the excuse of youth is running out. He is young and has a lot of learning to do. But playing careers are so short, you can't afford to waste time in taking those lessons on board ...

Gascoigne was only 24 when he lost control and injured his knee ligaments in that infamous tackle in the FA Cup Final and he was never quite the same player or person again ... That's why it made me wince to see Rooney lose control as he did against Villareal on Wednesday night. In the end, the only person he will hurt is himself and us fans who marvel in his talent ...

I'm sure David Beckham, Steven Gerrard, Sven Goran Eriksson and Sir Alex Ferguson are on at him the whole time to control his temper and over-exuberance. But in the end, it must come from the player himself. No amount of watching videos of his behaviour or strong guidance from Sir Alex and encouragement from his team-mates will do the trick on its own. Those things will help, but only Wayne's self-awareness and self-determination will end it all. If I'd have been sent off as a player, my father would have been waiting for me when I got home and branded me a disgrace. Being sent off was the worst shame a footballer could have. The game has changed, but the difference between right and wrong hasn't. Car drivers can't go down a one-way street just because their vehicles are more powerful. And no footballer, however rich or popular, can swear or mimic the referee because it is flouting their respect.

There is a suggestion that Wayne will lose half his ability if you restrict him to playing within the rules. That's a myth. In fact, he will become twice the player once he's learned discipline and control. It is possible to be aggressive on the pitch while retaining respect for your opponent and the match officials ...

Graham Taylor, too, was struck by the likeness between Gascoigne and Rooney. In his *Daily Telegraph* column, Taylor commented:

In 2002 Gascoigne's career was over while Rooney's was just starting, yet the similarities between the two are so blindingly obvious: a massive natural talent, expectancy from supporters and the media that neither player could or can maintain, and backgrounds that could, without any disrespect, be termed as off the street ...

A prodigious talent such as Rooney's is crucial to the welfare of any team. You need him onside with you. Alongside his talent comes a short fuse as regards temper and foul language. I do not want to join the long list of hypocrites who denigrate Rooney for losing his rag and using foul and abusive language without having any knowledge of his background or the lad himself.

I would want to get to know why he behaves as he does and what triggers it all off and whether he wants to change this aspect of his character, bearing in mind that, if he doesn't, it could become a telling factor if or when his career starts spiralling out of control ... Of course, every effort has to be made to improve his volatile reactions on the field, but I am sure that with the proper home and club environment allied to good personal management this will occur naturally.

Why should we expect 19-year-old footballers to be role models without firstly helping them to understand and appreciate the standing they hold in society? Some of the criticism levelled at Rooney is the result of envy and a class system that still exists in our country, people who find it impossible to either accept or understand that a lad from the blue half of

Liverpool can be much wealthier than them just by being an outstanding footballer.

Some of the points made by Taylor were echoed independently by former Busby Babe Wilf McGuinness, who when his playing days were over continued at Old Trafford as coach, then manager. However, McGuinness preferred to draw a parallel between Rooney and George Best in terms of behaviour and talent. 'George liked to play with a smile,' he told me, 'but even he would snap now and again. He'd do things that people would say were stupid. You know, he'd kick mud at someone or knock the ball out of his hand. We had all this. George got suspended for knocking the ball out of [referee] Jack Taylor's hand in the semi-final of the League Cup, as it was then. He got something like an eight-week ban, I think it was.

'It happened in our day, but perhaps the media coverage wasn't anywhere near as good. In a man thing, swearing happens; cursing and turning on refs used to happen then as it does now. Sometimes, they [the refs] just ignored it and got on with the game. We used to say to each other, "What a great ref, hey? He told me to piss off!", or something. But the microscope of the media is on these people now.

'The thing is, there's this competitive streak in footballers and sometimes it goes over the top – that's why we have referees. You're put in a position by your talent, and the media, who love this type of thing, try to make you the man they want you to be, and you can't necessarily be, overnight. If you're handled right and guided in the right way, most of the time you behave; but there's always going to be that streak – not a wild streak, but a competitive streak – in you because that's what helps you to be a better player.

'You want to play within the laws of the game, but sometimes you overstep the mark. We've not got to ignore or excuse that kind of thing, but we have got to try and understand it and not rip people apart in the media. Don't let the offenders get away with it, but do try to show a bit of understanding for people who are still growing up. God, footballers! We're still a bit immature in our thirties. It's only when we get to 50-odd or 60 that we mature!'

Differences of temperament also come into the argument, insisted McGuinness. As we have heard already from Gary Lineker, who managed to go through the whole of his career without being booked or sent off, some players are better able constitutionally than others to control their feelings. 'Duncan was lucky,' recalled Edwards' former team-mate. 'He had a temperament so calm that it was quite untrue in somebody so talented and strong. It was very rare that I saw him lose his temper; in fact, I can only remember two occasions when it happened.

'One was in a game against Real Madrid at Old Trafford, when he tried to lift or drive one of their players off the field because he was just time-wasting and not really injured. The other time was when Aston Villa's Peter McParland flattened Ray Wood in the [1957] FA Cup final and broke his jaw. Duncan didn't know then that Ray's jaw was broken, but he looked as though he was going to go up to McParland and do or say something. He took two steps towards him, then just steadied down. You can see that in the televised recording of the match. You think, "Oh, no. What's Dunc going to do?" It was a surprise. But then he turns and looks at Ray.'

Interestingly enough, McGuinness revealed, Matt Busby actively discouraged swearing. 'It was a lot different in those days,' he said. 'Matt would most probably allow the odd player to say something without thinking, like coming out with a swear word. But if it continued, he would say, "Excuse me, we've had enough of that. I don't want to hear that again."

'In our day, of course, it wasn't the done thing to swear. You'd never hear it on the radio or television. You heard it with a group of lads, just the lads together. Maybe one or two would express themselves more fully, but the language wasn't like it is now. Today, it's part of everyday life, part of television, part of everything.

'What about that bloody [former United player] Harry McShane's son, the [Ian] McShane in that bloody western on television – what do you call it? *Deadwood*, I think. I don't watch it often because the bad language in that is just unbelievable. But that's what they want in it, and that's what they get. Because it's so easily used, unfortunately they [players, I think he meant] use it in the wrong place sometimes.

'Referees have said they are not going to have people swearing at them, and you can understand that. But that sort of language on the field is not uncommon, is it? In fact, it's very common. You swear because you are hurt, you swear because something's gone wrong, you swear at a team-mate – and that's before you get to the opposition! It's not meant for everybody to hear, but it's done. You do things on the field that you don't want people to see, and you do them because it's just an instinct. But the more cameras there are there, the less players will do it, I think. Or, at least, they won't get away with it.

'Wayne Rooney has got what it takes to become one of United's all-time greats. He's just got to mature in his playing more than mature in his character. I mean, he'll sort that out, I'm sure. I can understand the things he does, but other people can't and they've branded him with a title. I think that can all be sorted out when he realises that everybody's expecting him to be better behaved. I hope so, because a lot of us would like to see Rooney playing as often as possible for England as well as United.'

Sir Bobby Charlton certainly would. And he believes the youngster will learn the hard way how to behave. 'He'll learn, he'll learn,' insisted Sir Bobby. 'I think he'll realise that he hates not being on the field, not playing. I always remember Jimmy Murphy saying to me, "If you fall foul of the referee, for whatever reason, and you get sent off, the only person you're doing is yourself. You really want to play football, right? Then you've got to use your brains; you've got to count to ten. As a forward, your job is to avoid players. As a defender, it's the opposite. So, if somebody hits you, forget it, get on with it, turn the other cheek." Wayne Rooney will learn that. He will learn it because he loves playing. In fact, it's because he loves it so much that he keeps falling foul of other players and the referee. He feels he's been done, been stopped doing what he wanted to do. When you are as good as he is and you know exactly what you want to do with the ball, then somebody clips your heel, your blood boils. Initially, you think, "You ****!"

'And, because he's such a great player, he seems to be the guilty party all the time. Nobody has any sympathy for him because he's so good. I have to say I was really disappointed with Sven-Goran Eriksson when he took Rooney off [against Spain]. He blamed him for what was happening, which was outrageous. But Wayne wants to play for England, he wants to play on the big stage, he wants to be with the best. So you've got to look after him.

'I know he's our player, and maybe people will say I would protect him, I would stick up for him. Well, I would simply because you need good players in this game. People want to see the best players; they don't want to see them sitting in the stand. Wayne's just got something that you can't take away from him, and the referees should study the personalities of players as well as teams' patterns of play, which some of them do. That way they could find out whether they are really mean or really nasty.'

Rather more controversially, Charlton believes that Rooney, and other players, suffer these days as a result of the celebrity culture that seems to have affected some leading referees, too, since they became full-time professionals – another of the major changes the game has seen since the war. Clearly, too, he laments the passing of the time when players and referees could communicate forcefully with one another without offence being taken. 'In the old days,' he recalled, 'referees would swear at you. They would say, "Sod off!" or "F*** off!" if you challenged their decisions. And if one of them sent you off, he would say, "Get off, you kid, you big baby!" And you would go. But now, if there are high-profile players involved, you can just see them [referees], can't you, with their little struts as they tick them off. They want to be stars as well, some of them; but I don't know of one person who's paid to go to a football match to watch the referee, do you? There are rules, and people have to abide by them, but if I went to a football match and the best player in the world wasn't playing because the referee had a little bit of an ego, I'd be cheesed off.'

These issues aside, Charlton is convinced that Rooney's discipline on the field is improving. 'Well, he's not chasing other players any more,' he pointed out. 'To begin with, if somebody fouled him he'd be after them.' And it is true that Sir Bobby's theory about his learning the hard way how to behave seems to be taking hold to some extent. 'On the pitch,' Rooney told *FourFourTwo* magazine in November 2005, 'you don't want any silly bookings, like last season when I got suspended for pushing the Bolton lad [Tal Ben Haim] over. That was silly. I'm trying to cut that out, so if I do get booked it's for tackling and not dissent or something stupid like that. If you look at any match, every player's doing it. But it gets highlighted a lot more because of who I am.'

Rooney is smiling more than he used to, too. He even managed to share a joke with Liverpool's Sami Hyypia during Manchester United's 1–0 FA Cup defeat at Anfield in February 2006, a match as notable for its poisonous atmosphere as for ending Liverpool's 85-year wait for a victory over United in the competition. At the same time, however, Rooney was also accused of provoking the Liverpool supporters by kicking the ball at them and kissing the hated United badge on his shirt.

It is certainly not true, as he claimed in the *FourFourTwo* interview, that his number of bookings has gone down each season. In 2002/03, his first full season with Everton, he picked up eight yellow cards and one red. In 2003/04, the total in all competitions rose to twelve yellows. There was a drop in 2004/05, his first season at Manchester United: it went down to just ten yellows. But it was back up again in 2005/06, Rooney having collected twelve yellows and one red before breaking his foot near the end of the season.

Sadly, such figures hardly suggest he is learning the lesson that bad behaviour means missing matches. Before his sending-off in Manchester United's Champions League match at Villareal on 14 September 2005, he had been booked three times. After that dismissal, he picked up another nine yellow cards; and, even allowing for the greater amount of playing time following the sending-off than before it, the general trend was not encouraging. Indeed, former Premiership referee Jeff Winter warned of dire consequences for Rooney and England at the 2006 World Cup if he tried the patience of foreign referees with his naturally aggressive style of play and liking for dissent.

With an autobiography to sell, Winter issued his warning after England had clinched their place in the finals by beating both Austria and Poland in their final two qualifying fixtures. The Austrians proved more difficult to dispose of than expected, and England won only 1–0 at a packed Old Trafford thanks to Frank Lampard's penalty after 25 minutes. It was no thanks at all to captain David Beckham, who stupidly got himself sent off for two yellow cards and left his team to play for the last half-hour with only ten men. A far cry this from the heroic performance against Greece with which Beckham had dragged England into the finals of the previous World Cup practically single-handed. No example, either, to set the suspended Rooney.

What nobody has really addressed is the reason for the boy wonder's frequent outbursts of bad behaviour. It is not enough to say he's a tough kid from a tough neighbourhood, although his social background does come into it. The puzzling thing about Rooney is that, like some other famous professional footballers, he appears to have two quite separate and distinct personas: one for off the field and one for on it. His record of misbehaviour before graduating to the Everton first team, too, was nothing like as bad as it became afterwards.

Ray Hall, manager of the Everton academy, is certainly anxious to put the record straight so far as the upbringing he received from them is concerned. 'I've got to be careful here because I don't want to embarrass anybody,' he said, 'but when we took Wayne on tour, it did more to develop his social skills than it did his football. It isn't just the football development that academies cater for, it's development of the whole young man. Because of Wayne's behaviour subsequently, therefore, you could say that we didn't do a very good job. But I would question that because, while he was within our academy, he didn't sneeze without people knowing about it. And he was no problem at all on or off the pitch: he was an absolute model of good behaviour. In fact, he was shy and, in some ways, introverted. I remember taking him to Dallas in Texas, where he had to stay with a family, and they were quite concerned because they couldn't get him to talk. Yet, suddenly, the world and his dog expected Wayne, at seventeen, to be a role model for everybody.

'It certainly wasn't a case of a lack of discipline on our part, and never more so than when he was under Colin Harvey's charge. I remember seeing a game at Crewe when Wayne was fifteen, I think, but playing for the U-19s. I was watching the U-17s, but when I turned round to watch the other game, Colin had him running round the pitch while the game was going on! He'd done or said something Colin didn't like, and he didn't do it twice.

'I don't know what causes him to behave badly now; I'm not a psychologist. All I know is that I remember saying to his mum and dad on the weekend he scored *the* goal against Arsenal that his life had changed for ever. And, you know, I said it with a kind of concern because he can't leave his front door any more without somebody wanting a piece of his life. So where does he go for his own solace?

'I'm almost getting into areas I don't know a great deal about. But I've been in the industry of developing young people for a long time, because I was a teacher before I joined Everton, and Wayne Rooney would have been a star pupil at anything. It just happened to be football that motivated him most and kept him where he wanted to go. So anything related to football was fine. But I think the pressures financially, from the media, from everybody, mean he's walking on eggshells every time he goes out.'

These are valid opinions; and Hall may have got close to the heart of the matter in an earlier chapter when he pointed to the two years of personal development Rooney missed at the academy by forcing his way into the Everton first team so quickly. Colin Harvey, too, has an interesting take on the subject as a former professional footballer of high quality himself, a senior youth coach at Goodison and a former manager of the club. 'Off the field,' he said, 'Wayne is very quiet. Not introverted, but quiet. But he's one of those who, once he goes on the field, he knows how good he is. He's very competitive and, sometimes, if he's not playing particularly well, it gets to him. It's like a form of frustration.

'When he was a boy, I never had a problem with him. I always found him top class. I think that in all the time I dealt with him, there was only one occasion when I had to reprimand him for something he'd done on the field. It was just a case of holding a player back while he tried to win back a ball he'd lost. But it's not premeditated when he goes on the field that he's going to do something or get involved with the referee. I think it's a form of frustration that things are not going right for him or the team. It's not malicious, put it like that.

'I had him in the U-18s from when he was fourteen, so he played for two or three years with lads four or five years older than him because, physically, he could handle it. He's always been physically strong, and temperamentally there were very few problems with him. I think it was a little bit later on, when he first made his breakthrough to the first team, that he had one or two problems. But, then again, it was just frustration.

'He'll have to come to terms with that, though. There's always going to be moments in his career where he's going to overstep the mark, but I think they will get less and less as he gets older. I certainly hope so, because if there's a better player out there then we'd like to watch him every week, wouldn't we? I used to say to Wayne that he's one of the few young players I'd pay to go and watch. As a fan, you get excited when certain players get on the ball. You can put him alongside Ronaldinho and people like that. As soon as they get on the ball, you know something's going to happen.'

In passing, it is worth mentioning that Harvey so disapproves of players swearing at the referee he believes their punishment should be an automatic red card. 'I don't care who they are, what sort of game it's in or whatever level it's at, they should be sent off immediately,' he said. 'I'm sure the penny would soon drop then. If you are getting sent off and not playing games, your team-mates are not going to put up with it, are they? I'm not talking about Wayne in particular; I'm talking about anyone who swears. It should be just a matter of course that you learn to bite your tongue and go back ten yards. You know, if they really clamped down on it at every level, particularly the younger level, they'd kill it all in a couple of weeks.'

Quite clearly, then, no one can accuse Everton of having encouraged Rooney's liberal use of the expletive.

The *enfant terrible* was back for that last qualifier against Poland, again played in front of a 60,000-plus crowd at Old Trafford, where the FA had chosen to stage England's most important matches during the six years Wembley was being rebuilt. Rooney did not score in a game his team needed to win, but he contributed fully to the 2–1 victory secured by Owen's goal just before half-time and Lampard's late winner. As a result, England sneaked ahead of the Poles by a point at the top of Group Six and qualified automatically for the finals of a World Cup they were regarded as one of the favourites to win.

CHAPTER 10

THE WORLD AWAITS

WHEN, only six weeks before England's first game in the 2006 World Cup, Wayne Rooney broke his right foot for the second time in his short career, he plunged the nation into despair. 'We're in Rooins' wailed the *News of the World* the day after the Manchester United striker fractured the fourth metatarsal in his foot towards the end of his club's 3–0 defeat at Chelsea. 'Rooney out of World Cup ... and Owen's a Doubt Too' yelled the *Sunday Times*, encompassing the equally depressing news that England's only other world-class striker, Michael Owen, had suffered a setback in his lengthy attempt to recover from a broken foot.

The prospect of England trying to win the World Cup without Rooney was bad enough; the possible absence of Owen as well made it little short of bleak. The unfortunate events of that last Saturday in April underlined not only the importance of Rooney and Owen to the side, but the lack of outstanding back-up for them. The obvious candidates – Liverpool's Peter Crouch, Charlton's Darren Bent, Tottenham's Jermain Defoe, Crystal Palace's Andy Johnson and Everton's James Beattie – had enjoyed varying amounts of success at club level but had done nothing in international football to make the other World Cup finalists quake in their boots.

The situation appeared to worsen a few days later when a scan was said to have revealed a 'cluster' of fractures in Rooney's foot. Now, it seemed, there was absolutely no chance he would recover in time. Pointing out that the Manchester United striker was the ninth England player to be struck down by the curse of the fractured metatarsal in the space of four years, the newspapers gloomily informed us that the healing time of the others had varied from nine weeks to five and a half months. David Beckham had recovered the quickest, but he still lacked full match fitness at the finals of the 2002 World Cup.

Throughout all the doom and gloom, though, England manager Sven-Goran Eriksson remained defiantly upbeat. 'I will bring Rooney to Germany and the World Cup, no matter what,' he declared only the day after he had seen his outstanding player crocked. 'I will give him every chance to be playing for England, and I think he will do so. Even if the chances are small I have to give him the opportunity to be able to recover. We're talking about Wayne Rooney. He's one of the best players in the world. He is extremely important for us. If we think that he has a chance to get fit during the World Cup, of course we will pick him. Maybe he can be playing for us later on in the competition.' In other words, Wayne Rooney was considered so vital to England's hopes of winning the World Cup that Eriksson was quite prepared to take him to Germany even if it meant he could play only in the later stages of the tournament, perhaps only in the final itself. This, too, despite the painful personal experience of knowing a similar gamble on the fitness of England captain David Beckham had backfired badly in the quarter-finals of the previous World Cup, against Brazil.

Sure enough, when the England manager announced his squad of 23 on 8 May Rooney was in it, as was Owen. But the inclusion of the two invalids was overshadowed completely by another of Eriksson's choices. Alongside the names of Rooney, Owen and Peter Crouch was that of Theo Walcott, the seventeen-year-old Southampton striker in whom Arsenal had invested £12 million but who had yet to play in their first team. It was a selection completely out of left field, and one totally out of character for the cool, phlegmatic and (in football terms at least) habitually conservative Swede, who confessed he had never actually seen Walcott play a competitive match; he was going on the recommendation of Arsenal manager Arsène Wenger and what he had seen himself of the jet-heeled boy in training. Pressed for a more detailed explanation, the England manager said memorably, 'It's probably not logical to go for Walcott, but you do it by feelings.

I'm excited about him and can't wait to start working with him. I've thought a lot about it over the last couple of months. You might think I'm crazy; but if you talk to other football managers, I don't think they will think I'm crazy. Yes, it's a big surprise. Yes, it's a gamble. Yes, it's illogical. But sometimes when there is no logic it can work very well.' Most pundits, however, did think Eriksson was crazy to take Walcott – either crazy or just 'demob-happy'. Some even went so far as to suggest that England's first foreign manager was trying to get his own back on his adopted nation for the rough treatment he had received at the hands of the English media.

What prompted such outlandish thoughts was the fact that Eriksson's scheduled departure from the job – his £5 million-a-year contract stretched until 2008 – had been brought forward to the end of the 2006 World Cup by the so-called 'fake sheikh' scoop run by the *News of the World* in January 2006. The Sunday tabloid lured the England manager and his agent, Athole Still, to Dubai with the false promise of a lucrative coaching opportunity in the United Arab Emirates, then duped them further by having its celebrated investigations editor Mazher Mahmood don Arab robes once more. Mahmood, who had famously led Newcastle directors Freddy Shepherd and Douglas Hall down a similar primrose path in Spain some years earlier, allegedly coaxed all manner of indiscretions out of Eriksson over a seafood meal and champagne in one of Dubai's most luxurious hotels, and between numerous bottles of Dom Perignon on a 72-foot yacht in the marina. As the champers flowed and tongues loosened, the Swede reportedly tried to persuade his new Arab friend to buy Aston Villa and install him as manager on £5 million a year net, plus bonuses. It was said that he bragged he could 'tap up' David Beckham and get him to move from Real Madrid to Villa. According to the *News of the World*, Eriksson 'also poured scorn on some of Britain's best-known players. He even attacked some of England's team, describing one as lazy, criticising another's upbringing, and saying a third was not worth his transfer fee'. The three players in question were said to be, respectively, Rio Ferdinand, Wayne Rooney and Shaun Wright-Phillips, whom Chelsea had bought from Manchester

City for £24 million. Of Rooney, Eriksson is claimed to have replied 'It is his temper ... He's coming from a poor family, a very rough neighbourhood' when asked what the Manchester United player was like as a person. In addition, the England manager appeared to hint that Michael Owen had joined Newcastle from Real Madrid just for the money. More serious than all that gossip was Eriksson's alleged claim, reported the following Sunday by the *News of the World*, that corruption was rife in English football.

Although the Swede was determined to pursue a legal action against the paper for publishing his words in a 'distorted and shameful way', the Football Association had clearly had enough. Having stood by their man throughout all his perceived scandals – alleged dalliances with Manchester United and Chelsea, and sexual shenanigans with TV personality Ulrika Jonsson and FA secretary Faria Alam – and even having upped his salary after one of those stories, the ruling body decided it could stand the bad publicity no more. On 23 January, the day after the second instalment of the *News of the World* 'exposé', it was announced that, in return for a pay-off in the region of £2.5 million, Eriksson had agreed to stand down following the 2006 World Cup finals.

The agreement set in motion a chain of events that descended into farce as the FA went looking for a successor to the Swede. New chief executive Brian Barwick, eager to make sure the right man was appointed, put together a small committee to wrestle with the problem. Consciously or not, it was the complete opposite of the methodology used by Barwick's more autocratic predecessor, Adam Crozier. Obliged to find a replacement for Kevin Keegan in October 2000, Crozier and Arsenal vice-chairman and FA board member David Dein had been responsible virtually on their own for the appointment of Eriksson.

The FA's search for Eriksson's successor soon began to suffer from all the weaknesses of choice by committee. Their deliberations were leaked to the press on a regular basis, with the result that the message coming through loud and clear was they could not agree on any one candidate. That was hardly surprising, given the number of names in the frame. Guus Hiddink, the Dutchman who had taken South Korea to the semi-finals of the 2002 World Cup, was an early front-runner, as was Luiz Felipe Scolari, the Brazilian who had won that tournament with his native country before taking Portugal, at England's expense, to the runners-up spot in the European Championship two years later. In both the committee and the media, however, there was a strong element of support for the appointment of a British manager: a country of England's history and standing in the football world, it was argued, ought not to have a foreigner in charge. Therefore, the names of Bolton's Sam Allardyce, Charlton's Alan Curbishley and Manchester City's Stuart Pearce were thrown into the mix. So was that of the much-coveted Ulsterman Martin O'Neill, who had resigned as the successful manager of Celtic to look after his sick wife.

If the FA wanted some continuity – never a major consideration for them previously – the most obvious choice was Middlesbrough manager Steve McClaren, who had worked as Eriksson's right-hand man during the Swede's six-year tenure of office. But McClaren was tainted by association with England's questionable tactics and strangely passive attitude when losing to a ten-man Brazil in the quarter-finals of the 2002 World Cup, and to Portugal in the last eight of the 2004 European Championship. So he started the process as something of an outsider.

There followed more than three months of uncertainty during which all the major candidates were interviewed and the FA failed laughably to keep their activities a secret. At one point they resorted without success to ferrying people, believed to include 'Big Phil' Scolari, to and from a country house in blacked-out cars in order to escape the notice of the media. As the peerless Hugh McIlvanney put it in the *Sunday Times*, 'The FA's emphasis on strings of interviews was seriously disproportionate to the objective being pursued, more in keeping with a hiring agency's hunt for highly qualified secretaries.' The search's potential for embarrassment was realised fully when Barwick flew to Lisbon to meet Scolari towards the end of April. Although the FA's chief executive insisted subsequently that his trip was just part of the selection process and that he wanted only to discuss Scolari's 'potential involvement', it was pretty clear Barwick had gone to Portugal to offer 'Big Phil' the England job. Unfortunately for the FA's headhunters, Scolari withdrew abruptly from the negotiations a couple of days later. Confronted suddenly by a pack of slavering English newshounds, he cited fears about intrusion into his private life as one reason, and as another a reluctance to agree to anything before the World Cup had taken place.

So, with the start of the finals little more than a month away, the FA were back at square one in their ham-fisted quest for Eriksson's successor. Scolari's withdrawal would not have mattered so much had the FA not gone on record as saying they were eager to make an appointment before the finals began. Their reasoning was that the new man should be given as much time as possible to prepare for the European Championship qualifiers that followed the World Cup; but all they succeeded in doing was to make a rod for their own backs.

In the end, the problem was solved by giving the job to the rank outsider, Steve McClaren, at the beginning of May. Although the Middlesbrough manager was clearly not the FA selection committee's first choice and enjoyed little support among the England fans, it was a logical, if uninspiring, step. As Eriksson's trusted lieutenant, McClaren offered continuity in terms of both a relationship with the players and planning for the coming European Championship. 'It is not an issue for me,' he said defiantly of the negative reaction to his appointment. 'It's not a matter of first choice, second choice. I am the choice of the FA, and I sit here as the next England manager ... I am here to do a job and win football matches and make sure England over the next four years can win a major tournament. If I do that, I am sure my popularity will rise.'

One of the few interesting aspects of an underwhelming appointment was the trouble McClaren had taken to prepare for this pivotal moment in his career. Expensive dental work and three years of coaching in the art of relaxing in front of the television cameras were only part of it. Knowing there was a skeleton in his cupboard the red tops would salivate over, England's new manager-to-be consulted

Max Clifford, the PR expert who specialises in clearing up messes in the private lives of people in the public eye. At Clifford's behest, McClaren admitted to an extramarital affair he had had while separated from his wife, and the problem was nipped smartly in the bud.

The necessity for such elaborate precautions was a sign of the changed times, of course. Fifty years earlier, the last thing Walter Winterbottom, England's first manager, would have worried about was how he looked on television or whether there was something in his private life the newspapers might use to embarrass him or call into question his suitability to do the job. But that was in a much simpler and more innocent age, an age when footballers and managers were not so far removed financially and socially from ordinary folk that they became fair game for the scandal sheets.

Any fears Wayne Rooney might have had about becoming public property must have been confirmed by a *Daily Mail* exclusive that revealed, just a couple of months before the World Cup finals, the staggering extent of his betting habit. According to the newspaper, he had run up debts of £700,000 gambling on horseracing, greyhounds and football matches with Goldchip Ltd, a private bookmakers set up by Steve Smith, a business associate of Michael Owen, to accommodate the wealthy England players who liked a flutter. According to the *Mail*, the problem had caused a rift between Rooney and Owen, although that was denied by the FA after they contacted representatives of the two players. A few days later, Rooney was said to have settled his 'outstanding issues' with Goldchip following stern warnings from his management company, Proactive, and Manchester United manager Sir Alex Ferguson.

Neither the earlier brothel creeping nor the reckless gambling affected the thrilling young player's popularity with the general public. No doubt he was doing what a lot of England fans would have liked to do themselves. As for the kids, they just loved him for what he could do with a football. Not long before Christmas 2005, Wayne Rooney was voted the world's second most famous person after God, no less, in a survey of 2,500 British under-tens by the promotional group Luton First. Jesus came third, with David Beckham, once the undisputed icon of English football, trailing some way back in fourth place. Understandably, Rooney was held in high esteem by his peers, too. Four months after giving God a run for his money in the fame game, the Manchester United and England striker was voted Young Player of the Year by his fellow professionals for the second consecutive season. Rooney was also on the PFA shortlist for Player of the Year, an honour that went to fellow Scouser and Liverpool captain Steven Gerrard.

Coleen McLoughlin, too, was flourishing alongside her high-profile fiancé. Derided a short time earlier as a fashion disaster and criticised implicitly for doing little but spend Wayne's money on expensive shopping trips, she suddenly emerged as a beautiful, smartly dressed young woman courted by the women's magazines. Fashion shoots for *Vogue*, *Hello!* and *You* magazines confirmed the startling transformation from not-so-ugly duckling into better-than-your-average swan. A fitness DVD, a television documentary and a fashion contract with Asda were not long in accompanying those notable successes as Coleen, at nineteen, began to prove she was quite capable of earning a good living herself, thank you very much.

Not that any of this mattered much to the millions of England supporters caught up in the 'will he, won't he?' saga of Wayne's bid to recover from his broken foot in time to play some part in the 2006 World Cup finals. It developed into one of the most extraordinary episodes in the history of the England football team, with Manchester United manager Sir Alex Ferguson and Eriksson fighting like cat and dog over the striker and his availability for the finals.

Early in the argument, it seemed that Ferguson, convinced his prize asset had no chance of recovering in time to play for his country, was determined to keep him at home at all costs for the treatment the player needed to be fit for the start of the 2006/07 domestic season. On 1 May, seven days before the England manager was due to announce his World Cup squad, Ferguson dismissed as 'folly' Eriksson's determination to take Rooney to Germany in the belief that he could be fit for the quarter-finals of the tournament. 'We have to make sure we don't build up people's expectations too much, which is what is happening at the moment,' he said. 'Sven-Goran Eriksson saying that he will take Wayne to Germany fit or not was something we didn't want to hear. This club will do absolutely everything to get the boy there; but if he is not fit he is not going to go. Sven is going on saying he will take the lad and then in six weeks' time he will have another two weeks to get fit enough to play in the quarter-finals. That is a wild dream.' Eriksson's surprisingly defiant response was to say he was prepared to take Rooney to Germany even if he was fit enough only for the final of the World Cup itself. To which Ferguson retorted, 'I don't want any complications with Wayne's broken foot, especially with a bandwagon gathering pace to get him to the World Cup, come hell or high water. Let's get it straight: for the sake of the boy and for England, United will do everything to get him fit in time. But I am not going along with this half-baked idea of him going to Germany 80 per cent fit and then finding him being pressured into playing before he is ready. That was the experience of David Beckham in the last World Cup and it was a disaster because he wasn't right. Wayne is young and, in the environment of a World Cup, it would be easy to persuade him to play despite not being fully fit.'

Undeterred by Ferguson's disapproval, Eriksson promptly named the player in his squad of 23 for the finals. Conscious of the risk he was taking over Rooney, the England manager included two strikers, Jermain Defoe and Andy Johnson, in his stand-by list of five. But even that choice was tinged with controversy: few could understand why he preferred Johnson, who had had a moderate season with Crystal Palace in the Championship, to Charlton's Darren Bent, the leading English scorer in the Premiership.

Defoe and Johnson were also insurance against any further problems with the recovery of Michael Owen from his broken foot. The Newcastle striker had complained of a 'dull ache' after completing the last half-hour of a Premiership game at Birmingham on 29 April, his first senior outing since sustaining the injury at the turn of the year. And even if Owen could overcome the problem, there were understandable worries about whether there would be time for him to regain match fitness and his old sharpness in front of goal in the six weeks before the start of the World Cup finals. But Sven, in his new, carefree mood, airily dismissed these concerns as of no consequence.

The England manager's seemingly blind optimism about his two first-choice strikers began to look less odd when news began to filter through about the remarkable speed of Rooney's recovery. First, not much more than a week after the injury, there were pictures of the player going about his business without the special surgical boot in which his foot had been encased initially. Then, a few days later, the boy wonder was shown merrily cycling around Manchester United's Carrington training ground, a broad smile on his face.

While Eriksson and United continued to exchange broadsides over which of them would decide whether Rooney was fit to play in the World Cup finals, the player's recovery continued to gather pace. Then, on 24 May, came a shock. Mike Stone, the popular and highly respected United doctor overseeing their star striker's rehabilitation, was sacked abruptly by the club. The official reason given by United was 'a difference of opinion on a non-footballing and non-clinical issue', but those of a suspicious nature could not help wondering whether Stone's dismissal was related directly to the sudden flood of good news about Rooney's recovery. It was speculated that Stone, who had been liaising closely with the England team doctor, Leif Sward, had been passing on too many optimistic updates about Rooney's progress for United's liking. A few days earlier, certainly, Sward had been quoted as saying that 'everything is pointing to Wayne making a perfect recovery'. It was a claim backed up by the slightly worrying news that the youngster had been dancing uninhibitedly at the £500,000 celebrity charity bash the Beckhams threw as a World Cup send-off for the England squad. Rooney himself was said to be furious over the dismissal of a doctor he trusted and regarded as a friend. For his part, Stone assured everyone that the recovery process, which was to be taken over by his assistant, Tony Gill, remained in good hands.

The disagreement between United and England over Rooney reached another flashpoint the next day. A scan on the player's foot suggested he was at least two weeks away from even kicking a ball in training, which hardened United's belief that he had no chance of playing in the three opening group games of the World Cup, the first of which now lay only sixteen days ahead. But Eriksson, of course, had said that he was prepared to take Rooney to the World Cup even if he could play in only the later stages. So he was not unduly perturbed by the latest news.

In the end, it was decided the striker would travel to Germany with the England party on 5 June and return to Manchester on the 14th for another scan to determine whether he was fit enough to return to full training. That arrangement was hardly an admission of defeat by Sir Alex Ferguson, who continued to strive hard to keep control of an argument he knew he could not win if FIFA took Eriksson's side. 'Obviously, we're making progress,' said the United manager. 'The fracture is not completely healed, but it's going exactly to the timetable we said at the beginning – six weeks. We've been right all along, and we say this because there's been so much wild exaggeration. We've kept an even keel because there is an inclination to be too optimistic . . . I'm praying he'll be fit for the World Cup. I said all along we'd get him there and we would do our very best.

'We have had to deal with a lot of nonsense damaging to the club. There seems to be a perception we don't want him to go. If you think about it, the one player we want to go is Wayne Rooney. Getting the experience of going to a World Cup will benefit the player and ourselves. But obviously there has to be a complete recovery because it's not an easy injury. Hopefully, the fracture will heal by 14 June completely. If not, then it's impossible. We mustn't rush him back.'

A 14 June scan was of little or no use to England, however. Since 9 June was the cut-off date for calling up replacements, Eriksson needed to know before then whether Rooney was fit enough to play in the World Cup. So, again flexing the administrative muscles nobody dreamt he had, the England manager demanded the scan be brought forward a week to 7 June. It took place at the Whalley Range Hospital, where Wayne arrived with Leif Sward, FA executive director David Davies, FA media officer Mark Whittle and a security guard following a flight on a private plane from Karlsruhe airport. They were met at Manchester airport by Paul Stretford, Rooney's agent, and Manchester United's medical team of doctor Tony Gill and physiotherapist Rob Swire, all of whom also accompanied the player to the hospital. Sward and Gill examined the results of the scan independently, before events made any announcement of their findings unnecessary. Shortly before eight o'clock that evening, Rooney walked out of the hospital, was whisked to the airport and then flown back to Germany. 'The big man's back in town!' he was alleged to have said (but denied later), as he was reunited with FA officials at England's luxurious Black Forest base, the Buhlerhohe Schlosshotel.

By this time, England had played three warm-up games against undemanding opposition on their way to the finals. They lost a B international against Belarus 2–1 at Reading's Madejski Stadium on 25 May; beat Hungary 3–1 at Old Trafford five days later; then rounded off their preparations by thumping Jamaica 6–0 at the same venue just a couple of days before flying out to Germany. What emerged from those games was a mixture of the good and the bad. On the credit side, Tottenham's Aaron Lennon proved against Belarus that he had the pace and trickery to trouble international defenders down the right. By scoring a hat-trick against Jamaica, Peter Crouch, too, suggested he had what it takes to be an international footballer. Not only that, but his now famous robotic goal celebration turned him into a cult figure with the England fans at the ground where previously he had been jeered by them. In addition to Lennon's pyrotechnics, the Belarus friendly was notable for the senior England debut of Theo Walcott, who thus succeeded in playing for his country before having made a first-team appearance for his new club. He came on for Owen after 62 minutes, but the young striker could not claim to have supplanted Wayne Rooney as England's youngest ever player until he was used as a 65th-minute substitute for Steven Gerrard in the full international against Hungary. At that moment, Walcott was seventeen years and 75 days old, or 36 days younger than Rooney had been when he made his debut against Australia in 2003.

Walcott replaced Gerrard because the Liverpool captain had been tried as a partner for Owen in what was clearly an attempt to find a like-for-like alternative to Rooney while the boy wonder was regaining full fitness. But although Gerrard scored the first of England's three goals, the experiment was hardly an unqualified success. As Liverpool had found when using their skipper as a second striker, this attacking midfielder is not comfortable playing with his back to goal. He tended to drop deep and leave Owen, still out of touch after his long lay-off, isolated. Nor, in Eriksson's opinion, did Jamie Carragher cover himself in glory. Despite having given the back four plenty of protection as an experimental midfield anchorman, the versatile Liverpool defender was switched to right-back in the second half as a replacement for the injured Gary Neville, the then unpopular Owen Hargreaves taking over from Carragher to a chorus of boos from the crowd.

For the first time, too, doubts were beginning to grow about David Beckham's overall contribution to the team. The England captain had been one of the few veteran *galacticos* not dragged down by Real Madrid's collective deterioration, but his natural lack of pace was becoming more of a handicap as the ageing process took him past 30. While Beckham now offered little or no penetration down the right, however, his mastery of the cross and the dead ball, not to mention his celebrity status, made it difficult for Eriksson to drop him. Against Hungary, for example, England's first two goals were scored from the skipper's pinpoint centres.

With the 6–0 victory over Jamaica fresh in their minds and an *en fête* nation seemingly convinced that winning the World Cup was just a formality, the England squad flew out confidently to Germany. Their spirits rose even higher when, shortly before his make-or-break scan on 7 June, Rooney was seen to be kicking a ball freely in training with that problematic right foot. Then, of course, came the boost of the boy wonder's clean bill of health. Rooney's progress impressed Eriksson so much that, to Manchester United's reported fury, he began talking about playing him in one of the three group games – a risk United believed the England manager had agreed not to take. Once again, though, the mouse roared. 'The good news,' said Eriksson, 'is Wayne Rooney has no more injury. He is injury-free. Now it's up to us to get him match-fit. I'm prepared to listen to everyone and discuss with them about Rooney, but the last say in this story is Rooney's and mine. I am doing this in the best interests of Rooney, the England team and 40 million England fans.' In other words, Sir Alex Ferguson and Manchester United could mind their own business.

Rooney was not match-fit enough to play against Paraguay on 10 June in Frankfurt, of course. Even so, he was stripped and sitting on the substitutes' bench as England stumbled to a 1–0 win secured by a Paraguayan own-goal early in the match. Only two minutes and 45 seconds had gone when the South Americans' captain, Carlos Gamarra, inadvertently glanced one of Beckham's wickedly struck free-kicks into his own net with his head. But there were few other attempts on goal as England's explosive start petered out in the 30-degree heat of the Waldstadion. So much of a struggle did it become for them in the second half that the frustrated England fans chanted 'Roo-ney, Roo-ney' and Eriksson had to bring Hargreaves' defensive qualities into midfield to prevent Paraguay equalising. Owen, who partnered Crouch up front in Eriksson's favoured 4–4–2 formation, did not finish the game. Again looking a long way short of full match fitness, England's most prolific striker was replaced by Joe Cole in a positional switch after Stewart Downing had come on for Owen in the 55th minute. Eriksson said he had made the change because the team were not holding the ball sufficiently in attack – one of several criticisms the manager made of England's performance. 'We have to play 90 minutes the way we did the first 35 if we want to win the World Cup, which is the target,' he said. 'We have to play better foot-ball, and we will.'

No doubt Eriksson's confidence was based on his calculation that Rooney was much closer to playing than most people imagined. To remove all doubt that the player's broken foot was now fully healed, the England manager again acted with surprising assert-iveness. Angus Wallace and Chris Moran, the two professors from the Queen's Medical Centre in Nottingham who assessed Rooney's

7 June scan, had said originally he would not be fit until after the group stage. They had been persuaded by England's medical staff to change their minds and look at him again before the final group game against Sweden on 20 June; but now Eriksson insisted Wallace and Moran fly out to Germany on 14 June, the eve of the second match, against Trinidad and Tobago in Nuremberg, to conduct their examination. Their conclusions were positive – although Eriksson was in the mood to defy them anyway – and Rooney duly made his return to the England team as a substitute for the labouring Owen after 57 minutes of the 2–0 victory over the game West Indians. Astonishingly, it was only six weeks and five days after he had been written off as a non-starter for the World Cup, although subsequent information did suggest the injury had not been quite as serious as first thought.

But even the uplifting introduction of Rooney, who had been straining at the leash to get into the action, could not disguise another disappointing performance by England. Astutely organised by their wily old Dutch coach Leo Beenhakker, and led intelligently by the former Aston Villa and Manchester United striker Dwight Yorke, now operating as a midfield playmaker, Trinidad and Tobago so frustrated England that they were forced to fall back on their instinctive, archaic tactic of pumping long balls to a tall target man, in this case Peter Crouch. It did not work until the 83rd minute, when Crouch rose above Brent Sancho – partly with the help of the Gillingham centre-back's dreadlocks – and headed Beckham's high, floated centre under the bar. The opening had been made for the England captain by substitute Lennon, whose chested pass was but one example of the major difference his zesty contribution made to England's attacking play in the last 33 minutes. Then, in stoppage time, Steven Gerrard recaptured some of his Liverpool form to whip home a 25-yarder with his left foot and underline the strange and worrying inability of Frank Lampard, a proven goalscorer with Chelsea and England, to achieve anything remotely similar.

Those two late goals were nothing like enough to protect Eriksson's team from mounting criticism of their style of play. English footballers have always been regarded as being over-reliant on the long ball, and now the rest of the world saw them as just reverting to type. Even Gerrard agreed that England had no chance of winning the World Cup unless they improved on their performances in the first two group games. However, no matter how scruffy the victory over Trinidad and Tobago, a tiny nation making its first appearance at the finals, it was enough to guarantee England a place in the last sixteen. That was because they had maximum points from their first two games while Sweden, the other major force in Group B, had dropped two points in a goalless draw with the Trinidadians. So, all that remained to be decided in the final group game between England and Sweden in Cologne on 20 June was which of them would top the mini-table and face the runners-up in Group A, Ecuador, in the first knockout stage. To do that, the Swedes needed to win. England, on the other hand, could afford to draw.

What they could not afford to do was lose one of their main strikers in the first minute of the match. Just as he was trying to play a simple pass inside from the left touchline, Michael Owen's legs collapsed under him and he was stretchered off with what proved to be a ruptured anterior cruciate ligament in his right knee. That kind of damage not only put Owen out of the World Cup, it condemned him to at least six months on the sidelines at Newcastle, who were not best pleased at losing their £17 million striker for so long in this way and, understandably, made all sorts of threatening noises about compensation from the FA.

But England were not exactly ecstatic at this cruel turn of events either. It meant they were down to three strikers, one of them a novice whom Eriksson seemed strangely reluctant to use after making such a song and dance about taking him to Germany. The other two, Wayne Rooney and Peter Crouch, now found themselves in tandem, Rooney having started a World Cup game for the first time and Crouch having come on to replace Owen in a 4–4–2 formation. But Crouch's introduction was an undesirable change, in that he and Steven Gerrard had been left out initially to avoid their collecting a second yellow card, which would have prevented them from appearing in the next game. In the event, both Crouch and Gerrard played in the match without incurring further penalty.

Gerrard replaced Rooney after 69 minutes, a substitution which infuriated the recuperating young striker. Clearly believing he was fit enough to last the 90 minutes, Rooney stomped off the field, kicked a water bottle, punched the Perspex roof of the dugout, threw himself down on the substitutes' bench, tore off his boots, chucked them away and seemed to ignore Gary Neville's attempt to calm him down. Here, sadly, was another unedifying example of his volatility and immaturity. As he has admitted, frustration at not having been able to recapture his very best form was the reason. Although he played reasonably well, Rooney was completely overshadowed by the excellence of Joe Cole on the left flank – which, it is easy to forget, used to be England's problem position. The Chelsea player, who terrorised right full-back Niclas Alexandersson throughout the first half with his darting runs and elusive dribbles, scored one of the outstanding goals of the tournament to put England ahead after 34 minutes. Waiting for a headed clearance by Alexandersson to bounce, Cole trapped the ball on his chest before sending a dipping volley into the far corner of the Swedish net from 25 yards out.

England lost that lead early in the second half. Clearly fired up by coach Lars Lagerback at half-time, Sweden overwhelmed England for a time with the force, intensity and intelligence of their attacking play. Marcus Allback, one of several members of the side who had failed to make the grade in the Premiership, equalised in the 51st minute from an accurate near-post corner by Tobias Linderoth. Catching England napping, the former Aston Villa striker stole in front of Beckham and sent a glancing header flying into the far corner. From then on, there was panic in the England defence whenever Sweden were awarded a corner, a free-kick or even a throw-in near goal. Goalkeeper Paul Robinson, regarded before the tournament as the epitome of calm, was now a bundle of nerves who had lost all judgement of crosses. Centre-back John Terry, so commanding in the air for Chelsea, also seemed powerless to deal with this rigorous examination of what had been regarded as England's great strength

– their rearguard. Nor did matters improve when Rio Ferdinand, Terry's defensive partner, had to go off with a groin strain and was replaced by Sol Campbell, a player so lacking in confidence and form after a traumatic season at Arsenal that it was embarrassing watching him try to cope with international football.

Despite all of this, and further Swedish attacks in which they struck the woodwork twice and had a shot cleared off the line, England managed to regain the lead five minutes from the end. Gerrard made a clever run round the back of the Swedish defence and Cole found his head with a lovely chipped pass. A first victory over the Swedes for 38 years seemed assured until the England defence collapsed again in the last minute. The second equaliser was pure slapstick, Terry completely mistiming his jump as he attempted to head clear a long throw by former Tottenham Hotspur left-back Erik Edman. Startled by this failure on the part of somebody normally so reliable in such situations, Campbell froze as the ball bounced in the England goalmouth. While he and Robinson hesitated, the predatory Henrik Larsson saw his chance and got enough of a touch on the ball to steer it into the bottom corner.

The result did not matter – England needed only a draw to finish top of the group and meet Ecuador in the last sixteen instead of the rampant Germany on home soil – but even so, their poor passing, persistent use of the long ball, lack of inventiveness and, now, defensive fallibility promised little further progress. After each game, Eriksson and his players would admit they hadn't played well, then promise it would be better next time. The trouble is, it never was. Ecuador may have beaten Brazil and Argentina in qualifying, but that was largely because they play their home games at altitude in Quito. Down at sea level, they were a much less threatening proposition. A 3–0 defeat by Germany in Group A proved a better guide to their modest ability than their victories over Poland and Costa Rica. Yet England struggled once more to dispose of spirited but undistinguished opponents.

They did so only narrowly, thanks to one of the deadly free-kicks with which David Beckham made his name as a footballer, but which are becoming less common now. Striking the ball some 25 yards out after an hour's play, the England captain bent it expertly over Ecuador's defensive wall and just inside goalkeeper Cristian Mora's right-hand post. Not long afterwards, Beckham, who had been feeling unwell before the kick-off, went to the touchline and threw up. Dehydration in the stifling summer heat was thought to be the probable cause. The winner might have been just an equaliser, though, but for an astounding piece of defending by Ashley Cole. Only eleven minutes into the game, another mistimed header by John Terry left striker Carlos Tenorio with the England goal at his mercy. Somehow, Cole's speed enabled him to make up 20 or 30 yards in time to deflect Tenorio's delayed shot against the crossbar with an outstretched leg.

Terry's slip, it has to be said, was more typical of England's shoddy performance than Cole's miraculous intervention. Once again, much to Frank Lampard's unjustifiable annoyance, they were roundly criticised by press and television pundits alike for the sloppiness and stodginess of their play. But England were now heading for the quarter-finals and a chance for revenge against Portugal, the country who had knocked them out of the European Championship at the same stage two years earlier, and that, as far as most of their supporters were concerned, was all that mattered. Apologists for the team's constipated form of international football tried to draw parallels with the 1966 side's unconvincing progress into the last eight of that historic tournament. But it was all so much whistling in the dark.

Reduced now to Wayne Rooney, still only 80 per cent match-fit, and Peter Crouch because of Owen's unfortunate injury and his own continuing refusal to take a chance on the seventeen-year-old Walcott, Eriksson decided to persist with Rooney as a lone striker in the unfamiliar 4–1–4–1 formation that had not worked particularly well against Ecuador. The intention, so far as one could gather, was to play a holding midfielder to protect the back four and release Gerrard and Lampard forward in support of Rooney. It sounded a reasonable idea in theory. In practice, however, it was far from a resounding success. For a start, Rooney's particular gifts as a footballer are not suited to playing on his own up front: his formidable ability to run at defences and either shoot at goal or create openings for others is best used when he plays as a second striker and comes from deeper positions. Not only that, but he received poor support from Gerrard and Lampard, both of whom failed to live up to their considerable reputations on this occasion. Man of the match Owen Hargreaves strove heroically to take up the creative slack, but his passing lacked the accuracy and imagination of Michael Carrick, the player he had replaced as midfield anchorman in another of Eriksson's abrupt and unsettling changes of mind. With Joe Cole and Beckham providing little from the flanks, it was not until the nippy Lennon replaced the injured captain on the right after 51 minutes that England's play showed some real urgency and penetration.

Eleven minutes later, though, came the game's defining moment. Having wrestled for possession of the ball with Ricardo Carvalho and Petit, Rooney was sent off for allegedly stamping on the genitals of the prostrate Carvalho. Subsequently, he pushed his Manchester United team-mate Cristiano Ronaldo away angrily when he rushed over to the Argentine referee, Horacio Elizondo, in an apparent attempt to inflame the situation; but Elizondo confirmed afterwards that it was for the alleged stamp he had issued the red card.

In which case Rooney did not deserve to be sent off, in my opinion. Most pundits were quick to seize on the young striker's poor disciplinary record and excoriate him for yet another failure to keep his temper in a trying situation. And, in truth, it did look as though Jeff Winter's pre-tournament warning about Wayne's volatility and the low tolerance levels of World Cup referees had been vindicated. But if that was a stamp, what rugby union players get away with in a ruck amounts to attempted murder. As Martin Jol, Tottenham Hotspur's Dutch manager, said in the *Sunday Times*, Rooney may have trampled on Carvalho, but he did not do it on purpose. So sure was the England striker that it had been an accident, he refused to issue the public apology for his sending-off some demanded. The FA thought a spot of contrition might persuade FIFA to punish Rooney less harshly, but typically he was determined to come out fighting. 'I remember the incident clearly and have seen it several times since on

TV,' he said in a statement he made two days later. 'I am of the same opinion now as I was at the time, that what happened didn't warrant a red card. If anything I feel we should have had a free-kick for the fouls committed on me during the same incident.

'I want to say absolutely categorically I did not intentionally put my foot down on Ricardo Carvalho. He slid in from behind me and unfortunately ended up in a position where my foot was inevitably going to end up as I kept my balance. That's all there was to it. From what I've seen in the World Cup, most players would have gone to ground at the slightest contact, but my only thought then was to keep possession for England. When the referee produced the red card I was amazed, gobsmacked.'

It is a version of events with which I agree totally. I thought at the time England should have been awarded a free-kick for Carvalho's challenge, and that Rooney had trodden, not stamped, on the Chelsea and Portugal defender accidentally. I still think so after watching several replays of the incident. Just stop for a moment to consider this point: if Rooney had been guilty of deliberate stamping, would it not have been in his interests to issue a grovelling apology? That way, he might have softened the wrath of FIFA a little. But no, he chose to protest his innocence at the risk of a long suspension from international football. As it turned out, just a two-game ban and a fine of £2,400 suggested FIFA, too, thought he had been harshly treated.

Had Rooney been sent off for pushing Ronaldo, it would have been a different matter. Technically, the referee would have been correct to dismiss him for raising his hands to an opponent. Mind you, the flashy young Portuguese winger is such an irritant that it must be very difficult for opponents to keep their hands off him at times. Indeed, former Newcastle and England striker Alan Shearer predicted on BBC TV that Rooney would 'stick one on' Ronaldo when they reported for pre-season training with Manchester United, while the even more militant *Sun* claimed he intended to 'split him in two'. At the time of writing, however, both parties were trying to patch up their differences, with Ronaldo and Rooney insisting they were still good friends. The Portugal winger claimed Rooney had congratulated him after the match and wished him well in the World Cup, a claim backed up by Rooney. How much prompting there had been by Manchester United manager Sir Alex Ferguson, it was difficult to tell. Ferguson, of course, was anxious they should kiss and make up because the last thing he wanted was a major rift between the two young stars around whom he was building a team to challenge for the highest honours in the 2006/07 season. But Ronaldo's desire to leave United for Real Madrid, expressed more than once during the World Cup, had already put those plans at risk. Frankly, it looked as though the Portuguese player, seen winking conspiratorially at his bench as Rooney was sent off, had gone out of his way to make himself unpopular enough in English football to be unemployable there.

The repercussions of Rooney's dismissal were certainly damaging for England. Down to ten men in the draining conditions of German heatwave, they tried without success to win the game in the remaining 28 minutes. Peter Crouch, on for Joe Cole, came closest as he showed why he would have been a much better bet than Rooney as the lone striker. With Portugal, lacking the suspended Deco and Costinha, incapable of breaking down this depleted, heroic but toothless England, a game of poor quality drifted into extra-time and the dreaded penalties.

Four times before, England had gone out of major tournaments on spot-kicks, most recently against Portugal in the quarter-finals of the 2004 European Championship. So could they reverse the outcome this time? No chance. Although the teams were level after three penalties, Simão and Hargreaves having scored and Lampard, Gerrard, Viana and Petit all having missed, Portugal accelerated away when Postiga scored and Carragher's twice-taken kick was saved by Ricardo. Then – the cruellest cut of all – it was Ronaldo who stepped up to drive home the decisive fifth penalty, give Portugal an unassailable 3–1 lead and claim the glory of sending them into the semi-finals.

And so the World Cup England's 'golden generation' of players was strongly fancied to win ended in tears and recriminations well short of the target. Quite rightly, Eriksson was criticised severely for not making more of the talent at his disposal. He stubbornly refused to concede the point, but the expedition was flawed from the start because he chose to take only four strikers, two of them half-fit and one an untried kid.

As for Rooney, the tournament came just a little too soon to regain full match fitness and the sureness of touch that had promised to make him one of the stars of the competition: he was never really at his sharpest at any time before England went out. It was astonishing that he managed to appear in the finals at all, given that his foot had been broken just six weeks earlier, but it was not only a matter of fitness: Eriksson's bewildering changes of formation, tactics and players did Rooney no favours. Playing as a lone striker plainly did not suit the most gifted support striker England have had for a generation. Yet Eriksson forced him to play there twice, partly because, even at that late stage, the manager could not solve the Lampard-Gerrard-Beckham-plus-holding-player conundrum in midfield. So, uncomfortable in the position and frustrated by his inability to impose himself on matches in the way in which he longed to, Rooney built up the head of psychological steam that led ultimately to his dismissal against Portugal. Even so, I still don't think he stamped on Carvalho.

Eriksson and the FA were also taken to task for allowing the players' wives and girlfriends, otherwise known as the WAGS, to live in close proximity to the team hotel throughout. It was the first time the England squad had been allowed such familial freedom at a major tournament abroad, and it contrasted sharply with the arrangements at the 1962 World Cup in Chile, where the players were billeted in bungalows at a small mining settlement 2,500 feet up in the Andes. There was a golf course, a cinema, a bowling alley and tennis courts, but none of the sophisticated delights that expensive Baden-Baden's shops, cafés, nightclubs and persistent paparazzi could offer the occasionally unruly and ultimately distracting WAGS.

Above all, there was the sense of a great opportunity missed. This was supposed to be the finest collection of footballers England had possessed since 1970, yet they had failed miserably to entertain, never mind reach the final. Was that solely the fault of an overrated manager? Or was it just that the players themselves were overrated?

Perhaps the flooding of the Premiership with foreign footballers was responsible? Graham Taylor, the former England manager, went so far as to cite Scotland's steep decline as a national team as a warning to England about the consequences of allowing too many players from abroad into your domestic league. But that is a matter of opinion we shall discuss next.

CHAPTER 11

EXTRA TIME

JUST about the only features of English football that haven't changed in the past half-century are the shape of the ball, the size of the goals and the layout of the pitch. In most other respects, the game Wayne Rooney plays today is unrecognisable from the one Duncan Edwards was familiar with back in the fifties. For one thing, it is much faster, more athletic and more demanding physically, mentally and psychologically than it was then. This is not to say that Edwards would have been any less of a force in the modern game: such a strong, talented and dedicated athlete would have had little trouble adjusting to the greater physical and mental demands. The point is made simply to underline the ability of Rooney to stand out in such a taxing environment.

It is necessary also to reflect on the extent of the administrative plastic surgery that has altered the face of the game almost out of recognition during the 54 years since Edwards first signed for Manchester United as a fifteen-year-old school leaver. The many nips and tucks include the advent of regular floodlit football and the League Cup; the removal of the maximum wage and gradual destruction of the retain and transfer system; the introduction of substitutes, three-up and three-down promotion and relegation, and three points for a win instead of two; plus the replacement of goal average with goal difference. Then there is the once-forbidden pleasure of professional football on a Sunday, the growth of sponsorship, the arrival of play-off matches to decide promotion and relegation and, last but not least, the expansion of the European competitions open to English clubs.

All of these we now take for granted. Above all, though, we must elevate television, the formation of the Premier League and the

Bosman case as the major engines driving change in English football. Nothing, arguably, has shaped the modern game more than those three factors; and, of course, they are all relatively recent. Regular television coverage has been taking place since 1964; but it was not until the medium was compelled to pay serious money for the privilege less than twenty years ago that it began to play a significant part in its development.

Barely a day goes by now when there is not a match to watch on the box, be it from home or abroad. Sky, the major operator in this field, presently offer their subscribers 138 Premiership matches a season, plus Coca-Cola Championship fixtures, FA Cup and Carling Cup ties, international football, Champions League clashes and games from Spain's equivalent of the Premiership, La Liga – all of them live. It is absolute bliss for the football addict and an almost unimaginable advance on the recorded highlights of English First Division football with which BBC Television's *Match of the Day* began the whole process so modestly back in 1964.

The technology for covering games has also improved and multiplied significantly since then. It seems hard to credit now, but the most famous game in the history of English football, the final of the 1966 World Cup, was transmitted to the nation and the rest of the world by just eight cameras in black and white. Thirty-four years later, 66 were installed in and around Wembley to record the last England international at the famous old ground – also against Germany – in pin-sharp colour and enhanced sound. Today, up to 25 cameras are used routinely to cover a Premiership fixture.

Television, in fact, is the cement that holds the whole shimmering, top-heavy edifice in place. In the beginning, the Jeremiahs said it would be the ruination of the game, and maybe that will still turn out to be the case. But the argument that expanded coverage of the game would stop people going to watch matches live has been blown out of the water by the consistent growth of attendances in all divisions since the advent of the Premiership in 1992.

At the moment, the main cause for complaint is that television's freedom to cover matches on various days of the week plays havoc with kick-off times and, consequently, the plans and habits of fans. Sky challenge this perception of them as wreckers of the old routines for their own purposes by claiming they merely comply with the requests of the various football authorities. Were Duncan Edwards somehow brought back to life now, though, he would be bewildered to see Premiership matches beginning at lunchtime or 5.15 p.m. on a Saturday, never mind being played on a Sunday or a Monday.

Sacrificing the traditional three o'clock kick-off on a Saturday is part of the price English football has had to pay for its economic prosperity and, in many cases, survival. The fact is that the game could not get by now without the money television pumps into it, the Premiership in particular. Indeed, the transformation from Edwards' game into Rooney's game could be said to have started as late as 1988, when ITV, BBC and the new boys on the block, British Satellite Broadcasting, struck four- and five-year deals totalling £74 million that took in everything from live Football League games to the FA Cup final and England internationals. That was a massive jump in income for the game because, since the regular televising of football had begun in the sixties, English football had received less than £5 million a season from television. Now it was £17 million and rising.

What changed the situation was the arrival on the scene in 1987, thanks to the deregulation of the industry, of BSB. Previously, without any other rivals to worry about, BBC and ITV had operated a cosy cartel that kept the payments to football as low as possible. But the emergence of BSB, another commercial station, compelled ITV to dig deep for the exclusive right to screen live league matches. The process was completed in 1992, when Rupert Murdoch's Sky satellite station, which had swallowed up BSB and become known officially as BSkyB, agreed to pay £304 million for the exclusive rights to screen Premier League matches live over a five-year period. It was a staggering sum of money, and a typically bold and audacious move by Murdoch that not only turned round the fortunes of Sky but changed the face of English football at the stroke of a pen.

Sky, then said to be losing money at the rate of more than £1 million a day, desperately needed more subscribers, and Murdoch realised that the best way of getting them was to outbid everybody else for Premiership football. In a bitter battle for the contract, Sky, in what some regarded as an unholy alliance with the BBC, outbid ITV by more than £40 million. By 2001, Murdoch's station was flourishing to the extent that it could pay as much as £1.1 billion for a three-year deal and, suddenly, English football was really in the money. Correction: the Premier League was in the money.

Sky's investment in football now totals more than £3 billion. The English clubs who have benefited most from this head-spinning injection of high finance are those who are, or have been, members of the elite league which grew out of the old First Division after it had broken away from the Football League in 1992. Since the 22 First Division clubs had been complaining for years about being held back financially and administratively by the 70 other members of the Football League, the split was not entirely unexpected. But it both shattered a 92-club structure that had held good for 42 years and emphasised the growing divide between the haves and have-nots.

The new-found wealth of the twenty Premier League clubs (two members of the old First Division having been offloaded in 1995) had profound effects on English football. Rolling in television money, plus sponsorship and advertising income inflated by increased television exposure, they were able to offer players salaries as good as, and often better than, any they could find elsewhere in the world. As a result, there was an explosion in footballers' rates of pay and a dramatic increase in the number of foreign players attracted to the Premiership by the rich pickings to be had there.

In *Living to Play*, a fascinating study of the development of the footballer since the legalisation of professionalism in 1885, authors John Harding and Gordon Taylor show just how dramatically earnings increased post-1992 and the creation of the Premier League. Taking Tottenham Hotspur centre-halves as a case study, they reveal that Maurice Norman, a member of the team that did the century's first league–FA Cup double in 1960/61, was paid £1,040 per annum, or £20 a week (the same as Duncan Edwards in 1958). By the early seventies it had not gone up by much at all. Mike England, allegedly, was earning only about £1,560, or £30 a week. But there had been a substantial increase by the 1980s, Paul Miller's annual pay rising to £27,000, or £519 a week. That was dwarfed in the early nineties by Gary Mabbutt's £120,000 p.a. (£2,307 per week), but the best was yet to come for the likes of Ledley King and Michael Dawson. Thanks to Jean-Marc Bosman, as well as the cascade of television money, Premiership footballers' salaries took off like rockets.

Bosman, of course, was the Belgian player who won the profession the right to complete freedom of movement when he persuaded the European Court of Justice in 1995 that, out of contract with his club, RFC Liege, he should be able to join a new club without a transfer fee being paid. Theoretically at least, professional footballers now had the freedom, like an employee in any other walk of life, to change jobs whenever they wanted. The only difference was that a transfer fee had to be paid if the move were made during the player's period of contract. In practice, however, it wasn't quite that simple. As Arsenal's Ashley Cole discovered to his cost, the rules still did not allow players to listen to overtures from other clubs while still under contract to their existing employer. The main effects of the Bosman ruling were visible in the length of contracts and the size of wages. Knowing they could not expect a transfer fee for their better players if they moved on when out of contract, clubs tried to sign them for as long a period as possible and then kept renewing the contracts long before they were due to expire. In both cases, a lot of money had to be offered to persuade the players to put their signatures on the dotted line. Hence the explosion in footballers' wages.

In 2000, less than a decade after Mabbutt had been earning £120,000 a year at Tottenham, a survey carried out jointly by the *Independent* and the Professional Footballers' Association produced some eye-popping statistics. Basic pay for top players over twenty years of age had risen above £400,000 a year (nearly £8,000 a week), it claimed, and about 100 Premiership players were earning £1 million or more per annum. Even below the Premiership, according to the survey, there was serious money to be made. Senior players in the First Division (now the Championship) were said to be on an annual average of £128,000, and their counterparts in the Second (now League One) and Third (League Two) Divisions, £52,000 and £37,000 respectively. However, the survey's findings were challenged strongly by players from the lower divisions, who insisted they were getting nothing like the money quoted. That could well be the case, but there is no getting away from the fact that since 2000 salaries at the top end of the scale have almost gone off the radar. Nobody turns a hair now when it is announced a Premiership footballer is earning £100,000 a week, or £5.2 million a year, and more. In May 2006, Chelsea signed Michael Ballack, the Bayern Munich and Germany midfielder, on a contract said to be worth £130,000 a week, or £6.76 million a year.

The seemingly inexorable rise in footballers' pay was confirmed in April 2006 by the latest PFA survey. It revealed that the average Premiership player earned £676,000 a year, or £13,000 a week. This worked out as an increase of 65 per cent on the weekly wage of £7,800 they were getting in 2000. They were better off in the lower leagues, too. In the Championship, the average wage had gone up to £195,000 a year – a rise of 53 per cent. Even in League One (£67,850) and League Two (£49,600) the players were earning as much as middle management in business and industry.

The strange thing is that very few of the footballers of Duncan Edwards' poorly-paid generation seem to resent the riches that are poured into the bank accounts of their modern counterparts. In his second autobiographical book, *Return of the Clown Prince*, the late Len Shackleton admitted his wife thought today's top-of-the-range wages obscene. But he, one of the most outspoken advocates of better pay for professional footballers, hastened to add that it was not because he had been denied that kind of money. Writing in 2000, he said, 'I'm certainly not aggrieved about what the lads get today, because it's certainly the commercial outcome of a long-fought and now past struggle.' Similarly, Sir Bobby Charlton replied, 'No, not at all,' when asked whether he begrudged today's players the king's ransoms they were being paid. 'If you're in the football business, you've got to pay football prices; that's the way it is. Unless, that is, they get a bit ridiculous.

Then clubs have got to say, "Well, no, we can't do that."' And Charlton was echoed in *Living to Play* by Nigel Gibbs, the former Watford defender. Gibbs, who insisted his pay was 'nowhere near' the £409,000 average annual wage for the Premiership in 2000, was all in favour of players earning whatever they could. 'Good luck to them,' he said. 'If the clubs are willing to pay it, the player should try to get it. They only have short careers. The clubs can always say "no", anyway.'

In fact, the only slight note of dissent came from Wilf McGuinness. 'I always believe that if you're top at whatever you do, you deserve to be paid top money,' he said. 'But there's a lot of players who've been very fortunate in getting top wages. Nowadays, pretty average players are multi-millionaires. Now that agents have come in, they might have guided players in the right way, but they're taking a big chunk of money out of the game. I don't think we would have taken that much money out of the game in our day.

'It's all gone a little bit too mercenary. And when people are willing to pay that kind of money to try and get success, there's a price to be paid. The spectators pay it and the clubs, too, in the end, because it won't last for ever. In the past, it was difficult to make a really great living out of the game, but that's something we had to live with. I never look back, though, and say, "Oh, we were badly treated!" At the time, everything was great.'

Everything is also relative. The difference between the 1950s, when footballers did not earn enough to set them up for life, and now is illustrated vividly by Bobby Charlton's recollections of that early post-war period. 'Your future was certainly not settled in those days,' he said. 'If you were 30 or over and lucky enough to be still playing, what everybody ever thought about was what they were going to do when they were too old to carry on. The big issue was security for the future. When I first started, one of my cousins had a grocery shop and I thought he was unbelievably wealthy because of it. I remember saying to him, "I'm going to play football. What would your business cost to set up?" He said, "Oh, about £2,000," and I thought if I saved about £100 a year I should be able to do that, because I was convinced I was going to play for twenty years. It never entered my mind that I wouldn't. But the whole thing was, what were you going to do afterwards?

'There were no lists of back-up staff then like you get now: coaches, physiotherapists, masseurs, nutritionists and everything else. At that time, there was the trainer and his assistant, and that was it. They had to do the kit as well, you know, so it has changed a bit! Even then, I think, you could accumulate money through the PFA pension scheme if you paid a little bit into it, but it wasn't very much. Today, you're set fair for the rest of your life if you're good enough and you play in the Premiership for any length of time and have put some pension schemes away. Schemes like that weren't available until I was 29 [in 1966]. I was that age when my accountant came and said, "There's a bit of a breakthrough for you." When I asked him what he meant, he said, "You can now put some money from your wages into a pension scheme and you can claim it when you're 35, which is classed as the retiring age for a professional sportsman." So I had to start putting everything I had into the pension scheme and, at the end of it, it gave me something like £28 a week for the rest of my life. Twenty-eight pounds a week! Nowadays you see some of the lads are earning in one week what my whole pension scheme is worth. It's unbelievable!

'But I don't panic, I don't worry. It's not in my nature. I've managed financially and I've done it on my own. I've not done it with football particularly, but I'm quite satisfied. Security is a big thing. I'm lucky, maybe, because I come from a footballing family. My uncles were footballers, and they used to say, "You've got to look to the future because you're going to be playing for maybe less than half your life. It's not going to go on for ever."'

This, remember, is one of England's most famous footballers talking: a World Cup winner, a European Cup winner, England's record goalscorer, a player whose name is synonymous all over the world with the best the English game has to offer. Yet it was impossible for him to earn enough during his twenty-year career (1954–74) to settle into a comfortable retirement. He tried management, at Second Division Preston, but it didn't work out; and, in any case, clubs of that modest stature were certainly not paying then the sort of salaries that make millionaires of some of today's managers. Charlton had to find other ways of earning a decent living. His methods included using his savings, his name and his expertise to set up the now famous Bobby Charlton Soccer Schools, of which David Beckham is the most celebrated graduate. He owns a travel agency as well and has travelled the world himself representing sponsors at the finals of the World Cup and other major football events. He is also, of course, a director of his beloved Manchester United.

None of this should be used as an excuse to complain about the size of today's Premiership salaries; and, as we have seen, Sir Bobby certainly does not. Rather, it is an indictment of the criminally low rates of pay footballers received until television began to pump significant amounts of money into the game a few decades ago. If you accept that footballers are entertainers on a par with actors, opera singers and ballet dancers – and, all the obvious jokes aside, it is difficult to see how else they can be categorised – then they should be remunerated accordingly. Not only that, but the battle for salaries commensurate with the income generated by the players through the turnstiles, television and sponsorship has been so long and hard, it is difficult to begrudge today's generation their Ferraris and palatial homes.

Excesses there have been; excesses there always will be where there is an abundance of money. Killing or injuring themselves, and others, in fast cars; 'roasting' young women in expensive hotels; drinking far more than an athlete should; fighting with nightclub doormen; scandalising American tourists with drunken behaviour post-9/11; trying to coerce your club into increasing the size of an already gargantuan salary after they have stood by you following your failure to take a drugs test – all of these well-documented aberrations are genuine reasons for concluding that today's footballers are grossly overpaid, greedy for more and totally out of control. But let us keep a sense of proportion. We are talking here of the game's youthful lunatic fringe, some of whom have seen the error of their ways. The vast majority of the profession are upstanding members of society who will use their wealth to provide themselves and their families with financial security for life once their short careers as footballers are over.

The long march towards the financial and contractual freedom they now enjoy began during Duncan Edwards' era, the fifties. Until 1961, when the PFA succeeded in forcing the Football League clubs to abolish the maximum wage they had imposed for years as a mutually convenient way of keeping costs down, professional footballers could not earn more than £20 a week. But the union's vigorous campaign against this iniquitous wage cap finally succeeded in blowing it off three years after Duncan had died.

'It was £20 a week then,' recalled Bobby Charlton, 'and it used to go up in twos. Then, suddenly, from £20 the PFA asked for £24. The Football League said that was outrageous and that's what made the PFA threaten the strike action that changed the whole thing. When we got the maximum wage lifted, Matt Busby called everyone in at United and said, "I propose to give you what you're entitled to." And I thought to myself, "That's twice as much as I've been getting!"

But, with the notable exception of Johnny Haynes and his £100 a week at Fulham, the pay of very few players shot up appreciably once the maximum wage had been abolished. As John Harding and Gordon Taylor point out in *Living to Play*, the clubs operated private maximum schemes and, at first, the top rate was £30 a week. But George Cohen, the Fulham and England full-back, is quoted as saying his wages went up to about £45 in 1961 (no doubt this had something to do with the Haynes effect). Then, when Cohen made the England squad in 1963/64, his pay jumped to £80. This basic, apparently, was far more than Nobby Stiles, his England team-mate, was getting at Manchester United, although the bonuses were better at Old Trafford.

It was not just a question of wage restraint having to be cleared out of the way: professional footballers were chained to their clubs by the archaic, and seemingly immovable, retain and transfer system. Hence the accusatory description of players of the time as 'soccer slaves'. Sir Tom Finney was a notable sufferer in that respect. One of the finest and most versatile forwards England has ever had, in that he could play brilliantly on both wings and at centre-forward, Finney was made the offer of a lifetime in 1952 when he was 30 years old and twelve years into his long and distinguished career with Preston North End. While on tour in Italy with England, Sir Tom was astounded to hear Prince Roberto Lanza di Trabia, the millionaire president of the Sicilian club Palermo, promise him a signing-on fee of £7,000, wages of £130 a month, bonuses of between £30 and £100, a Mediterranean villa, a new, top-of-the-range car and free travel to Italy for his family. All of this for a footballer who, famously, had worked as a plumber for £5 a week just after the war and was earning only £9 more than that when Prince Roberto invited him to enter a dazzling new world of infinite promise.

But, as Finney had half-expected, the Preston directors woke him from his daydream when he returned home and told them of the offer. Even though Palermo were prepared to pay North End a £30,000 transfer fee, they flatly refused to sell their star player. They even went so far as to issue a pompous, patronising statement in which it was reported that the chairman had received an approach from 'T. Finney' regarding an offer from an Italian club for his services. 'Unanimously agreed,' the statement continued, 'that the player be informed that we could not accede to this request. This player has been retained with the FA and was expected to re-sign for season 1952/53 on his return from holiday.'

A modest and decent man, Finney chose not to challenge the board's decision, partly because he did not see any point in fighting the system and partly because, deep down, he did not really want to leave Preston, his home town, and the plumbing business he had there. No doubt he was keenly aware, too, of the failure two years earlier of seven British international footballers in their attempt to walk out on their clubs and join a new professional league being set up in Colombia, which was temporarily outside the jurisdiction of FIFA, the governing body of world football.

Aston Villa and Wales centre-forward Trevor Ford, Stoke and England centre-half Neil Franklin and Manchester City and Wales wing-half Roy Paul were among the British rebels who flew out in secret to Colombia to investigate the lucrative terms on offer. Most of them did not like what they saw and soon returned home. In fact, Charlie Mitten, the Manchester United winger, was the only escapee to stay for the complete season. On their return, the majority of those who had dared challenge the retain and transfer system were suspended by their clubs, then transferred. As John Harding and Gordon Taylor said of the failed escape attempt, 'The story has been recounted many times but, from any angle, it was a pathetic event. Professional men scurrying to and fro across the world like boarding-school boys breaking out of the dorm for a midnight feast and having to face the headmaster the following morning. In the event, they all took their "six-of-the-best" and shook the hand of the prefect administering the blows.'

The repercussions of the abortive Bogotá affair were less fresh in the mind when, thirteen years later, the Players' Union finally found a footballer who was willing to go all the way and challenge the retain and transfer system in court. The honour, if that is the right word, fell to George Eastham, a gifted little inside-forward, who had made numerous attempts in 1960 to persuade Newcastle to release him from his contract. Newcastle refused repeatedly to let him go, so Eastham finally lost patience, walked out and took a job outside football working for Ernie Clay, the future chairman of Fulham.

That was in April 1960, and he remained out of the game until the November, when Newcastle accepted a bid of £47,000 for him from Arsenal. Understandably, Eastham was reluctant then to take the matter any further; but Cliff Lloyd, the hard-working and influential secretary of the union, persuaded him it was in the interests of all professional footballers to pursue his case against Newcastle, which had been set in motion in October 1960, alleging unlawful restraint of trade. No doubt Lloyd's words were given added force by the union's success, in 1961, in getting the maximum wage abolished.

At all events, the case finally came to court in June 1963. In the face of fierce opposition from the Football League, Cliff Lloyd proved to be the most impressive witness and the judge, Mr Justice Wilberforce, eventually ruled in favour of Eastham. In his historic summing-up,

Wilberforce said, 'It is claimed that those who know best consider it [the retain and transfer system] to be in the best interests of the game. I do not accept that line of argument. The system is an employer's system set up in an industry where the employers have established a monolithic front and where it is clear for the purposes of negotiation the employers are more strongly organized than the employees ... I conclude that the combined retain and transfer system as existing at the date of the writ [1960] is an unjustifiable restraint of trade.' Wilberforce, however, did not condemn the system outright, only the retain part of it. So Eastham's courtroom victory was just one step, albeit significant, towards the complete freedom of contract footballers enjoy today.

The consequences of the step became evident the following April, when negotiations between the Football League and the PFA produced important changes to the procedure for employing and transferring players, which had been in force since just after the formation of the Football League in 1888. The essential difference between the old and new systems was that every contract was to be freely negotiated between club and player. Moreover, a player at the end of his contract could not be offered new terms worse than those already in force. And if his club did not wish to take up their option to re-employ him, he was free to leave without a transfer fee being paid instead of becoming stuck in a kind of limbo on reduced wages waiting for another club to make an offer for him. Players were also given the right of appeal, first to the Football League Management Committee and then to an independent tribunal.

Those concessions were improved still further in 1978, when, after a lot of haggling between the Football League and the PFA, it was established that a player would be free, at the end of his contract, to seek employment with another club provided a transfer fee could be negotiated between the buyers and sellers. If they could not agree, the matter would be settled by the independent tribunal. However, George Davies, the PFA's solicitor, struck a note of caution. 'The new regulations,' he said, 'do attempt to provide more equality to the bargaining position. Time will tell whether the arrangements spelt out in the new regulations offer a reasonable freedom for your members ... Legally, perhaps, we are still only at the half-way house.'

Davies was right, of course. It took another seventeen years before professional footballers, thanks to Jean-Marc Bosman and his legal action against RFC Liege, won the complete freedom of contract the English PFA had been aiming at for at least 35 years. Actually, it would be more accurate to call it freedom of movement because, as already mentioned, unlike an employee in most other walks of life, a professional footballer cannot listen to job offers from other employers while still under contract to his club unless given permission to do so.

Over the past half-century, plainly, the balance of power in English football has shifted decisively from the clubs towards the players. The PFA were instrumental in pushing it in that direction, as was the ever-increasing income from television, advertising and sponsorship. But so, too, were agents. Most of that extra money would have gone into the clubs' coffers were it not for the hard bargaining done by agents on behalf of their footballer clients. And that hard bargaining did not really become possible until 1978, when the PFA won their members the right to negotiate contracts freely with their clubs. Now, the agents are regarded as the villains of the piece, greedy bloodsuckers draining huge amounts of money from the game that it can ill afford.

Needless to say, they do not agree with the description, and fight their corner fiercely. Take Geoffrey Irvine, once assistant to Bagenal Harvey, the man generally regarded as the pioneer who launched the profession in England in the 1940s. An agent for 40 years, Irvine has worked for some of the biggest and most powerful sports agencies in Britain and the world. His opinion, therefore, is worth hearing. 'Some agents have been good for the game and some haven't,' he said. 'But what I object to, perhaps because I have been an agent, is the idea that it's the agents who are causing the problems. The agents only exist because the clubs allow them to. All this money swilling round, and the money that agents get paid is only paid because people are prepared to pay it. If clubs don't like it – if football doesn't like it – they could do something about it. But they won't because they are all swilling around in it. The current argument is about "backhand-ers" and bungs and what agent is doing this or that; but a much more significant question is which club people are getting these bungs. So I really object to agents getting the hammer for this when I'd like to see some of the football clubs exposed.'

Irvine may get his wish if the latest 'probe' into the game's alleged corruption is successful, although he should not hold his breath in anticipation. Bribes, backhanders and 'bungs' are as old as the game itself. Inducements offered by clubs to the parents of promising young footballers, mysterious brown envelopes changing hands to influence results, and fivers shoved into the boots of 'amateur' foot-ballers are part of its racy folklore. However, the problem remains the same: acquiring sufficient evidence to prove the corruption. As Simon Inglis says in his history of British football scandals between 1900 and 1965, *Soccer in the Dock*, 'Sometimes there have been crimi-nal intentions, often there have been allegations of the most serious nature, but always, always, always there has been the major prob-lem of finding evidence. Not just rumours or anonymous letters, but concrete evidence, good enough for a judge. Throughout our history there are examples of players and officials providing information one minute then refusing to acknowledge or put it in writing the next. "If you repeat this conversation I shall deny it ever took place" has, unfortunately, been all too common a cry.'

Yet, in the 50 years this book is examining, wrongdoers have been caught and punished. In the late 1950s, just as Duncan Edwards' career at Manchester United was gathering pace, Sunderland were thrown into disarray by the severity of the punishments imposed on them by the Football Association for making illegal payments to their players at a time when the signing-on fee for a purchased footballer was, even then, a paltry £10. Chairman Bill Ditchburn was banned from football, as were other members of his board, and Bill Murray, who had spent 28 years at Roker Park as player and man-ager, resigned after being fined £200 – a considerable sum in 1957.

Then, in 1965, three prominent First Division footballers, Peter Swan, Tony Kay and David 'Bronco' Layne, were sent to prison for four months for being part of a widespread match-fixing operation uncovered by the Sunday newspaper the *People*. Swan, Kay and Layne, all players with Sheffield Wednesday when the offences were committed, also found themselves banned from English football for life on the completion of their sentences. It was a high price to pay, particularly in the case of England internationals Swan and Kay, for receiving £100 each, their reward for throwing a match against Ipswich to facilitate a betting coup.

If the Sunderland and Sheffield Wednesday affairs were caused partly by what you might call a lack of money, the next big scandal was very definitely a matter of excess. In 1995 George Graham was sacked after eight and a half very successful years as manager of Arsenal for being found guilty by an FA Premier League Inquiry of taking £425,500 in under-the-counter payments from Norwegian agent Rune Hauge. The money was Graham's cut from the transfers to Arsenal of the players John Jensen and Pal Lydersen from Danish and Norwegian clubs. Subsequently, he was banned from the game for a year.

Graham, however, was the only prominent figure to be punished as a result of the inquiry's findings. Some thought that unfair because the practice of managers taking a cut of transfer fees was believed to have become widespread within English football. Brian Clough, then retired, was the only other manager at whom an accusing finger was pointed, and Peter Leaver QC, the chief executive of the Premier League at the time, concluded that 'Overall I believe the work of the Inquiry team confirms the view that football is essentially a "clean" industry. However, it is clear that some of the practices present in transfer transactions, most notably in the early part of the 1990s, did require investigation and are unacceptable to the modern game. It is the duty of everyone in football to understand that and act accordingly.'

That rather Panglossian view of financial matters was echoed in a report commissioned by the FA in an attempt to find a way forward out of the mess caused initially by Tottenham chairman Sir Alan Sugar's courtroom allegation that Spurs' manager Terry Venables had told him Brian Clough liked a 'bung' when it came to transfers. 'Certainly,' concluded Sir John Smith, a former commissioner of the Metropolitan Police, in said report, 'there is a generally held view that there is not too much wrong with football ... it's a well-ordered game which is properly regulated ... If there's not much wrong with it then why seek to fix it by establishing these mechanisms which will be costly and perhaps intrusive and perhaps damage your opportunity to develop the game?' Smith answered the question by criticising the FA's inability to enforce compliance with its rules and emphasising the need for a permanent 'police force' to root out wrongdoing at clubs and ensure 'the sort of financial probity that all good businesses must have'. To their credit, the FA did set up a compliance unit in response, but its influence gradually withered away through a lack of co-operation and work that persuaded its head, Graham Bean, to resign in frustration.

The subject is back on the agenda, though, following allegations by Luton Town manager Mike Newell of continued corruption involving club officials and agents, and the apparent corroboration of that claim by England coach Sven-Goran Eriksson when lured into a number of indiscretions by the *News of the World*'s 'fake sheikh'. Now it is another former Metropolitan Police commissioner, Lord Stevens, who has been charged with the truly Herculean task of cleaning English football's Augean stables. Since the FA and the Premier League, who commissioned the inquiry and are seeking to take over more and more of the FA's powers, are already squabbling over the terms of reference, the prospects of a successful outcome are not good.

There is no doubt that FIFA, the governing body of world football, are struggling to control the activities of the mushrooming number of agents around the globe. Responding to media exposés of murky transfer deals, FIFA brought in a licensing system. Under it, agents were compelled at first to pay a bond of 200,000 Swiss francs (£80,000) to obtain a licence; now it is evidence of a suitable insurance policy and the ability to pass an exam. Clubs and players using unlicensed agents were to be subject to heavy fines. But it does not seem to have made much difference. Unlicensed agents appear to operate still with impunity, and the FIFA rule that agents should be paid by only one party in a deal is flouted constantly.

'In the early eighties, as foreign players came into the English game, there was an influx of continental-type agents, who were brokers, and that is actually where the problem started,' claims one of the most successful and respected English agents, Jonathan Holmes. 'Football refused, for a long time, to acknowledge there were such people as agents, but they came in and flooded the game. So then people started going around blowing the whistle and saying, "Oh, you've got to start doing something about this!" Unfortunately, they didn't know what it was they were trying to police. They didn't know whether they were trying to police brokers and agents or people who represented players.'

Holmes began his career as an independent financial adviser to Leicester City players in the 1970s, made his name as Gary Lineker's agent, and is now chairman and chief executive officer of one of the major sports agencies in the world, the SFX Sports Group. With that weight of experience behind him, he added, 'It was a progression from there onwards. The culture was pretty corrupt and it was obvious that managers were taking backhanders and all sorts of things – outrageously so in some cases. Having refused to acknowledge it, football then brought in some kind of policing, which was hopeless; and, from then on, it's been consistently hopeless. They have never adequately prosecuted anyone. The only person they got was Rune Hauge, and that was the result of newspaper pressure.

'Although the *Sunday Times* have done quite strong pieces from time to time, the newspapers have been pretty pathetic in pursuing it as well. At great expense, the *News of the World* got their man to impersonate a sheikh just to get the astounding admissions out of Sven-Goran Eriksson that he would take another job at the end of the World Cup and that English football was corrupt! I can remember talking to [investigative journalist] Tom Bower, and he said the great thing about writing about football was that he knew nobody would do anything about it in the end. Which is what's happened, really.

'It's a complete mess. And, I suppose you would have to say 'twas ever thus in English football. The game's always been about sweeping stuff under the carpet for its own amusement. You can go back to the betting scandal of the sixties, to Sunderland in the fifties, or even further back to the great Herbert Chapman, who was found guilty of making illegal payments at Leeds, wasn't he, before he became famous as the manager of Huddersfield and Arsenal.'

The root cause of English football's current problems, though, is not unscrupulous agents or greedy club officials; it is too much money chasing too few good players at a time when the players hold the whip hand. In the Premiership, the competition to catch the gravy train of European football, or even to stay where the living is a lot easier than in the Championship, is so fierce that clubs will pay almost any price to get the players they want. And, for that, they need agents – licensed or unlicensed – as much as the agents need them. It is disingenuous to argue, as Geoffrey Irvine and many others do, that agents make a lot of money only because clubs are willing to pay it to them. The clubs have little choice in the matter if they want to be successful.

Jon Holmes is honest enough to put it like this: 'Agents work on the time-honoured principle of what they can get away with. This is Wild West capitalism, this is. It's not some kind of regulated gentlemen's club, and never has been. If you ask me if the money agents earn is justified, I'd have to say probably not. But what else is justifiable in terms of what people earn? Can you justify what mobile phone salesmen make as against the wages of people who work in mental hospitals? The simple truth is that the game is awash with money and has chosen to lash out in the various ways that it does.

'People say what the players earn is outrageous; but it's never been part of my job to stop clubs making outrageous offers to my clients – quite the reverse. But I've always believed that if you look after the game, the game will look after you. Therefore, if the players behave themselves and enhance the game, more money is available for the game as a whole. It's a question of being careful not to kill the goose that lays the golden eggs.

'As for the effect agents have had on English football, I would say that they, like the militant trade unionists of the eighties, drove wages up and were successful in obtaining greater rewards for their members. Looking back, where did all the money go from those massive gates in the forties and fifties? So agents have enabled players to take a greater share of the goodies coming out of the game. Whether that's a good thing or a bad thing is for people to judge.'

The clubs need a vast network of scouts to check on players recommended by agents or to spot talented youngsters before their rivals do. Manchester United, for instance, employ about a hundred people to keep an eye on developing talent and to submit reports on opposing teams. Compare this with the little group of eight chief scout Joe Armstrong used to recruit the Busby Babes from all over the country back in the 1950s.

These days, though, the ground rules have changed radically with regard to the recruitment of young players. Because clubs are allowed to sign only boys who live within an hour or an hour and a half's travelling distance of their grounds or training grounds, some 40 of United's scouts are concentrated in the Manchester and district area. Theoretically, therefore, United would be unable to sign Duncan Edwards today unless his family were prepared to move house from the Midlands to the north-west.

This restriction came in with the academies most of the clubs in the Premiership and the Championship now have. The academies were the brainchild of the FA's former technical director, Howard Wilkinson, who introduced them in 1998 as part of his Charter for Quality, an intended solution to a perceived decline in the quality of England's young players. The academies were designed to replace or complement the more modest centres of excellence brought in by Wilkinson's predecessor, the long-serving and controversial Charles Hughes, in 1992.

There are vast differences between the two concepts. For one thing, the academies are a great deal more expensive. Whereas the centres of excellence could be set up for next to nothing in a club's existing ground or training ground, the academies had to be purpose-built.

United's, erected at their swish new training ground at Carrington, just outside Manchester, cost £8 million and takes nearly half of that a year to run. For such an outlay the youngsters get state-of-the-art facilities and expert coaching in how to cope with the modern game on and off the field. In addition to improving the boys' football technique, the academies offer a course in life skills. That means advice on anything from drug, alcohol and gambling abuse to financial direction and how to handle the media.

'If you've got a player, the technical qualities are an amazing ingredient within the make-up of that player,' says Ray Hall, manager of the Everton academy where Wayne Rooney was schooled for six or seven years, 'but there are a whole load of other things that are part of his development. He needs physiological development, he needs psychological development, he needs mental training, he needs social and intellectual development. What makes a player isn't just his technical qualities. In fact, when a player's technical qualities are outstanding, everybody talks about his mental approach to the game as well as his technique. They all say, "He's a winner! He wants to win! That's what separates him from the rest." Now that's not a technical thing to do with his feet, that's part of his make-up, and you would hope that we help in terms of trying to develop that, because it can be developed.'

Signed-on academy members range in age from nine to nineteen. There are 120 to 130 of them in that age group at Carrington, but United coach lads from as young as five or six as well because they need to sort out which of them are going to be talented enough to be taken into the academy at nine. Here is another massive change, since it was not so long ago that professional clubs were expressly forbidden to go anywhere near schoolboy footballers until they were fourteen. Even then, they were not allowed to coach them for more than one hour a week. But now, anything goes. 'We could take them at one year old, if we wanted to,' said Les Kershaw, director of United's academy, deliberately exaggerating the extent of the new freedom in this area. Compare this with the care Manchester United had to take not to sign Duncan Edwards until he had played the last

England schoolboy international of the season in which he turned fifteen, 1951/52.

The lifting of all age restrictions, in the face of what used to be fierce opposition from the English Schools FA, is something else for which the professional game should be grateful to Howard Wilkinson. As Kershaw added, 'The significant difference now is that professional football funds the game of football. When Duncan Edwards was young, everything revolved around schools football. In other words, the schoolteachers were in charge of the game until a boy left school. What Howard Wilkinson did – thank him or curse him – was the monumental thing of wresting control of the schoolboy game away from the teachers and putting it in the hands of the professionals. He has to be thanked a lot for that.'

The change nearly destroyed the ESFA, however. 'When the association lost access to the children,' recalled John Read, chief executive of the schools' governing body, 'the next battle was for the international schoolboy team, which was the U-15s. It wasn't so much just changing the team to the FA, it very nearly finished the English Schools FA for commercial and financial reasons. Basically, the whole of schools football was financed by three Wembley matches a year with the U-15s. We still run the U-18s to this day, but with an average crowd of between three and five thousand, it costs more to run the team than we get in income. So we rely very, very heavily on commercial sponsorship to the tune of £1 million a year. The FA, to be fair, now give us a compensation payment [the size of which he would not reveal because of a confidentiality agreement] for the loss of those U-15 fixtures back in 1996; but that doesn't really cover the income that we lost. It was quite generous at the time, but not now.

'The switch to the professional clubs changed the whole structure of English schools' football, in that our representative sides – I'm talking about districts and counties here – took a great big hit. They are still suffering, too, because the better boys and girls are now playing at the academies. What's also happening is that local village teams with four, five or six junior sides are now beginning to fight against the schools as well.

'It's a battle that's only just beginning, and it's one that I believe we will fight because, whereas we could see the academies with the professional coaches as a good thing for both football and the kids, we do see school football under the authority of a teacher or PE teacher as being more beneficial than some of the club teams. Their coaches are just interested parents, and it's the win-at-all-costs attitude that worries us. They don't necessarily know how to look after children, either. They don't know how to break the news to them that they've been dropped, or how to talk to them – all the child protection issues.'

Happily, the ESFA is thriving again after what Read describes as 'coming through the blitz a couple of years ago'. In the last five years, the number of inter-school competitions has increased from seven to seventeen and they now run a national competition, the FA Cup for Schools, for boys and girls in every age group from eleven to eighteen. But the question still nags: why on earth did the ESFA, for years dead set against letting the professionals anywhere near their children, suddenly relinquish control of them to Howard Wilkinson and the FA?

'The changes in the system began to happen when the FA decided to introduce their School of Excellence at Lilleshall in 1984,' explained Read. 'Certain schoolboys started going to Lilleshall and, when all that faded in the nineties and the individual clubs formed their own academies or centres of excellence, the age grouping changed. As a consequence of that, the FA set out rules and regulations for the academies and centres of excellence on education, on how to treat the kids, and were really taking over a little bit of the pastoral role the schoolteacher used to have. Even so, the membership of the ESFA were appalled by the change at the time. But I think now, some ten or fifteen years later, it is accepted that, at the top level, it is the best situation for the children. There was no option, really. The FA is the governing body of football and they dictated that's what would happen. It was the final giveaway, as it were, when the FA agreed to this compensation payment.'

No doubt Wilkinson impressed the ESFA with the research he had undertaken in preparation for the launch of the academies. 'Having been in management at Notts County, Sheffield Wednesday and Leeds, Howard had a fairly broad spectrum of experience already,' said Les Kershaw. 'What he did then was seek information from as many places as he could. I think he had trips to Brazil, France, Spain and elsewhere. I know for certain that he visited Clairefontaine [the French establishment near Paris that is held up as a model for all other national football centres] and I'm sure he would have had a look at what Ajax were doing in Holland. What he tried to do was take the best out of what he saw and put it all together.'

Wilkinson himself attributes the success of his ground-breaking negotiations with the ESFA to sheer logic. 'I persuaded them to surrender control by logical argument and talking about the best interests of the kids,' he explained. 'First, I persuaded the Football Association that, despite what they might think, the most important people on their agenda were players and coaches. Then I explained to the English Schools Football Association that the best interests of the kids was the first consideration that any educationalist should make. I also asked the question, "Can it be right that a talented player at fourteen or fifteen is playing 110 games a season, when we know that playing organised games where the main consideration is victory is not the way forward?" We won by, I think, the biggest majority ever seen in the council. I think everybody was for, and one abstained.'

When it came to putting Wilkinson's plans into practice, though, they did not work out quite as planned. 'The academies actually started in July 1998,' said Kershaw. 'The meetings with the professional football clubs had been going on for maybe twelve to eighteen months before that, but the season 1998/99 was the first time that clubs could seek a licence to run an academy. And I think Howard expected that, because of the rigours on facilities, staffing and so on, probably the upper echelons of the Premier League would be the only people who would be able to afford to run an academy.

'What's happened, of course, is that we've now got 40 and it's a very diluted system to what Howard actually anticipated and what was actually set out. There's been one or two comings and goings – Peterborough and Wrexham went out, for instance, while West Brom have recently come in – but 40 is far too many. I believe the intention was to set up academies on an elitist basis. Just as a schoolboy has to show outstanding potential to get into Oxford or Cambridge, you were looking for the kind of boy who had the ability to go to the very top of the game.'

Wilkinson confirms that the academy system was intended to be elitist, but only in the sense that it was designed to produce young footballers of the very highest quality, no matter the size of the club doing it. 'It is true,' he said, 'but not on the basis of you can only learn to swim if you can afford a swimming-pool in your back garden. Having done the research, having looked at youth development in other countries, having picked the brains of experienced people in this country, and having looked at other areas of elite development – whether it was the Royal Ballet School, whether it was RADA, whether it was Oxford, whether it was winning a gold medal in rowing – I was looking for a formula that develops the most talented people, that separates them from the rest, that takes their talent to the line. At its best, this sort of elite youth development costs, so the potential providers had to decide whether they could afford it. But don't let's get this wrong: the best school in the world is the one that has the best teachers, not necessarily the best facilities. I was trying to get the message over that you need both.'

The irony here is that the academies were seen as a replacement for the FA National School at Lilleshall, which was closed in 1999 partly because it had come to be regarded as too elitist. The alternative idea was to make it easier for a greater number of talented young footballers to receive expert coaching than was possible at the National School, given its limited annual intake of fourteen-year-olds on two-year courses. 'The clubs said, and I agreed with them,' explained Wilkinson, 'that they were the best places to develop the best players because of their expertise and their experience. Now that was a debatable point; but given that the concept of the school was only applying to eighteen kids a year, it was clear that to develop a group of boys that small was too narrow an approach. The concept of the school was brilliant, so how could we get twenty schools who offered the same provisions? How could we replicate Lilleshall in Manchester or London? That way, instead of twenty outstanding kids at Lilleshall, we'd have four hundred outstanding kids around the country. If you examine England teams over recent years, a lot of those kids at Lilleshall did make it to the very top [Michael Owen, Sol Campbell, Andy Cole, Nick Barmby and Ian Walker, for example]; but there are kids playing for England now who didn't go to Lilleshall.'

Not only that, but the National School was far from perfect, according to John Cartwright, its technical director for the first two years. 'Basically,' he said, 'it started off on the wrong foot because the kids were always selected to produce a team. So, as there were only sixteen players, you could only have one or two centre-halves, for example. There were maybe a couple of extra defenders and midfield players, but you didn't necessarily pick the best players in the selection process, and I always thought this was wrong. They had to play for the English Schools FA's England U-15 team as well, and if they didn't get selected for that there were tears and Christ knows what because they were supposed to be the best young players in the country. Then you might have five or six of them selected, and you didn't see them because they were going off to different games for the ESFA. So, the first year in, that was a problem. Then, in the second year, they were all doing their O-Level mock exams or their GCEs, or whatever they call them now, and that was on top of them all the time. So, it was a bad two years. There were so many things on top of them going into maturity and coming out of puberty, so it wasn't an easy period for the kids.'

Nor, as we have seen already, is the academy system without its flaws or its critics. The restrictions that, theoretically at least, shrink the area in which clubs can look for promising young players – up to the age of twelve, a boy must not have to travel for more than an hour to the academy from his place of residence; for those twelve and over, the time limit is extended to an hour and a half – are another bone of contention. As with most rules, however, there is usually a way round them. One obvious solution for the bigger clubs is to move promising youngsters to within their catchment area. Another is just to go out and buy them, as Arsenal did in the case of the outstanding young striker Theo Walcott. Southampton's compensation for losing Walcott could be as much as £12 million if the player develops into the world-class footballer Arsenal manager Arsène Wenger – not to mention Sven-Goran Eriksson, who included the seventeen-year-old in his World Cup squad – expects him to become.

'The one thing that comes from the travelling restrictions,' pointed out Manchester United's Les Kershaw, 'is a very parochial system, which is obviously not always suitable for internationally famous clubs. We also have our own in-house rule that we do not bring to this club any boy who lives outside the travelling distance until he has started his GCSEs. The trouble is that by the time they are four-teen boys are either in an academy already or have packed in play-ing. But occasionally, if we've found a lad who has got very good talent, we'll negotiate with his mum and dad about the fact that the only way he can sign for this club is if his address is in the catchment area. So what we do is put them with families. A boy will become part of a family that some call "landladies". We prefer the name "family providers", but they're basically a landlady. Like when you go to university, you either go into digs or a flat. So the boy goes and lives with the family and he attends our partner school, which is Ashton-on-Mersey School. We take over his complete educational programme from fourteen to leaving school, and he does the GCSE programme at Ashton-on-Mersey School. He is classed as an Ashton-on-Mersey schoolboy, not a Man United boy. But he trains with us in the evening.'

This arrangement is not so far removed from the digs Duncan Edwards and other members of the Busby Babes were put into with Mrs Watson at 5 Birch Avenue, just round the corner from Lancashire Cricket Club's Old Trafford. Nor is it unlike United's attempt to pro-vide their young recruits with an alternative occupation, in Edwards' case carpentry, should they not make it as professional footballers. It is a million miles away, though, from the £3 million home Wayne Rooney and fiancée Coleen McLoughlin were having built to their own specifications at fashionable Prestbury, just south of Manchester, as their base in the area. In fairness to Wayne and Coleen, though, times were already beginning to change around 1970, when George Best, first of the well-paid celebrity footballers, finally moved out of Mrs Fullaway's digs and into his own £35,000 custom-built house at Bramhall, south of Manchester and not too far away from Prestbury.

But there is no disguising the fact that Manchester United resent the timing restrictions that hamper their recruitment of young players in a way Sir Matt Busby could never have imagined. 'The sad part is that they don't apply to sports such as swimming and athletics,' argued Les Kershaw. 'The Premier League hides behind the words "child protection". They say it is not in a child's interests to travel more than one and a half hours to training, and they've said they've sought opinions from people well versed in children's issues. But, obviously, it hasn't applied to swimming because kids go up and down motorways at six o'clock in the morning to get to a swimming pool.

'I'm not saying it's right or wrong. What I'm saying is there's got to be more than one way to skin a cat. You know, if David Beckham was twelve or thirteen now, it would be very, very difficult for him to sign for Man United. That can't be right, can it? Because all Beckham wanted to do was to play football for this club. And, with the rules as they are now, we might not even have known that, living down in London, he wanted to play for Man United. That's the problem! The same goes for Duncan Edwards from Dudley. Duncan would have been tied up maybe with Wolves or West Bromwich Albion or one of the other West Midlands clubs. His choice would have been restricted. Take a kid now in the south-west of England. He's got Plymouth, who have a go [at coaching youngsters], Torquay, who have totally abandoned kids, and Exeter, who if they don't join the league this summer [2006] have been told that the funding of their centre of excellence will be stopped. So what chance does a kid have in a small country like this if he happens to be born in the south-west? We can't go down and open a centre there because it's outside our area and we're barred from doing it.

'I've got to believe that what academies do is definitely for the good of the game; but whether they're for the good of Manchester United is a different question. The one thing we're doing now is producing players who are far more gifted technically than ever happened in the past. We've put a lot of expertise and money into coaching boys between the ages of seven and twelve and it's paid dividends because we're producing a lot of very skilful young players. It doesn't mean they'll ever play for Man U, but they can all manipulate a football, which we haven't had in the past. But we can only do it with kids who live in Manchester and District, which is hardly satisfying for a club that has a worldwide reputation for giving youth a go. That's the problem we face.'

Unsurprisingly, Kershaw is supported in his frustration by the Manchester United manager, Sir Alex Ferguson, who bemoans not only the time restrictions on youth recruitment, but the fact that United are one of seventeen clubs of varying status vying for the best boys in the north-west, the country's most congested football area. 'At the end of the day,' he said, 'we're operating a parochial system for a club that's got expectations to win in Europe. Before the academy system, I think we were the most successful club at recruiting players from all over Britain.' Ferguson is so unhappy with the current system, in fact, that he does not think it is working. 'I definitely don't think so,' he said. 'I think what it's done is cost a lot of money. It costs us £3.6 million a year, for example. And, because of the pressure the system puts on finances, there's a lot of clubs who used to have two teams, U-17s and U-19s, who've cut it to just one team, U-18s. Now they're talking about a lot of teams wanting to get rid of reserve football, and it's all down to finance.'

This is not to say that Sir Alex is thinking of abandoning United's proud tradition of producing their own players, a tradition he has done much to extend and enhance. Far from it, in fact. Ferguson knows only too well how self-financing, profitable even, the process can be. 'The door's been shut a bit, and we're not happy with that, but we've still got to produce quality through our own ranks and we're still very successful at that,' he said. 'If you look at the academy system here for the last eighteen or nineteen years – since we started to try and produce players – you would have to say that it's absolutely grown since then. You can't place values on Ryan Giggs and Paul Scholes [this was before Scholes developed his eye problem]. If I sold either of them at any given time, it would pay for all the money we've spent on academies in those nineteen years. And, if you look at it that way, David Beckham, Phil Neville and Nicky Butt were sold for over £30 million in all. Over £30 million for just three boys who went through our academy system!'

Ray Hall, Everton's academy manager, also complains about the system but presents a similar justification to Ferguson for continuing with it. 'The investment that goes into academies is enormous,' he said, 'but does the system work? It's the envy of the world, but I'm not so sure we're getting enough outstanding players from it. What I'm trying to say is that, because of the restrictions on who we can recruit, we are not getting the same number of talented players that we did before the academy system came into being. There wasn't as much investment then, so it seems quite strange or ironic that the more investment that's gone in, the fewer talented players you can sign. So that's the problem, and I'm not sure what the solution is. I listen to some people in similar positions to my own, and they say we should go back to a free-for-all. Rightly or wrongly, that's OK. But if I were the head of Bury Football Club's academy and I had a talented player I'd worked with for three or four years, I wouldn't want him going to Everton or Manchester United or Manchester City.

'Another thing to consider is that the Premier League have raised the bar in terms of the players. It is now far more difficult for a young player to get into a first team in the Premier League because of the number of foreign players playing in England now. There used to be time to develop young players, but that time has gone. You almost have to be a Wayne Rooney to get in the side.' So why persevere with academies, then? 'For one reason – a Wayne Rooney,' replied Hall. 'Somebody's got to develop him, and why shouldn't it be Everton? He cost the club very little – it was just wages and a new contract right at the end – and he left the club for nearly £30 million. That's more than a decent return on the investment. I don't think there's any other part of the club, including the stadium, that is worth that kind of money.'

It is worth pausing here to recognise the fact that nearly all the players quoted by Ferguson and Hall as having been sold at a massive profit were recruited locally. Phil Neville and Nicky Butt come from Manchester and District, as do two of the other former youth players Sir Alex talked about, Ryan Giggs and Paul Scholes. Phil Neville's brother, Gary, is another local boy from the freakishly talented United youth team of 1992 who graduated to the first team. In fact, of that talented sextet, David Beckham was the only one to hail from another part of the country, Giggs' Cardiff birthplace notwithstanding. And Wayne Rooney, when he joined Everton, could not have been more of a Scouser.

So could it be that the clubs protest too much about the restrictions on recruitment imposed by the academy system? Howard Wilkinson certainly thinks so. 'It's like anything else,' he said. 'You bring something in and not everything is going to be right. It has to be reviewed and, as a result of the review, you take the good and make it better; you get the not-so-good and ask yourself if you can improve it; and the bad you throw out.

'The time restriction came about as the result of three things. One was child welfare: people said you couldn't have kids in a car for two hours there and two hours back, three times a week, because that's not in the best interests of the child. Secondly, the clubs themselves said they wanted some protection from their wealthier brethren. "Why should we spend money," they said, "and have the big boys come and nick our kids?" The third factor was time to practise. How the hell do you practise if you're a boy in Torquay and you're an Everton player, say? But it's one of those things only the clubs themselves can resolve. It's a consensus thing.

'I know clubs are now moving boys, and even parents, from one part of the country to another to make them eligible for their academies. I scratch my head over that one. The crucial thing is that a kid's got to be developed. If he's not been developed, he's not going to maximise himself. Somehow or another, you've got to do that. Then there's got to be a consensus on how. I didn't have a problem with satellites [branches of academies being set up in other parts of the country], but the clubs did.'

The crowning glory in Wilkinson's Charter for Quality, his ambitious attempt to bring the technique and organisation of English football up to the high standards set by France and other western European countries, was supposed to be a new National Football Centre near Burton-on-Trent in the Midlands. Set in 352 acres of parkland designed by Capability Brown, the centre was intended to supplement the academy system by providing a much-needed focal point for every level of the English game from the humblest parks player right up to Wayne Rooney and company. It was, in short, to be the English Clairefontaine.

Launched during the expansive regime of former FA chief executive Adam Crozier, the project received enthusiastic backing from the governing body at first. So much so that £20 million was spent installing the infrastructure for the centre. This consisted mainly of laying eleven pitches, two of them synthetic and the others with under-soil heating, plus drainage, floodlighting, etc. But a financial crisis brought on by the problematic £757 million Wembley Stadium project and general overspending persuaded the FA to mothball the proposed National Centre in 2003, a year after Wilkinson had left as technical director.

To say he was unhappy about the decision is an understatement. 'It was a major blow to me professionally, one of my biggest disappointments,' he admitted in an interview for this book, 'particularly as it had been so wholeheartedly endorsed by the FA as part of the Charter for Quality. The charter was a vision, a practical document, a philosophy, designed to change the direction of English football in a fairly radical way. One part of the document was academies, but the document addressed every level of English football from grassroots right through to the England team. The National Centre was at the heart of that philosophy. It was going to be the headquarters, in practical and symbolic terms, of all that the document enshrined. At the elite level, in terms of players and coaches, my idea was for this country to start to turn out coaches who were, for example, [Jose] Mourinhos and beyond. It was a place where I also saw a heck of a lot of research going on. I saw issues of county football associations being addressed there, at their new headquarters. Girls' football, boys' football, disabled football, international minor competitions – all of them could have been housed there. It would have had a sports science research unit, a sports medicine unit, a human performance unit, an indoor hall, and all sorts of technological equipment that would enable us to stay ahead of our rivals.

'I read an article by [Chelsea chief executive] Peter Kenyon where he said Mourinho is more into technology than any manager he's ever seen or talked to. I'm not saying that technology and its interpretation are what generally makes a good manager; what I am saying is that the FA owes that to football in this country because we are the most famous association in the world and the strongest football country in the world. Unfortunately, too many decisions in that building [FA headquarters at Soho Square] are made from a very self-interested point of view and are increasingly dominated by the rich and famous.'

Wilkinson's anger and despair may be premature, however. At the end of 2005 it was announced that Umbro, kit suppliers to the England team for more than twenty years, had agreed to partner the FA in the development of the National Football Centre. What it means in practical terms is that Umbro will pay £12 million towards the total cost of the project, estimated by Wilkinson to be in the region of £65 million, and have their name incorporated in its title. Judging by the joint FA/Umbro statement, it looks as though other sponsors are being sought to defray the cost. 'This stand-alone contract,' it said, 'will see the FA and Umbro work together to develop the Burton-on-Trent site further, subject to the successful conclusion of various partnership arrangements and all permissions being granted for the project to be concluded.' It looks, too, as if the partnership means business in more ways than one. 'Umbro's investment,' the statement continued, 'will be used to aid funding of superb facilities including changing rooms, a fitness and treatment area, a gym and ball-court, a hotel and golf course. The investment will play a key role in helping establish the status of the National Football Centre as the FA's football development and education hub.' A hotel was also part of Wilkinson's plans; so if the partners remain true to their word, the finished centre may not fall too far short of the idealistic vision the reforming technical director had for it. We shall see.

Whether there is actually a need for such a swanky establishment is another matter. Many of the Premiership clubs, who wield increasing power within the FA and demanded economies at Soho Square, do not believe there is; they feel their academies are already doing the job of improving the quality of England's young players. In addition, there are those like John Cartwright, former technical director of the FA National School, who argue that state-of-the-art facilities are no good unless the coaching in them is of the very highest quality. And, as things stand, he is not convinced that would be the case at Burton-on-Trent.

There are certainly no restrictions on the number of foreign youngsters who can be inducted into the academies of English clubs once they are aged sixteen. Manchester United, for instance, have a Finn and two German boys in their youth teams. Another two boys, one from China and one from Guinea, are farmed out to Royal Antwerp, the Belgian club with whom United have established an alliance mainly for the purpose of aiding the development of their young players, English and foreign. Similarly, boys from Scandinavia and western Europe can be seen among the 160 aged between nine and nineteen at Everton's academy. Disturbingly, Les Kershaw claimed that, because United are not allowed to recruit from the whole of the country, the best players at their academy are not English. 'I think that's sad, and the manager thinks it's sad,' he reported. 'But we have to fight with the rules that we have put in front of us. Nobody can tell me that Giuseppe Rossi is not going to be a great player, but we've rooted him out from Italy and he's not had his education in

Manchester. Gerard Pique – we rooted him out from Barcelona. So we spend a lot of time and money scouting Europe and further afield.'

So successful has United's scouting operation been that 23 nationalities are represented in the club, a large proportion of them in the first-team squad. Goalkeeper Edwin van der Sar and striker Ruud van Nistelrooy are Dutch, defender Mikael Silvestre and striker Louis Saha are French, left-back Gabriel Heinze is an Argentine, winger Cristiano Ronaldo is Portuguese, utility player Quinton Fortune is South African, goalkeeper Tim Howard is American, Rossi is Italian and Pique Spanish. To this list have to be added the likes of Ryan Giggs (Wales), John O'Shea (Republic of Ireland) and Darren Fletcher (Scotland). In fact, Wayne Rooney, Rio Ferdinand, Wes Brown and Gary Neville were the only Englishmen assured of a starting place in the first team in the 2005/06 season. This does not take account of the worrying eye problem that sidelined Paul Scholes or the horrifying ankle injury suffered by Alan Smith, but it is still a disturbing statistic at a club that always prided itself on producing talented young players from the British Isles.

It is certainly an enormous change from the days of the Busby Babes, eight of whom were English. The only regular members of the side who were not were Harry Gregg and Jackie Blanchflower (Northern Ireland) and Billy Whelan (Republic of Ireland). English football was not without its foreign players in the 1950s, of course. The Chilean Robledo brothers, George and Ted, at Newcastle; Bill Perry, the South African who scored the winning goal for Blackpool in the final of the 1953 FA Cup, the 'Matthews Final'; and Bert Trautmann, Manchester City's ex-German POW, immediately come to mind. For the most part, however, the non-Englishmen were drawn from other parts of the British Isles – from Scotland mostly, but also Ireland, north and south, and Wales. And, traditionally, there were plenty of them.

Still, Sir Alex Ferguson's United, with four or five English regulars in their team, look positively patriotic alongside Arsenal, who often field a first team containing not a single Englishman. A growing sense of unease in the game about the overwhelming number of foreigners in the Gunners' side found a voice when West Ham manager Alan Pardew expressed disappointment that, in the absence of the injured Ashley Cole and the psychologically disturbed Sol Campbell, there was not one British footballer, let alone an English one, in the Arsenal team that knocked Real Madrid out of the 2005/06 Champions League. 'We are losing the soul of English football,' claimed Pardew, who felt Arsenal's progress was not necessarily a triumph for the English game.

Arsène Wenger hit back angrily, accusing Pardew of racism and regressive thinking. 'When you represent a club,' thundered the Arsenal manager, 'it's about values and qualities, not about passports ... I try to choose the best player and my pride in my career is not to choose somebody because of his passport.'

But Pardew defended himself strongly. Insisting that he admired Wenger greatly and had had no intention of trying to belittle Arsenal's Champions League achievement, the West Ham manager issued a statement:

> When I said it was disappointing that there were no British players in the Arsenal team that went through to the last eight in the Champions League, I was not being racist or xenophobic, as Arsène Wenger has suggested. A manager who is married to a Swede and has signed players from Ireland, Wales, Argentina, Israel and France, while giving trials to players from Japan and Poland, cannot be called racist. Our multi-cultural approach to our squad is something I'm proud of. But I care passionately about our game and will always give my views honestly and from the heart.
>
> My view is that if we're to have strong British national sides – and success at that level boosts crowds and revenue in our domestic leagues – then we need to have young British players coming through ... I maintain we need to protect our young talent for the greater good. It is a view I know is held by the Professional Footballers' Association, other managers and indeed FIFA, who are considering introducing a quota system.

Jose Mourinho at Chelsea has said he will build success at Stamford Bridge with a backbone of English players ...

There was more than one dimension to this revealing spat between two Premiership managers. On the most obvious level, Pardew was expressing the widely-held view that English football is in danger of becoming swamped by foreign players, a process that threatens the integrity and future of the national team. But Wenger took the argument to a deeper, more worrying level when he stated quite openly, and with unusual peevishness, that he could not give a fig for international football. 'I find silly this rule of six,' he said, referring to the number of home-grown players UEFA, the governing body of European football, would like teams to include in their squads. 'It's more to protect the national teams than to make football progress. If it makes the national team progress I don't care, because international football is low, not the best quality.' Then, looking forward to the second leg of Arsenal's Champions League tie with Real Madrid early in 2006, Wenger added, 'Who minds on Wednesday night if Roberto Carlos is Spanish or not? You paid £50 to watch a football game, you want to see quality. We're not in 1950. People can see the best football when they like – just switch on the button. Real Madrid against Arsenal has been seen by more than a hundred countries in the world. They don't care where people come from.'

So there you have it: another serious outbreak of the age-old conflict between club and country. If Wenger's argument were followed to its logical conclusion, there would be no World Cups or European Championships, no international football of any kind. Just wealthy clubs refining the art of the game, and certainly making lots of money from it, by playing each other over and over again each year with teams of talented, well-paid mercenaries.

Which is exactly the potentially boring prospect the powerful, eighteen-strong G14 group of leading European clubs – of which Arsenal are a member – appear to be pursuing. The Gunners' fans do not seem to mind at all, which is hardly surprising given the success Wenger has brought to the club and the heavenly quality with which his teams have enhanced the Premiership. It's harder to stomach if you don't happen to support one of the eighteen chosen few, but do get a buzz from following your national team around the world – witness all those flags from Bradford, Darlington, Tranmere and other underprivileged outposts at England matches. Not only that, but it is a proven fact that any success enjoyed by the national side boosts attendances at club matches the following season.

We may not be in 1950 any more, as Wenger points out, but some things have not changed since then. One of them is Britain's love of international football. It may be a thinly veiled excuse for displays of nationalism, but it definitely matters to the average football fan. Think back to all those joyous, and not so joyous, outbursts when Scotland, Northern Ireland and Wales succeeded in beating the hated English. Why else, too, did the Lightning Seeds sing of 'thirty years of hurt' at Euro 96 and strike a chord in every English heart? Because England had not won any major tournament since the World Cup in 1966, that's why.

Perhaps it is because Wenger is obsessed with perfection that he does not seem to grasp this salient feature of English football. Yes, everybody loves to see a high-class Champions League match between two teams packed with world-class players; but, by and large, the English also like to be able to identify with one of the teams they are watching. And that, more often than not, means having some English or British players in them – a practical step, if nothing else, given the physical, combative nature of Premiership football, and a requirement recognised by the Portuguese Mourinho at Chelsea, the Dutchman Martin Jol at Tottenham, the Spaniard Rafael Benitez at Liverpool and the Frenchman Gérard Houllier before him.

Wenger, it must be said, can do a lot more than point to the production of Ashley Cole and the purchase of Sol Campbell as evidence of his faith in English footballers. He held on to George Graham's redoubtable English back five or six for as long as he could, and he invested heavily, though unsuccessfully, in the promise of Francis Jeffers and Jermaine Pennant. More recently, some questioned his sanity, never mind his judgement, when he agreed to risk £12 million on

Theo Walcott, the then sixteen-year-old Southampton striker hailed as English football's next boy wonder.

In any case, as Liam Brady points out, it has never been Arsenal's principal concern to produce players for the England team, hard as they have tried to do so along the way. The former Arsenal legend, who now runs the club's academy, also claims that the Gunners have probably provided the Premier League with more players than any other club since the academy system started. 'There's four at Reading, who won the Championship by a street,' he argued. 'There's Jay Bothroyd and Jerome Thomas at Charlton, there's Julian Gray and Neil Kilkenny at Birmingham, there's David Bentley at Blackburn. We haven't got them in the Arsenal team because we get them in the Arsenal team at a very high standard.' In other words, only the very best will do for Arsenal, regardless of nationality.

Duncan Edwards would have found it very strange to see foreign managers in charge of English clubs, never mind foreign footballers playing for them. In his last season, 1957/58, nearly two-thirds of the managers in charge of the 22 clubs in the old First Division were English, and the rest were Scots. That majority looks overwhelming alongside just over half of the twenty Premiership clubs who were run by Englishmen in 2005/06. Five of the remainder were in the care of men from the British Isles, but only two from Scotland – Manchester United's Sir Alex Ferguson and Everton's David Moyes. Four clubs – Chelsea, Liverpool, Tottenham and Arsenal, all of them in the top five – had foreigners in charge.

The growing tendency for England's leading clubs to look overseas for managers was something seized upon by Gordon Taylor, the outspoken chief executive of the Professional Footballers' Association. Taylor, who supported Pardew in his row with Wenger and has often supplied a rare voice of sanity in the game's many disputes, said, 'It's interesting that Sepp Blatter, [president] of FIFA, has said there should be five or six national players in each club team; but whether that could be got through because of legal reasons, I don't know. It's this battle of club v. country. It came to a head, I suppose, with the Alan Pardew–Arsène Wenger bust-up. I had a great deal of sympathy for Alan when the race card was thrown in because he was just being patriotic and saying, "No, Arsenal are an English club, but you can't say they're flying the flag for England; they're flying the flag for Arsenal and for the Premiership if there's not one player in the team who could play for England."

'When there are English players in there, like Jamie Carragher and Steven Gerrard at Liverpool, John Terry, Frank Lampard and Joe Cole at Chelsea, and Wayne Rooney, Gary Neville and Rio Ferdinand at Manchester United, you do feel there is a link that enables the club to be identified genuinely as English. This is not a criticism of Arsène Wenger, because he's got a job to do as Arsenal manager. Foreign managers are much more cosmopolitan, and are inclined to look abroad first for players. Although, in fairness, for Rafael Benitez to have put his faith in Peter Crouch was quite a strong commitment.'

The argument between Pardew and Wenger spread to include the quality of the young English players being produced by the academies. Wenger's apparent reluctance to make any of Highbury's English graduates, with the notable exception of Ashley Cole, regular members of his first team was approved tacitly by England manager Sven-Goran Eriksson and the FA's director of football, Sir Trevor Brooking. Both of these luminaries came to the conclusion that it was difficult to promote young Englishmen because, as Brooking told the *Daily Mail*, 'The harsh fact is that many clubs feel our teenage hopefuls are a long way behind the technical skills of their European counterparts.' Sir Trevor backed up this view by revealing the startling fact that, as the 2005/06 season entered its final phase, only about 40 per cent of the 300-plus first-team players in the Premiership were English. This compared unfavourably with Spain's equivalent, La Liga, where home-grown footballers represented 65 per cent of the total number of players. Unfortunately, too, with the last season of the old First Division, 1991-92, when over 76 per cent of the 553 players used were English.

Yet what of places like Middlesbrough, where their academy is turning out top-notch English youngsters in increasing numbers? And doing it simply by scouring their immediate area in the north-east for talent. Middlesbrough may not have fared very well in the Premiership in 2005/06, but youngsters such as James Morrison and Lee Cattermole – not to mention Stewart Downing, already capped at international level – helped their unfashionable club reach the final of the UEFA Cup and identified themselves as potential senior England internationals. What, too, of the fact that every member of the England squad going to the finals of the 2006 World Cup, and with such high hopes of winning it, was a product of the country's academies?

Nor, by any means, has the influx of foreigners been wholly bad for English football. When players from abroad began to flood in, it was argued that the native youngsters could learn a thing or two from them (not including 'diving'). That has undoubtedly proved to be the case, and never more so than with Eric Cantona and the graduates from Manchester United's outstandingly promising youth team of 1991/92, who worshipped and copied the gifted French maverick and perfectionist. Without question, too, many of England's young footballers have benefited from having to compete with the foreign imports for a first-team place. The cream will always rise to the top, they say, and you do not have to look much further than Terry, Lampard and Cole at Chelsea, Gerrard, Carragher and Crouch at Liverpool, and Paul Robinson, Ledley King, Michael Carrick, Michael Dawson, Jermaine Jenas, Jermain Defoe and Aaron Lennon at Tottenham to see that the old cliché remains as true as ever.

What we should remember, perhaps, is that organised English football has never been played purely by the English. William McGregor, founding father of the Football League, was a Birmingham businessman who came from Perthshire, and he was joined in his creation over the years by thousands of players from Scotland. Indeed, Liverpool once fielded a team completely made up of Scotsmen. They did not go quite that far in the 1950 FA Cup final against Arsenal, but there were still three Scots and three Welshmen among the 22 players on view.

It would be interesting to discover how the proportion of Scottish, Irish and Welsh footballers in the English game 50-odd years ago compares with that of the non-British now; but the figures are hard to come by. However, Gordon Taylor assured me that the vast foreign legion of today easily outnumbers the Scottish, Irish and Welsh contingent of old, which has shrunk dramatically over the years. 'There's a very limited number of Scots and Welsh players now,' he said. 'The Irish representation has kept at a pretty reasonable level, but from the Republic of Ireland, not Northern Ireland. The influx of foreign players has been so great, though, that there are a lot less in the Premiership who qualify to play for England now than when they were competing with the Scots, Irish and Welsh for first-team places in the old First Division. You look at the England U-21 side and you hardly see a lad in first-team football. Yet there are some good players among them.

'Back in 1978, when [Argentina's] Ossie Ardiles and Ricky Villa joined Spurs, there was some concern over work permits for players from non-European Union countries. But, since Bosman in '95, there could be no restrictions on EU players in the European economic area. So now we must have some 25 countries that are permit-free. There's also been some relaxation for non-EU countries in that, to qualify for a move to English football, a player just needs to come from a country that's in the top 70 in the world rankings and to have played in two-thirds of their international games.

'There's also been the growth of agents, to the extent that there's now an international network of them. You can make what you want of that, but it's one of the reasons there's been an inquiry because you can have three, four or five agents involved in one transfer, particularly with some of the South American players, and not all the money's going to clubs. Then there's the weak excuse for not buying British that home-grown players are too expensive. But that's a real dichotomy when you think that all the Premier League clubs are keen to expound their belief in youth development.

'Even stranger is the fact that English clubs, with the support of the FA, have been lobbying against the latest UEFA criteria that suggest next season (2006/07) clubs should have at least four in a squad of 25 who are developed at the club or in the country. It's a token gesture by UEFA, a tilt at a windmill, because they are not saying those four have to be on the pitch; they only have to be in the squad. But it shows the extent of the problem we've got when England and Italy were against it.

'I feel it's a terrible indictment of the FA's structure for football if they cannot bang the drum in the best interests of our young players, particularly when, apart from the FA Cup, their income and their status comes from how well England does internationally. It probably shows how much they are in the grip of the Premier League.'

The full title of the Premier League is the *FA* Premier League, of course; and it could not have come into being in 1991 without the backing of the FA. If it had lacked the approval of the governing body of English football, the Premier League would have been shunned by FIFA and UEFA and, as a result, stillborn. But, like a cuckoo in the nest, the Premier League then set about taking over the governing body by demanding reforms, dominating its boards and committees, and even seeking control of the England team.

Ironically, the chief obstetrician at the birth of the biggest structural change in the history of English football was a former secretary of the organisation that would suffer most from the secession of the old First Division – the Football League. As chief executive of the Football Association, Graham Kelly put his former employers, the body which had established organised football in England 103 years earlier, at risk. He did so with the best of intentions. As he revealed in his autobiography, *Sweet FA*, the rationale for the formation of the Premier League was as follows:

- fewer games for the top clubs and players;
- better preparation for the England players;
- stronger commercial activities;
- better arrangements for developing young players;
- compulsory qualifications for managers;
- and the end of the power struggle between the FA and the League.

In other words, it was an attempt not only to end the tiresome, debilitating squabble between the FA and the League over who ran English football, but to improve England's chances of winning major tournaments, raise managerial standards, pave the way for the academies and enable the clubs to raise the money required to modernise their stadiums.

It should be remembered that the Premier League was formulated in the aftermath of Lord Justice Taylor's report into the dreadful disaster at Sheffield Wednesday's ground, Hillsborough, in April 1989, when 95 Liverpool supporters were killed (sadly, one more died after being in a coma for four years) and another 200 were injured as a result of severe overcrowding crushing spectators against the perimeter fence at the start of an FA Cup semi-final against Nottingham Forest. Taylor's recommendations included all-seater stadiums, modified fences and new spectator offences of racist or obscene abuse.

His report had the effect of ushering in the modern era of English football – the era in which most stadiums have been modernised and more than twenty new, impressive, customer-friendly arenas have sprung up around the country (not counting the embarrassingly shambolic Wembley Stadium project). No longer, for the most part, are the fans treated like cattle and supplied with bog-standard facilities. Being all-seater, the modernised stadiums have also helped to discourage the hooliganism that used to thrive on the freedom of malcontents to range at will over the open terracing the seats have replaced. As a matter of fact, the containment of the hooligans has been one of the major successes of English football in the past twenty years.

The scourge of hooliganism, which had cast a blight on the domestic game during the seventies and eighties, reached its horrifying apogee at the European Cup final of 1985. Thirty-nine spectators, all but eight of them Italian, were crushed or trampled to death at Brussels' Heysel Stadium following a charge by Liverpool fans into a section of the terracing occupied by Juventus supporters. Another 437 people were injured, and the outcry was so great that Margaret Thatcher, then Prime Minister, threatened to bring in an identity card scheme for football supporters. That questionable solution was averted; but Heysel, which resulted in English clubs being banned from European football for five years, did concentrate minds wonderfully on the underlying problem.

The clubs, the football authorities and the police worked so hard on finding an answer that, despite the absence of the perimeter fences that contributed so fatally to the Hillsborough disaster and which had been erected to prevent pitch invasions, crowd disturbances are rare inside grounds these days. Outside them, too, the police have reduced the number of clashes, often pre-arranged, between rival gangs of hooligans. Nobody dares to say the problem has been eliminated, because they know it could resurface at any time; but at least it does seem to be under control.

Nor is the containment of hooliganism English football's only success story. Against all expectation, the rump of the Football League is thriving despite having been dumped by the elitist Premier League clubs. Cut off from the big bucks pouring in from Sky (they receive just 5 per cent of the Premiership's TV income), the Football League also had to survive the shattering collapse in 2001 of their £315 million deal with ITV and Ondigital for the coverage of league and League (Carling) Cup matches. It left them owed £178 million, yet none of the 72 Football League clubs has gone out of business, as had been feared. Anything but, in fact.

One of the reasons the lower divisions have beaten the odds is that Sky stepped into the gaping hole left by ITV and Ondigital and picked up the Football League TV rights for £95 million. It may have been a bit of good business, in that they got them on the cheap, but there is no denying that it was an act of rescue as well. As Barry Fry, then just manager of Division Three Peterborough, said at the time, 'Sky are football's biggest friends, and they alone are responsible for saving between 30 and 40 clubs from going to the wall.' The PFA have also played their part by paying the wages of clubs fallen on hard times, a regular and harrowing experience that has left its mark on chief executive Gordon Taylor. 'It's certainly richer,' he said, trying to sum up the state of the game. 'It's certainly bigger, inasmuch as it's front-page, middle-page and back-page news. Footballers have taken over the celebrity status of pop stars and film stars. What isn't healthy is the imbalance of the money towards the Premiership, with the rest struggling to hold on to their coat-tails.

'But what illustrates the tremendous strength of the [football] structure in this country is the vibrancy of the Football League, where attendances have increased for about twenty years on the run. And then you have the [Nationwide] Conference, which we opened up into the League when we introduced one-up and one-down in 1986, since when it's become two-up and two-down. Now, half the teams in the Conference are operating on a full-time basis.

'So the strength in depth in England is unbelievable. Everybody predicted that it would have to contract, that you'd have to chop off dead wood, every time we helped clubs in administration, clubs like Middlesbrough and Charlton who are now thriving in the Premiership. I can give you a long list of clubs who were threatened when coming to terms with the new financial situation and were over-stretched. But they've all survived, and it's an incredible success story.

'The game is also more comfortable to watch than it's ever been. Our stadiums are the finest in the world. Our average attendances are still the highest in the world. We have more professional clubs than any other country in the world. We've also handled the hooligan factor that threatened the game's existence, though you can never become complacent about it. But we've been a role model in dealing with that. Again, we'll provide more players for the 2006 World Cup teams than any other country; and the coming-together here of so many players from so many different countries has been a springboard for us to initiate very successful anti-racism policies and set an example to other countries, such as Spain, who are clearly lacking in the knowledge we've gained.

'Some of us have lived through the times when the game was going to be closed down or you needed identity cards. Some of us have lived through the horrors of Heysel, Hillsborough and the Bradford fire. I've had the administrator calling at the door every other week with a new club ready to fold. So when you consider all that, you'd have to say the game has never been in a healthier state financially, though the spread of that money is more unequal, possibly, than it's ever been.

'That raises the ultimate question for any sport: how do you retain a successful competition and make sure you don't win things just by being the richest and biggest? If a few clubs and a few countries have a monopoly on the game's success, then it's going to lose its appeal. It's one of the reasons you have a handicap system in horseracing and golf – to make the competition a bit more worthwhile.' Taylor's solution, clearly, would be to redistribute some of the Premier League's colossal wealth among the lower divisions.

He is uneasy, too, about the takeover of major British clubs in the last few years by foreign millionaires/billionaires such as Roman Abramovich at Chelsea and Malcolm Glazer at Manchester United. 'It's another big problem the game has got to deal with,' he said. 'I feel the authorities have to bring in a "fit and proper" rule that enables them to say to would-be buyers of clubs, "This is all well and good, but your balance sheet is not adding up; and if the competition is going to be affected we need it to add up. We also need to know that there's some long-term chance for the club if the individual benefactor pulls out." As to whether it's good to have your Dave Whelans [at Wigan] and your Jack Walkers [at Blackburn], you have to say the game's always been open, and should remain open, to that sort of approach so long as it's not a question of the plug's pulled and the club goes under if that particular person walks away.'

For all the unease about the bona fides of Abramovich and Glazer, it has to be said, at the time of writing, that they have done absolutely nothing wrong. The worst they could be accused of was putting *too* much money into English football and thereby distorting the market. This applied more to the super-rich Abramovich, although Glazer did not hesitate to back manager Sir Alex Ferguson in the transfer market, either. It would not be difficult to think of British interlopers who had done clubs far more harm.

Undoubtedly, too, foreign managers and footballers have improved English football in many respects. 'What the foreign influx has brought in,' continued Gordon Taylor, 'is great input with regard to diet, physiology, training, commitment and dedication. I'm not saying it wasn't there before, but they've brought in new ideas, just as David Beckham may have brought something to Real Madrid. John Charles was regarded as a god when he went to Juventus, so he obviously brought something new to them.

'It's that integration of different cultures and backgrounds whereby you can pick up and learn from the best. Rafa Benitez and Jose Mourinho would no doubt say they like to have the grit, character and will-to-win of the Jamie Carraghers and John Terrys of this world. So you hope that, with the definitive technical skills our youngsters can develop, we'll be getting the best of both worlds eventually. Interestingly enough, the English players have acknowledged the foreigners' skills by making people like Thierry Henry and Eric Cantona their Players of the Year.

'For those young Englishmen like Frank Lampard who make the grade, it's a white-hot atmosphere of talent; and if they can come through because of playing with such players, then they're even better for the experience. That's why, with the World Cup finals this year [2006], it will be interesting to see how we go on. If we don't do as well as we should, then you would begin to worry because the players we've got have been playing successfully at the very highest level.'

Taylor also welcomes the foreign footballers in his capacity as a trade union leader. 'They've been brilliant members of the PFA,' he enthused. 'When we've had industrial problems – maybe over TV money with the Premiership or the Football League or the FA – they've been very supportive. They've probably seen the strength of the PFA, unknown in their own countries, whereby they've got guaranteed representation and fair play, and their contracts are worth what it says on the paper. They've seen the amount of work we do for them. So when we've asked for their support, they've given it unquestioningly.'

As for the future of English football, one can only see the big clubs becoming bigger, richer and more powerful while the rest continue to bump along as best they can financially. Despite all the efforts of the European Commission to break BSkyB's virtual monopoly of football coverage in Britain, the game's television income is unlikely to decrease – just the opposite, in fact. That much was evident from the new TV deal concluded in May 2006. For the three years from August 2007, the Premier League will receive the staggering sum of £1.7 billion – or £28 million a year for each of the twenty clubs – for the rights to televise Premiership games. It is a 66 per cent increase on the previous contract and has been brought about by the European Commission's insistence that television companies other than Sky be allowed a slice of the cake. Thus Sky, who were expected to get five of the six packages of games on offer, had to settle for four and pay £1.314 billion for the privilege. The two other packages went to new Irish subscription channel Setanta, who paid £392 million for them.

The competition to broadcast matches involving English clubs is increasing all the time. It is not just Sky versus the BBC and ITV any more: Channel 5 cover UEFA Cup games, while both the BBC and ITV have been given more flexibility by the increase in their number of channels. Then there are satellite newcomers like Setanta, plus companies eager to transmit football matches and information to mobile phones and other wonders of modern personalised technology that so delight the youth of the nation. And where there is competition, there is money.

'Television keeps falling over itself to get games on screen,' said Gordon Taylor. 'The proposition that too much football on television would lead to a reduction in gates has proved a fallacy because it's turned out to be just the opposite. Of course there is always an ultimate point, and to some extent the change of fixtures, the change of days, the change of kick-off times is a worry for the hardcore supporters who like to go to the away games as well. Planning their calendar year is difficult. We should never make the armchair spectator the priority because down that road lies the emptying of stadiums, the lack of atmosphere and the very thing that makes the game so attractive. I cannot think of another game, another industry, that brings together so many parts of the community on a regular basis.'

If we take it as read that television companies will continue to fight to give the leading football clubs money, then it is difficult to see how footballers' wages can do anything other than continue to rise. The clubs could call a halt to the spiral tomorrow simply by refusing to pay the players what they want; but they won't do that because they don't want to lose their best players. For the same reason, the clubs will be reluctant to impose a wage cap, or have one imposed on them should the Independent European Sport Review of May 2006 find favour with the European Commission. The review, initiated by European sports ministers led by Britain's Richard Caborn, and backed by UEFA, sought, among other wide-ranging reforms, to restrain players' salaries and force clubs to field a minimum number of home-grown players. But the weight of opposition to it may be judged by the fact that the ink was hardly dry on the page before the Premier League were lobbying the Prime Minister to resist the review's 'damaging' proposals. Theoretically, the FA could override the Premier League with the 'golden' share they were allocated when the League was formed: it gives them the power to outvote their partners. But they did not use it to bring down the number of clubs to the preferred eighteen, and now, with the League calling the tune, it is too late. As for the players themselves, nothing would be more certain than the threat of a strike were any attempt to be made to restrict their earning power. And it must be extremely doubtful whether the clubs would be prepared to fight them over it. Maybe only market forces are capable of keeping footballers' pay within what the rest of society considers 'reasonable'. So far as one can see, such forces could be released only by a surplus of talented players, the disappearance of all agents, or a recession, none of which is very likely at the moment.

In any case, market forces can be overrated. Back in the mid-eighties, when aggregate attendances in English football's four divisions fell to 16.5 million – roughly half the total for Duncan Edwards' last season, 1957/58 – I was one of those who believed in natural selection and the survival of the fittest. It was my theory that the game, in trying to preserve its famed strength in depth, was struggling to keep more clubs going than the public wanted to support. Therefore, the weakest should go part-time or be allowed to fade away quietly. For me, it was a simple question of supply and demand.

But what do I know?

INDEX

INDEX